Invasion!

OPERATION SEALION, 1940

Martin Marix Evans

Harlow, England • London • New York • Boston • San Francisco • Toronto • Sydney • Singapore • Hong Kong
Tokyo • Seoul • Taipei • New Delhi • Cape Town • Madrid • Mexico City • Amsterdam • Munich • Paris • Milan

PEARSON EDUCATION LIMITED
Edinburgh Gate
Harlow CM20 2JE
United Kingdom
Tel: +44 (0)1279 623623
Fax: +44 (0)1279 431059
Website: www.pearsoned.co.uk

First edition published in Great Britain in 2004
© Pearson Education Limited 2004

The right of Martin Marix Evans to be identified as author of this work has been asserted by him in
accordance with the Copyright, Designs and Patents Act 1988.

ISBN 0 582 77294 X

British Library Cataloguing-in-Publication Data
A CIP catalogue record for this book can be obtained from the British Library

Library of Congress Cataloging-in-Publication Data
Marix Evans, Martin.
   Invasion! : Operation Sealion, 1940 / Martin Marix Evans.–1st ed.
      p. cm.
   Includes bibliographical references and index.
   ISBN 0-582-77294-X
   1. Operation Sea Lion. I. Title: Operation Sealion, 1940. II. Title: Operation Sea Lion,
1940. III. Title.

D771.M297 2004
940.54'211–dc22

                                                                                          2004044788

10 9 8 7 6 5 4 3 2 1
08 07 06 05 04

Set by 3
Printed by Biddles Ltd, King's Lynn

The Publishers' policy is to use paper manufactured from sustainable forests.

Contents

List of figures   vi

Acknowledgements   ix

Introduction   x

PART 1   1 September 1939 to 15 September
             1940: History   1

1   The fall of Norway and France   3
2   The defence of Britain   56
3   Planning Sealion   80
4   The gathering force   113
5   Controlling the sea and the sky   138
6   Assessing the terrain and the defences   148

PART 2   9 September 1940 to 29 September
             1940: Conjecture   165

    The invasion of England: introduction   167
7   Landing Area B – Hythe to Dungeness   173
8   Landing Area C – Rye Bay   191
9   Landing Area D – Pevensey Bay   204
10 Landing Area E – Rottingdean to Cuckmerehaven   214
11 The British reaction   228
12 The final round   236

Appendix   262

Sources   264

Index   270

List of figures

1   Coasts of Europe turned hostile; the British perception of their
    situation in July 1940   9
2   The track to Hollister Farm, near the Shere to East Clandon Road,
    guarded by a pillbox and anti-tank block   60
3   Map showing the principle lengths of coastline protected by
    'Emergency Batteries', the main 'GHQ' defence line and local 'stop
    lines'   61
4   A line of anti-tank pimples on the edge of the wood west of Port
    Lympne Wildlife Park   61
5   Spigot Mortar base and pit partly concealed by a garden fence
    alongside the A3100 north-east of Godalming   62
6   Second World War additions to the Norman castle at Pevensey   63
7   The seafront of Hastings in the holiday season from the German
    handbook to the South Coast of England   86
8   Detail of the 1:25,000 map updated to 8 August 1940 showing
    the area around Dover   88
9   Detail of defences map of 3 September showing Watling Street
    north-west of Dover with pillboxes surrounded with barbed wire
    and fields blocked with obstacles to prevent aircraft landing   105
10 Testing an assault boat launching system   115
11 A *Pioniersturmboot* in action, clearing an obstacle at speed   117
12 Training for landing in England. Camouflaged motor boats steady
    a barge while a primitive ramp is put together   118
13 Barges assembled at Rotterdam Meerhaven   119
14 A heavy bridge pontoon ferry with two 8.8cm flak guns
    undergoing trials   122

15 The German dispositions in the Channel, September 1940   143
16 British (M.I. 14) assessment of German aircraft ranges as
    calculated in August 1941.   146
17 The landform map from the Coastal Handbook   151
18 Landing area E on Map 41 of the Coastal Handbook   153
19 The geology of south-east England as shown in the Handbook   154
20 A detail from the original defences map of 3 September, showing
    Landing Area C, Rye Bay and north to the Isle of Oxney.   157
21 A detail from the *Übersichtskarte der Gewässerabschnitte in England*
    showing south-east England   158
22 Part of England, the detailed geological map   174
23 The part of the defences map of 3 September showing Landing
    Area B   178
24 A Panzer III (U) going ashore, trailing its breather tube and radio
    link   180
25 The drain running from the Royal Military Canal past Botolph's
    Bridge to the sea near the Redoubt   185
26 German troops under fire   188
27 The Rye Bay to Hastings part of the defences map, Landing
    Area C   193
28 The shore of the south-west of Rye   196
29 A substantial coastal strongpoint on the west bank of the
    sea-canal to Rye   197
30 German troops attempt to move forward with their rubber boats
    in readiness for crossing a water obstacle ahead   198
31 An aerial photograph from the Coastal Handbook showing the
    canalised River Rother to Rye Harbour   200
32 A composite based on two sheets of the defences map showing
    Landing Area D   206
33 The shingle beach in Landing Area D looking from
    Norman's Bay towards Bexhill   207
34 The Pevensey Levels seen from Norman's Bay   209
35 Steam trawlers ready to serve as tugs moored in Rotterdam   211
36 The section of the defences map covering Landing Area E   216
37 View west across Cuckmerehaven towards Seaford Head, with
    anti-tank ditch   219

38 On the valley flank a cylindrical Type 25 pillbox looks over the
River Cuckmere   220

39 The view towards Newhaven Redoubt and harbour mouth from
Bishopstone railway station, overlooking the shore   222

40 Bren-gun emplacements built into the tower over the booking
hall of the railway station   224

41 An aerial photograph from the South Coast Handbook of the port
of Newhaven with the Redoubt, harbour facilities centre and Ouse
delta   226

42 A column of bren-gun carriers on the move   241

43 German infantry working their way forward in the company of a
Panzer II   244

44 A horse-drawn German supply column in 1940   249

45 A snapshot made by a German soldier of armour crossing a
temporary pontoon bridge   251

46 The dark rectangle of a gun enclosure reveals the presence of a
pillbox covering a bridge on the Chilworth to Shalford road   254

47 The loopholed wall at River House Cottage overlooking the green
in Elstead   255

48 A pillbox on the banks of the Wey, north of Somertset Bridge, on
the minor road from Esltead to Peper Harrow   258

Acknowledgements

We are grateful to the following for permission to reproduce copyright material:

The Bodleian Library for their original maps, sections and adaptations of which are used for Figures 8, 9, 20, 21, 22, 23, 27, 32 and 36; Peter Schenk for Figures 10, 11, 12, 13, 14, 24 and 35, from his book *The Invasion of England: The Planning of Operation Sealion*, Conway Maritime Press Ltd, 1990; and the Tank Museum for Figures 26, 30, 42, 43, 44 and 45.

In some instances we have been unable to trace the owners of copyright material, and we would appreciate any information that would enable us to do so.

Introduction

In a year in which the sixtieth anniversary of the successful invasion of the mainland of Europe was undertaken by the Allies, it seems to me interesting to contemplate what made for success in such a venture in the middle of the twentieth century and to take as an example an invasion that never took place: the invasion of England. The resulting study is presented in two parts. Part One follows events in Europe from the attack on Poland by Germany in September 1939 to the Battle of Britain a year later and includes the details of the preparations the Germans made for Operation Sealion, as the invasion was code-named. Part Two consists of a conjectural narrative account of what events might have taken place had the decision to proceed with the invasion of England been taken. The strategy, tactics and events described in Part One provide the foundation for those portrayed in Part Two.

That Adolf Hitler prepared to invade England is incontestable and that his intention was serious is hard to deny. Immense resources were devoted to the project not only in gathering the forces required and the means of transporting them, but also in research and documentation. Machinery similar to that invented independently by the Allies and used in the invasion of Normandy was developed: the amphibious tank, the landing craft and the flame-throwing tank, for example. That this investment was a mere ruse is unlikely in the extreme. Much of the printed material survives and I have drawn on German Army handbooks in my personal collection and German maps in the collection of the Bodleian Library in Oxford to build a picture of the German perception of the terrain they planned to conquer. Dr Peter Schenk has made a detailed study of the plans prepared and the equipment assembled for Operation Sealion, as the invasion was code-named, and I have relied heavily on his scholarship. However, while the historical facts, as I understand them, have been respected, it is necessary to introduce decisions that were never made in order to have an event that did not happen in history occur in this book. The three crucial decisions that are fiction are:

- the German adherence to attacking airfields and aircraft production facilities instead of bombing London in September 1940;
- the British order to the RAF to withdraw from its airfields south of London; and
- the consequential decision made by the Germans to invade.

I have taken care to make it clear where fact ends and imagination takes over. Some incidents in Part Two are based on real events and those are mentioned in the notes. In Part Two the names of individuals are only used where a name was needed to make the text read comfortably and, unless a footnote glosses the text, my imagination is the only basis for assuming that the person mentioned might have acted in the way described. The photographs from the Second World War used in this part were not, of course, made in England but are used in the belief that they show what might have been seen had the invasion taken place.

It is said that the greatest of German fears was of the Royal Navy. It seems to me that they were mistaken and that the Royal Navy would have been deeply reluctant to be drawn into resistance of Sealion prior to landings in England and tentative about intervention afterwards. At the time the stated preference of the Royal Navy was to attack the enemy Navy, surface and submarine vessels alike, in order to protect the nation's supply lines. Not even the evacuation of Dunkirk can be seen as an exception; the beachmaster was a naval officer to whom the highest ranks of the Army were subservient. It was a triumph for the Royal Navy and no discredit is implied, but it was exclusively its operation. Later in the war, in the light of the outstanding examples of the campaigns of Admiral Chester W. Nimitz in the Pacific theatre, the British Senior Service condescended to combine in operations with other arms, but at this early stage the Royal Navy did its own thing – with valour and determination, but its own thing none the less.

The popular perception of the Germans is of a fighting force that possessed technical superiority in arms and tactics, considerable courage and determination, and superb powers of planning and staff work. The first two characteristics were demonstrated in Norway and France, as this account describes, but the planning and staff work is another matter. The Norwegian campaign was conducted against adversaries ill-prepared and poorly trained. The great advantage the Germans had was that they were capable of conducting all-service operations, combining the strengths of the Army, Navy and Air Force with flexibility. They were ready to exploit any room granted to them for manoeuvre and support one another spontaneously in the field. Both in France and in Norway supply problems were mitigated by the availability of fuel and food on the ground; people could live, to a significant extent, off the land.

In 1932 Captain Anton von Bechtolsheim of the German Army visited the US Army Artillery School at Fort Sill. He gave a lecture which presaged what was observed in World War Two.

All staffs are small, because we believe that only small staffs can work quickly. We believe that the more officers a staff has the more orders will be given, not because the orders are necessary, but because everyone likes to have a say and everyone likes to give orders.

The German Army has, of course, its principles as to what is to be done in war, but – please mark this well – no stereotyped rules as to how it is to be done. May it be well understood I am talking about tactics, not technique!

We believe that movement is the first element of war and only by mobile warfare can any decisive results be obtained. Our supreme tactical principle is therefore mobility. Mobility exists down to the organization of the infantry squad.

Mobility is aided by surprise, by the independence of the subordinate commander within the mission of the higher unit, and what we call tactics by mission.

Mobility means quick decisions, quick movements, surprise attacks with concentrated force; to do always what the enemy does not expect, and to constantly change both the means and the methods and to do the most improbable things whenever the situation permits; it means to be free of all set rules and preconceived ideas. We believe that no leader who thinks or acts by stereotyped rules can ever do anything great, because he is bound by such rules. War is not normal. It cannot therefore be won by rules which apply in peacetime. Situations in war change rapidly, and changing situations cannot be solved by rules. We do not want therefore any stereotyped solutions for battle, but rather an understanding of the nature of war. . . . You will now understand why I cannot give you forms for attack, defence or pursuit. We have no normal way of carrying out any form of battle.[1]

This declaration must be seen in the context of a staff officer of a former enemy army addressing an American audience; a circumstance in which prestige and pride may have been involved as well as, and perhaps in conflict with, academic integrity. The approach to tactical decision making was subsequently demonstrated in the campaigns of 1939 and 1940, but discussion of strategic and logistical considerations is missing from the report of the lecture. It does, however, appear from the history of what actually took place that the German reputation for methodical planning and meticulous attention to detail is not supported by the behaviour or philosophy of the German Army. They had no normal way of carrying out any form of battle, Bechtolsheim declared, and the elevation of this philosophy appears to have reduced the attention given to boring backroom labour. Almost every German campaign foundered with the over-reaching of supply lines, just as it had in the spring of 1918.

The invasion of Normandy by the Allies in 1944 made use of versions of machinery very similar to those invented for Operation Sealion. The American experience in the Pacific had contributed to the development of sophisticated and diverse types of landing craft and Major-General Sir Percy Hobart's 'funnies', the specially-adapted tanks, included the Duplex-Drive Shermans which were amphibious machines. Such devices are well-known and easily seen in film and photographs of the time, but what is less remarked are the provision of supply facilities without which the enterprise would most certainly have failed. The Allied landings in France were supported by artificial ports, the Mulberry Harbours. Two were planned but even when one was destroyed by a storm the remaining installation was able to ensure the flow of the massive amounts of matériel required to sustain the campaign. Fuel was pumped through 'Pluto', PipeLine Under The Ocean. By contrast the German plan to invade England assumed that Dover or Folkestone would be taken, and the landing of supplies on open beaches that British intelligence calculated was possible does not appear to have formed part of the German planning. This text gives them the benefit of the doubt and assumes that supplies would have come by that means. The provision for fuel was trivial. Petrol was to be shipped over in drums. No fuel tankers were allocated to the operation.

In the event, Operation Sealion was not put into action in the autumn of 1940. It was not formally cancelled either, but simply delayed for the time being before it was quietly forgotten in the aftermath of German failure in the Russian campaign. If it had gone ahead, it would have failed, not on the sea but on land. Neglect of the rules for carrying out a form of battle may be effective at a tactical level, but a tank without fuel is merely a badly built bunker. Armies neglect logistics at their peril.

I am grateful to Dr Peter Schenk both for the loan of archive photographs from his collection and for answering my questions. Dr William Kilbride gave me invaluable guidance in how best to search the Defence of Britain database. David Keough drew my attention to material I would otherwise have missed in the archives of the US Army Military History Institute in Carlisle, PA, and Jack Smithers and Michael French to events and locations I knew not of. The bulk of translation of *Wehrmacht* texts previously available only in German was undertaken by Angus McGeoch and additional help with translation was given by Chris Sylge and by Nigel Read; without them I would have been lost. The staff of the Map Room of the Bodleian Library, Oxford, were, as always, both helpful and patient. I am grateful to them for their tolerance and to the library itself for permission to reproduce maps based on those I found there. I have also been granted permission to make use of photographs from the Tank Museum, Bovington for which I return my thanks. The modern photographs are my own work.

Sources of quoted material are identified in the notes and I am particularly grateful to the people who allowed me to quote from unpublished works. The Hon. Caroline Ponsonby has given me access to the papers of her father, Major Lord Sysonby and Doug Swift has allowed me to borrow from his moving account of his experiences that in fact led to his capture in France, although I have moved the events to Kent. I have also had the benefit of examining papers and diaries held in the Second World War Experience Centre in Horsforth, Leeds and in the other institutions mentioned in the Sources section. Finally, I have transplanted a good deal of real history to the conjectural part of the text. The actual should not be confused with the invented, but I trust the latter benefits from being close to real life.

Martin Marix Evans
Blakesley, March 2004

Notes and References

1   Hamilton Howze Papers, US Army Military History Institute, Carlisle, PA, USA.

PART 1

1 September 1939 to 15 September 1940:

History

chapter 1

The fall of Norway and France

The Second World War began with an unprovoked attack by Germany on Poland on 1 September 1939. One and a half million troops struck from the north and the west with the benefit of air supremacy achieved by the destruction of the Polish air force on the ground as day broke. The advance was spearheaded by nearly 2000 tanks. By 9 September the greater part of the Polish army was surrounded and, in spite of a counter-attack on the River Bzura, German control was virtually complete by 17 September. On that day the USSR invaded Poland from the east. The last of the Polish resistance ceased on 6 October.

The lightning war, *blitzkrieg*, had been a dazzling success for Hitler's Germany. The German leader himself had visited Major-General Heinz Guderian, commander of XIX Army Corps, on 5 September 1939. They met near Plevno on Tuchel Heath and drove along the line of the advance. 'Our dive bombers did that?' asked Hitler at the sight of a shattered Polish artillery regiment. 'No, our panzers!' Guderian replied, and went on to report the cost in casualties for the seizure of the Polish Corridor, the access route to the Baltic Sea between East Prussia and Germany. The four divisions of Guderian's command had suffered about 150 dead and 700 wounded. The favourable impression on the German leader was followed up with advice to speed up the supply of Panzer III and IV tanks and also to upgrade their armour and guns.[1]

In 1937 Guderian had published his book *Achtung! Panzer!* It did not appear in English until 1992. Guderian had served much of the First World War in signals and became a radio specialist before becoming a staff officer to General E. Tschischwitz, head of Motor Transport Troops. He studied the use of motorised troop formations, being driven to conclude that, alone, they were useless, but with artillery, engineers and tanks the combination would be immensely powerful. Whether it was his background or his military genius that led Guderian to this vision of integrated operations involving tanks, artillery, engineers and mobile infantry is a moot point; but what is important is that Guderian's views were to mould the strategy and tactics of the Panzer divisions. He specified three tactical requirements: surprise, deployment *en masse* and suitable terrain.

Of surprise he said:

The rapid execution of the armoured attack is of decisive importance for the outcome of the battle; the supporting arms that are destined for permanent cooperation with the tanks must accordingly be just as fast-moving as the tanks themselves, and they must also be united with the tanks in an all-arms formation in peacetime.[2]

The principle of deployment *en masse* is, he stated, valid for all arms and as to terrain,

... the tank forces should be committed only where there are no obstacles that exceed the capacity of their machines; otherwise the armoured attack will break on the terrain.[3]

The achievements of the Panzer forces in Poland confirmed the validity of Guderian's ideas.

The phoney war

The attack on Poland triggered the declaration of war on Germany on 3 September 1939 by Great Britain and, just over five hours later, by France. It was upon France that Britain relied, for the British Expeditionary Force that set out for France comprised a mere five divisions, and only another five could be made available in the next few months. By contrast the French had 12 divisions of fortress troops to man the strongholds of the Maginot Line and another 72 divisions were already mobilised or ready to be mobilised.

The battlefield, it was assumed, would be on the French borders. The east, facing Germany, was already equipped with the sophisticated and secure complex of fortresses of the Maginot Line. Within a steel and concrete carapace, for the most part buried underground and with artillery-bearing turrets commanding the approaches, hundreds of men could eat, sleep, relax, exercise and stand guard to preserve the integrity of French soil. André Maurois wrote:

What has already, before the supreme test, deserved all the wonder and praise is the fact alone that generals and engineers have dared to convert into fortresses not only whole mountains, but a whole range of mountains, that they should have impregnated with fire every inch of the threatened ground all along our north-eastern frontiers and found government after government willing to give them the necessary millions. . . . The English never wearied of poring over the annotated photographs, the firing-maps, the drawings and the diagrams which mean that on a single telephone call of three or four figures, a storm of shells will rain on such and such a segment of wood B17, or such and such a section of territory 243. They were fascinated by the perfection of detail. . . .[4]

Between these strongholds, to avoid their being outflanked and by-passed as they had been in the First World War, mobile interval troops supported the static works. This impressive and expensive defence ran from the Swiss border to La Ferté, 24km (15 miles) south-east of Sedan. The 35 divisions of General G. Prételat's Army Group 2, a third of the French army, held that line. To the west of the last fort, a string of strongpoints, concrete bunkers and pillboxes, straggled along the Meuse and across northern France towards Lille where it petered out, partly because of insufficient funds, partly to avoid disrupting a region of immense industrial and commercial importance, and partly to avoid excluding the Belgians, allies in the last war and probable allies in the next. As the South African Deneys Reitz discovered, the Belgians excluded themselves, leaving a great gap in the line to which the Allies' eyes were drawn.

Reitz was an old soldier. He had first fought in South Africa, against the British, as an under-age member of the Pretoria Commando at the outbreak of war in 1899, when Winston Churchill was a war correspondent with Sir Redvers Buller's forces. He finished the war on the staff of General Jan Smuts, under whom he was to serve again in the First World War with the British against the Germans. He finished that war in command of the 1st Royal Scots Fusiliers on the Western Front. In 1939 he was the South African government's Deputy Prime Minister and in October set out for London from Durban by Sunderland flying boat to represent his country at a conference of the Dominions of the British Empire to consider the joint conduct of the new war. The journey, by one of the most advanced and sophisticated civil aircraft of the time, was long and emphasises the technological limitations of machinery at the outbreak of the Second World War. The first day took him from Durban to Mozambique where the night was spent in a house-boat. There they heard news on the radio, or wireless as Reitz calls it, of the sinking of HMS *Royal Oak* in Scapa Flow. The next day, 15 October, they flew by way of Lindi, Dar-es-Salaam and Mombassa to Kisumu on Lake Victoria, Kenya. The third day began with the flight across the lake to Fort Bell (now Port Bell) near Kampala, then on to Lake Albert and north along the Nile to Malakal and finally to Khartoum. The fourth day saw only one refuelling stop, at Wadi Halfa, before arriving in Cairo where Reitz delivered despatches to the British Commander-in-Chief of the Near East, General A. P. Wavell. On 18 October they flew on via Alexandria and Crete to Corfu, and from there, next day, to Rome and then Marseilles, where Reitz saw some swastikas painted on the walls and posters opposing the war. The final day's journey was by way of Lac Biscarross, south-west of Bordeaux, and then across the Bay of Biscay, Brittany and Normandy to land on Southampton Water. The train to London arrived in the blackout.[5] It had taken a week to make a journey that, by the end of the century, would take less than a day's non-stop flight.

Reitz describes the situation he found.

Next morning I looked out through my window on to Hyde Park and a clear sunny day. There were gun pits among the trees and scores of anchored balloons swung overhead like silver fish in the sky.

In spite of these warlike preparations there was an air of unreality about the situation. The Germans had overwhelmed Poland in three weeks, but since then there was a strange calm. Everyone had expected that France would immediately be attacked and that from the very start heavy air raids would be launched on Great Britain, more particularly on London. So certain was the government of this that nearly a million children had been evacuated to the country; elaborate arrangements had been prepared to remove all the civil service departments to the provinces; underground shelters had been excavated; churches, museums and art galleries had sent their treasures away and even the stained glass windows from cathedrals and guildhalls were taken down and stored in vaults, and every building in London was heavily sandbagged against bomb splinters. But, thus far, not a single German aeroplane had attempted to approach the capital and save for an occasional hostile machine over the Firth of Forth the war remained what the comic papers called a 'sitzkrieg' instead of the 'blitzkrieg' that was anticipated. So much was this the case that during the weeks I spent in London I gathered the impression that people were becoming bored....[6]

On 9 November the British Foreign Minister, Anthony Eden, led a party of representatives from the War Council on a tour of inspection of the front line in France. The Australian, Canadian, New Zealand and Indian delegates, and Deneys Reitz for South Africa went with him from Newhaven to Dieppe by night, steering a zig-zag course to confuse enemy submarines, and thence to Paris by car. The next morning they visited Vincennes to meet General Maurice Gamelin.

He spoke bitterly of the situation, saying that they had constructed the Maginot Line at vast expense, but the Belgian Government had raised objections to a continuation along their frontier, so it was only half a bulwark. Yet now they had been threatened with invasion, the Belgians were so intimidated by German threats that they refused to indulge in staff talks and he prophesied that either British or French troops would have to move forward of their works to go to their assistance.[7]

No reassurance was to be had from Reitz's experience of the politicians either. His party dined with French Cabinet ministers and in a series of private conversations each warned him not to confide in the others. It appeared to him there was more enmity between the Frenchmen than towards the Germans.

The party then went north, over country Reitz recognised from the previous war, to the headquarters of Lord Gort, commander of the British Expeditionary Force (BEF). From there they toured the line near Lille and were not impressed. The trenches were shallow and the concrete domes which were intended to form a string of gun emplacements had only a single anti-tank rifle in each of them and the loopholes gave only to the side, offering no frontal view at all. The tour continued eastwards as far as Metz where Reitz was confused to find that the Germans were looked upon with some favour. The fortress of Mont de Welshe in the Maginot Line did, however, impress.

If one can visualise a hundred and fifty miles of battleships buried bow to stern with only their turrets visible it will give some idea of this gigantic undertaking. . . . The tragedy is that it did not run the entire length of the frontier. . . .

During the time we spent up and down it, we saw heavy guns moved from the bowels of the earth at the touch of a finger; we watched ghostly electric trains running silent along endless corridors, with men and munitions, and we were hospitably entertained in bastions and bays.

Yet there was an air of unreality. I remember the last war, with never a moment without shells howling across or machine-guns rattling away. Now there was a deathly quiet and I did not hear a single shot fired in France though powerful armies stood face to face.

We were allowed to lower and raise the guns by pressing levers and swivels much as a child would be allowed to switch on the lights or press the button of the hooter in a motor-car, but when I suggested that I should be permitted to pull a trigger and fire a shell or two at the German lines across the way the French officers gazed at me as if I had uttered a blasphemy.[8]

On their return to London Reitz and Casey, the Australian minister, asked to see the British Prime Minister, Neville Chamberlain. After a good deal of evasion and mutterings about colonial interference, they were granted an audience with the great man and told him of their misgivings. Reitz went as far as to say that the Germans would go through the British positions like a knife through cheese. This was put aside with the remark that one cannot build shelters in muddy soil and shells bursting in damp ground did little harm.[9] It was obvious that first-hand observation was not going to be allowed to influence ivory-tower concepts.

While trenches were dug and concrete was poured into the flimsy extension of the Maginot Line in northern France, the action was taking place in Scandinavia.

The Scandinavian problems

The Baltic states had been allocated to the Soviet Union's sphere of influence by the secret provisions of the Ribbentrop–Molotov Pact of August 1939. The Soviets required Finland to yield up bases on the Baltic, the Karelian peninsula and near Murmansk on the Arctic coast but this was refused and at the end of November an excuse was manufactured to secure what was wanted by force. To the surprise of the world at large, the Finns did not collapse, outmanned and outgunned though they were, and they even mounted counter-attacks in the depth of winter. The Soviet response was to reorganise and by early March 1940 they overwhelmed Finnish resistance. Allied offers of support had, quite correctly, been deemed insufficient.

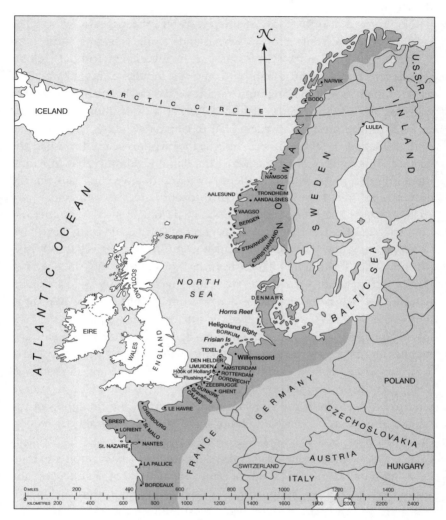

Figure 1 Coasts of Europe turned hostile; the British perception of their situation in July 1940. After *Coastal Command*, London, HMSO, 1943, p. 43

Through this period Germany, supporting the Soviet Union, had been able to prevent supplies reaching Finland other than by way of Norway and thence overland.

Norway was also the focus of interest in regard to the war at sea. The Leads, the coastal route protected by islands along Norway's shore from Stavanger to the North Cape, was in Norwegian territorial waters. Combatants could pass through but could not indulge in acts of war. This gave Germany a way to bring in merchant vessels safely and also to get her warships out into the North Atlantic. A further consideration was securing supplies of iron ore from Sweden. Half of Germany's needs had been met until September 1939 by imports from France while Sweden furnished the balance. The Swedish ore came across the Baltic in summer, but in winter the route through Narvik in northern Norway and down the Leads was the only one ice-free. Norway's importance to both sides was therefore very great, provided that the volume of ore shipped from Sweden in summer was not increased. The fact that the Swedish port of Luleå could easily have been developed to render Narvik redundant was known but neglected in British planning and thus the temptation to bring Norway into the Alliance or to violate her neutrality remained. Germany's best interests were in maintaining that neutrality and using her territorial waters for safe passage as long as the British did not jeopardise the situation. That did not prevent the loss of Norwegian ships and seamen, some 350 of the latter, to German submarines and mines by the end of February 1940.

It was while the Russo-Finnish war was still in progress, during February 1940, that the British made their plans to seize Narvik and Luleå in order to send troops to support the Finns in accordance with the resolution of the League of Nations. This would compromise Swedish neutrality as well as that of Norway, and so forces were to be sent there as well. The 5th Scots Guards was recruited from experienced skiers and sent to Chamonix to train as a mountain unit. It soon became apparent that neither of the Scandinavian countries intended for this special attention were inclined to cooperate and the plan was dropped. The stimulus for a change was anger at the British action in boarding the German prison ship *Altmark* in Jössenfjord, within Norwegian waters, on 16 February. The vessel, the former supply ship to the German 'pocket battleship' *Admiral Graf Spee*, which had been scuttled outside Montevideo, had been protected by a Norwegian flotilla when Captain Philip Vian's destroyers had attempted to intercept her. Vian then took HMS *Cossack* into the fjord and liberated 303

Allied merchant seamen to the joy of his countrymen and the fury of the neutrals. Neither was Adolf Hitler best pleased, but the crucial effect was to strengthen both British and Scandinavian convictions that British naval power was the dominant factor in this sphere. The British therefore had difficulty in conceiving of the idea of a German threat on any scale and the Norwegians considered that Britain was more likely to breach their neutrality than the Germans were to invade. Grand Admiral Erich Raeder had already sown the seed of an invasion plan when, the previous December, he had sent the young Norwegian Major Vidkun Quisling to see Hitler and expound his theory of an Allied invasion of Norway to threaten German shipping. Hitler had ordered the initiation of a plan for the conquest of Norway which had been put into intensive development under the code name *Weserübung* at the end of January. Now, on 19 February, Hitler ordered the work to be accelerated.[10]

The invasion of Norway

The challenge of Norway differed in the extreme from the land and air war carried to so satisfactory a conclusion in Poland. The key geographical characteristics were taken into account: people, commerce and industry were based on the coast or in the narrow valleys running inland and settlement was in a number of locations isolated from one another, the largest of which were the regions around Oslo, Bergen and Trondheim. The Norwegian army was, as a result of virtual disarmament in the previous 20 years, theoretically capable of mobilising only some 56,000 men and it was assumed that the heightening tensions since September 1939 would result in about 19,000 being in place at the time of invasion. The navy had only five modern vessels, destroyers and a minelayer, three small First World War destroyers, two coastal defence vessels and some 40 smaller craft. There were 16 modern aircraft among the 40 the air force possessed. The army's six divisions were based at Oslo (2nd Division) and Halden (1st Division) to the south-east of the capital; at Kristiansand (3rd Division) on the southernmost tip of the country overlooking the Skaggerak; at Bergen (4th Division) and Trondheim (5th Division) on the west coast and finally at Harstad (6th Division) in the Lofoten Islands off Narvik. These locations meant that hitting the Oslo region, Kristiansand and the two more southern of the west coast centres at the same time could result in the destruction of five-sixths of the army.

The German Navy recognised the massively superior strength of the Royal Navy and was therefore to rely on the element of surprise. The transportation of troops by warship was the answer and fuel and other supplies were to precede the attack, posing as innocent merchant ships. Two of the Tanker Echelon were destined for Narvik and one for Trondheim, arriving before 'W Day', while those for Oslo, Kristiansand, Stavanger and Bergen were timed to arrive at their destinations on the day itself. The ships carrying equipment and other supplies were called the Export Echelon, of which three ships were for Narvik, three for Trondheim and one for Stavanger. The Oslo region was to receive a flow of supplies by way of the other country targeted for conquest, Denmark. The 1st Sea Transport Echelon, of 15 ships, was to arrive in the target ports from Bergen round to Oslo on W Day while subsequent echelons were for Oslo alone. The Navy wanted all warships out of their destination ports as soon as possible but the Army wanted cover, while Hitler sat on the fence. The operation was to be covered by 28 submarines spread from the coastal waters off Narvik, across to the Orkney and Shetland Islands, and down to the western opening of the Skaggerak.

Of the six divisions allocated to the invasion, the Navy was to carry a first wave of a mere 8700 men to Norway. The Warship Echelon consisted of 11 Groups in all. Group 1 consisted of the battleships *Scharnhorst* and *Gneisenau* with ten destroyers, carrying 2000 troops for Narvik; Group 2, the cruiser *Admiral Hipper* and four destroyers carrying 1700 troops was for Trondheim; Group 3, for Bergen, had two cruisers, *Köln* and *Königsberg*, two service ships and eight torpedo boats with 1900 troops; Group 4 had a single cruiser, *Karlsruhe*, a service ship and ten torpedo vessels taking 1100 troops to Kristiansand; while Group 5, going to Oslo, had three cruisers, *Blücher, Lützow* and *Emden*, three torpedo vessels and eight minesweepers to carry 2000 troops. The remaining six echelons were for Denmark.

Air cover was to be provided by X Air Corps with various reinforcements. Up to then its operations had been bombing missions against British merchant shipping. It comprised 4th, 26th (with one group of 100th Bombardment Wing attached) and 30th Bombardment Wings. The latter was augmented with one dive-bomber group, two twin-engine fighter groups, one single-engine fighter group, a coastal reconnaissance and naval support group, and two long-range reconnaissance squadrons. The Transport Chief (Land) of X Air Corps disposed of seven groups of three- and four-engine transports and 1st Special Purpose Transport Wing which was to carry air-

borne and parachute units.[11] Transport Chief (Sea) had the 108th Special
Purpose Transport Wing of seaplane transports and three air-traffic safety
ships. Later British estimates[12] put the German air presence at 1000 aircraft,
of which 290 were bombers, 40 dive-bombers, 30 single-engine fighters, 70
twin-engine fighters, 40 long-range reconnaissance, 30 coastal and 500
transport aircraft. These figures appear to be on the high side as, for
example, the Messerschmitt Bf 110 units in X Air Corps had only 55 serviceable machines from an establishment of 64, rather than the 70 listed by
the British.[13] Nevertheless, German air superiority was massive. The major
problem was that of distance, for the range of the Ju 88, the versatile high-
speed bomber, limited it to operations over Oslo and Stavanger from the
Hamburg area and the He 111 could only reach Bergen. Operations further
north depended on acquiring airfields in Denmark and Norway. The Ju 87
'Stuka' dive-bombers and Messerschmitt 109 single-engine fighters were
limited to the Skaggerak and Kristiansand when flying out of Germany.[14]
The effective use of air superiority, therefore, depended on early possession
of landing fields in Denmark and Norway.

Neither Norway nor Britain was alert to the dangers of the situation.
Norway suspected that Britain might interfere with the freedom of shipping
in the Leads, which was indeed the case, and Britain thought not only in
terms of laying mines against merchant shipping but also of the seizure of
Narvik to prevent the enemy occupying that place should it appear likely.
Neither of them seriously contemplated a German invasion without an
event, such as the British landing in Norway, to trigger a reaction. Three
Royal Navy flotillas were organised. Eight destroyers were destined for
Vestfjord, the main approach channel for Narvik, four destroyers and the
minelayer HMS *Teviot Bank* were to mine the route between Trondheim and
Bergen, and a third force of two destroyers was to pretend to mine the haven
off Molde. In case of Norwegian resistance, the battlecruiser HMS *Renown*
and four more destroyers reinforced the northern group. The landing force
prepared lest the Germans invade was to be furnished by the 49th Infantry
Division and the 24th Guards Brigade, to be deployed in Bergen and
Trondheim and in Narvik respectively. Two battalions of the 148th Infantry
Brigade were assigned the destruction of Sola airfield at Stavanger. These
forces were to sail from Rosyth and from the Clyde. The focus of attention
was Narvik and the route of shipment of Swedish iron ore. It was assumed
that the Royal Navy would dominate the sea and that these eight battalions
would suffice. In the event 51 German battalions were to be the opposition.

General Nikolaus von Falkenhorst, in whose hands the planning of Operation *Weserübung* was placed in February, recounted the meeting he'd had with Hitler and at which the reasons for invading Norway were set out. First, it was to prevent the British doing so and turning the Scandinavian/Baltic area into a region of major conflict. Second, it was to permit the German fleet greater freedom of movement and third, there was the matter of Swedish ore.[15] Only the last of these was considered by the British.

So, as the British scheme for mining Norwegian waters trundled into action, the German action or reaction was scarce considered, except by Vice-Admiral Sir Max Horton. He was responsible to the Commander-in-Chief, Home Fleet, for submarine operations in the North Sea. On 29 March 1940 he ordered his captains to patrol Norway's southern approaches and so it was that 19 boats were there when the invasion began. Their orders were to sink German troop transport ships and many enemy vessels therefore passed unharmed under the flags of neutrals on the first day. Orders were then given for any north-bound ship to be attacked.

The secrecy on which the crucial factor of surprise rested was preserved by a mixture of German sound judgement and pure luck, generously augmented by the caution and mistakes of their enemies. W-Day, the day of action, was 9 April. On 3 April the first tanker left Hamburg and the first three ships for Narvik sailed. The warships loaded on 6 April and sailed during the night and 1st Sea Transport Echelon sailed that same day. The report from the Netherlands Military Attaché in Berlin, Colonel Sas, that he had information from a senior, anti-Nazi, German officer (possibly Colonel Hans Oster who warned the Dutchman just before the start of the operations of 10 May, *Fall Gelb*) about invasions of both Norway and of the Low Countries was rejected by the Danes as a German plant and by the Norwegians as not credible in the face of British sea power. Another report on 6 April said that the Germans were planning to land a division carried in ten ships to Narvik; that was put aside as unlikely. On 7 April the sailing of a convoy some 15 to 20 vessels strong a couple of days earlier out of Stettin (Szczecin) on the River Oder north-east of Berlin was reported to the Norwegians. It was assumed to have entered the Kiel Canal, its destination unimportant. That same day the *Gneisenau* and the *Scharnhorst* of Group 1 and the *Hipper* of Group 2 got under way with their convoys.

On 8 April the British mine-laying operation took place. On the same day the movements of German ships were reported by the British to the

Norwegians; the message arrived at 1900 hours. That afternoon the Polish submarine *Orzel* torpedoed the *Rio de Janeiro*, a vessel of the 1st Sea Transport Echelon bound for Bergen, off Lillesand. Numerous survivors were picked up by Norwegian fishing boats and the rescued men said they had been on their way to protect the neutral port from the British. The Norwegian naval commander did not believe them. At 1820 hours the Norwegians ordered a state of readiness for their coastal forts, but made mine-laying dependent on further orders. Minutes after they had reported being in action, the order was given at 0100 on 9 April for mines to be laid between the forts of Rauöy and Bolarne on either side of Oslofjord, but by then the German convoy had already sailed past. Mobilisation was ordered at 0230 hours, to come into effect on 11 April.[16]

Meanwhile the German convoys were hurrying northwards towards Narvik, Trondheim and Bergen. They had been observed by British reconnaissance aircraft on 7 April and attacked by Blenheim aircraft without success, but Vice-Admiral Günther von Lütjens was informed that British signal traffic between the Admiralty and C-in-C, Home Fleet, was intense; the British were certainly moving to oppose him. The weather worsened, formation was lost and speed slackened to a still-swift 22 knots. The British were underestimating the speed and mishandling the intelligence provided by aerial reconnaissance. Bomber Command's tuning signal had not been sent out and only one receiving station picked up the report from the squadron leader of the Blenheim formation; it failed to repeat.[17] Nevertheless, by 2115 hours Admiral Sir Charles Forbes had his fleet out of Scapa Flow and the 2nd Cruiser Squadron had left Rosyth. Then, in a remarkable display of inter-service insularity, the First Sea Lord, Admiral Sir Dudley Pound, ordered the 1st Cruiser Squadron to sea and the troops which were to have been taken to Norway should a German invasion take place were sent ashore in short order and much confusion. The contingency plan had been overthrown by the Royal Navy without consultation or communication even with C-in-C, Home Fleet.[18] Winston Churchill's account differs in saying that 'All these decisive steps were concerted with the Commander-in-Chief,' but as he was First Lord of the Admiralty at the time his view is not disinterested.[19] The evaluation of Pound by the historian of the war at sea, Captain S. W. Roskill, having set out his substantial capacity for work, his imperturbability and the world-wide extent of his responsibilities, includes the observation 'Admiral Pound [had] little time to keep his colleagues on the Board of Admiralty informed about current or projected operations.... It is certainly the case that he constantly overworked himself, but how far this was inevitable where one man had to carry such responsibilities it is hard to say.'[20]

The weather separated both British and German destroyers from their larger companions and in the morning, at about 0900 hours, the *Bernd von Arnim* saw a destroyer going in the opposite direction at speed and making a strange recognition signal. She opened fire and the unknown vessel turned in pursuit; she was one of the battlecruiser HMS *Renown's* screening group, HMS *Glowworm*. The British destroyer herself opened fire. The action was seen by the German cruiser *Hipper* which had been detached and sent back in support of the scattered destroyers. The cruiser's first salvo struck *Glowworm's* bridge and the damaged destroyer fired torpedoes and made smoke into which she disappeared. *Hipper* followed only to find her tiny enemy turning back towards her, determined to ram. The larger ship could not evade the collision and a great gash was torn in her starboard side as the destroyer was dragged half under the hull of her enemy. *Glowworm* was sinking, and a huge explosion finished her. One officer and 37 men were picked up by *Hipper*.

Lütjens realised that the action would have been reported to the British commander and he also learned that a Dornier reconnaissance aircraft had reported two battleships, a heavy cruiser and six destroyers steaming north. He therefore sent *Hipper* and Group 2 immediately for Trondheim while he sailed as cover for the Narvik-bound destroyers. They parted as the destroyers entered Vestfjord and the *Scharnhorst* and the *Gneisenau* turned away at first to the west and then north-west. There, on the morning of 9 April, they encountered HMS *Renown* and Vice-Admiral Sir J. W. Whitworth. The opportunity to destroy an important British ship was not taken; indeed, *Gneisenau* was hit by a 15-inch shell from *Renown* and suffered further damage from lighter ordnance while *Scharnhorst* suffered a flooded turret in the heavy seas. Lütjens's faster and more modern ships were able to draw away, content to have delivered the invasion ships to Narvik and Trondheim.

The experience of Group 3, charged with landing troops at Bergen, was initially trouble-free. It sailed from Wilhelmshaven in the early hours of 8 April and, with the good fortune of covering fog, escaped the attention of the British to make a landfall at about midnight and enter Korsfjord at 0200 hours on 9 April. The *Köln* was challenged but responded with a British recognition signal. As dawn approached the flotilla entered the final body of water on which Bergen stands, Byfjord, passing under the guns of Kvarven fort. Unfortunately the blackout of the town included the power supply for the searchlights and the back-up generator was out of service. Two merchant vessels were on the move and the gunners of the shore batteries forbore to fire. Guns jammed, torpedoes were defective and the Germans sailed on. Two of the service ships were slightly damaged and, eventually, as *Königsberg* came up to the Kvarven fort, effective fire met her and did real damage. German troops were soon ashore and the batteries on both sides of the fjord were taken. The admiral immediately put the navy's withdrawal in hand, leaving the crippled cruiser and the most damaged of the service ships behind. A transport and the supplies it carried was lost to a Norwegian mine the next day and another two transports were sunk before the channels were finally swept, but Bergen, too, was now in German hands.

The approach of Group 5 to Oslofjord was seductively peaceful. The plan was to have two detachments of troops of 163rd Infantry Division, two battalions from the sea and two air-landed at Fornebu after parachutists had taken it, capture the king and his ministers in a dramatic *coup-de-main*. The commander of this operation, Major-General Engelbrecht, his staff and one battalion of his division were aboard the powerful new heavy cruiser *Blücher* which led the force up the fjord. Here again searchlights were darkened by generator failure and the men of Oscarsborg Fort were striving to get it working. The guns were old but large, three 28cm (11 inch) guns, and there was a torpedo battery. The fort stood on Kaholm Island facing another fort, Kopås, on the mainland some 600 yards (550m) across the fjord, where there were three 15cm (6 inch) guns. The commander of Oscarsborg knew his guns would be slow to reload and the order to fire would probably be for the only shot the guns would be able to deliver.

In the half-light and haze the Germans assumed there was no resistance in the offing and they pushed steadily onwards at some 12 knots, coming within range of the fort's guns. The order was given to fire. Two 28cm shells struck *Blücher*, one below the bridge and the other astern, near the aircraft hanger. Fuel and ammunition being carried on deck took fire. More shellfire, with the smaller batteries joining in, put the steering gear out of commission and the ship had to be guided by varying engine speeds. The fire reached a magazine, which exploded, while the damaged cruiser had ploughed on into the arc of fire of the torpedo batteries and suffered two hits underwater. At 0700 hours the order was given to abandon ship and minutes later *Blücher* rolled over and sank. The burning oil that covered the water prevented the Norwegians from rescuing many who managed to escape from the ship. Perhaps 1000 men died, including most of the staff of the 163rd Infantry.[21] The command devolved upon *Lützow*, also damaged by Norwegian gunfire but less seriously, and she and *Emden* pulled back to land their troops at Sonsbukten on the eastern side of the fjord, south of the Dröbak narrows. The Luftwaffe supported the action with bombers and dive-bombers but it was not until 1900 hours that Dröbak was taken and the forts to the north did not surrender until the following morning. The German convoy finally reached Oslo at 1145 hours on 10 April. The airborne operation had not gone smoothly because of the fog. Indeed, the commander of 2nd Group, 1st Special Duty Wing, X Air Corps ordered his aeroplanes to put down in Denmark having lost two Ju 52s already. Captain Wagner of 2nd Special Duty Wing led the second wave of 53 aircraft. He heard the order to land, but did not accept it as genuine (he was, in any case, subordinate to the Transport Chief, Land, and not the Air Corps) and pressed on. He was killed by machine-gun fire as they came in to land at Fornebu but the rest of the flight came on and the field was taken by the airborne infantry instead of the parachute troops as had been intended. The weather cleared and the vanguard caught up in the afternoon, so that, at 1530 hours, the Germans marched to occupy Oslo.

The taking of Stavanger, by contrast, was almost a formality. The airfield defences at Sola were bombed by Ju 88s and a parachute company dropped to secure the field. It was opposed by two machine-gun posts which were soon overcome. The runways were cleared of the barbed wire strung across them and the two battalions of 69th Infantry Division landed as planned. The city was occupied without resistance and the whole area was secured by nightfall. The only problems arose from the sinking of the tanker *Stedingen* by the British submarine *Triton* the previous day and of the transport *Roda* of the Export Echelon by the Norwegian torpedo boat *Ægir* which was sunk in turn by attack from the air. The tanker had been carrying aircraft fuel, the loss of which restricted the use of Sola field until another tanker arrived on 11 April.

Group 4's experience at Kristiansand was informative. The approach was made in poor visibility. Thick fog obscured the coast at 0345 hours and by 0600 when it began to clear the presence of the Germans was known to the defenders. When the flotilla tried to enter the fjord the guns of Odderøya drove them back more than once, the *Karlsruhe* being unable to bring her guns to bear effectively. Air support was called in and the Luftwaffe delivered a heavy raid on the forts, so effective that, when troops were ferried ashore at about 1100 hours, the batteries offered no further resistance. The city was under German control in mid-afternoon. Here, as at the other landing-places in southern Norway, initial resistance had been overcome by effective use of air power, although the limitations in the case of poor weather were also made clear.

With the initial landings completed in broadly satisfactory fashion, the Germans had to maintain the momentum. The British and French, on the other hand, had to isolate and pinch out these incursions, a task in which they would have to depend excessively on Norwegian help. The German Navy was now committed to returning its principal ships to their home port and evading confrontation with the Royal Navy. Admiral Forbes was shaken by the German air attacks during the afternoon of 9 April when they were halfway between Bergen and the Shetland Islands. Fortunately Sola airfield was not available as a base and the 47 Ju 88s and 41 He 111s had to fly from Aalborg and from Germany, limiting their time to engage. A British destroyer was sunk, HMS *Gurkha*, and *Rodney* was lucky that a 500kg bomb failed to explode fully. Instead of proceeding to attack German ships in Norwegian ports, Forbes turned away to meet the carrier HMS *Furious* with which he planned to launch an air strike on Trondheim. *Furious* carried no fighters so even after she joined Forbes lacked air cover and he had added only 18 Swordfish torpedo-reconnaissance biplanes to his strength. The crews of the Fleet Air Arm were well worked-up and the quality of their air-manship was later to guarantee the destruction of the German battleship *Bismarck*, but the mission against Trondheim from *Furious* on 11 April failed notwithstanding. Even if fighters had been available, they would have been Blackburn B-24 Skuas, already at this time obsolete as fighters but effective as dive-bombers. Indeed, on 10 April a dawn attack by 16 land-based Skuas from Hatson in the Orkney Islands, enjoying the benefit of surprise because the Germans assumed the single-engine aircraft to be their own, sank the *Königsberg* at Bergen.[22] Where German air cover was lacking, at Narvik, the action of the Royal Navy was decisive, leading to the complete destruction of the German ships there.

In attempting to evade the Royal Navy, the Germans were only partially successful. On 10 April, at 2200 hours, the damaged *Hipper* left Trondheim, had the luck to miss the approaching British under Forbes, and made contact with *Scharnhorst* and *Gneisenau*, completing a great evasive sweep to the west, at 0830 on 12 April. They entered Willemshaven that evening. The *Köln* left Bergen on the night of 9 April with two torpedo boats as escort. She hid from British aircraft in a small fjord and was able to make it home safely on 11 April. The *Karlsruhe* was not so lucky. She left Kristiansand at much the same time on 9 April and was immediately torpedoed by the British submarine *Truant*. The damage was so severe that the German torpedo boats escorting her had to sink her. From the Oslo sector the *Lützow* set out on 10 April, in the evening, and was torpedoed by *Spearfish* the next morning. The steering gear and screws were smashed and she was towed back to Kiel. In all the Germans lost one heavy cruiser, two light cruisers and ten destroyers in the Norwegian invasion. British submarines also sank eight German transport ships in addition to those mentioned above; the deployment of British submarines had been a success. The challenge for the invaders was now to maintain supply and reinforcement transport.

The loss of two ships with 900 troops from 2nd Sea Transport Echelon caused the German Navy to decree that troops had to be carried either in warships or in fast, small ships. The men were taken to Jutland, where one of the most northerly Danish ports, Frederikshaven, is situated, and carried across the Skaggerak to southern Norwegian ports. They were soon speeding over at some 3000 men a day; between mid-April and mid-June 42,000 men were shipped over unharmed. From Skagen, even further north, small boats rushed ammunition and other supplies across the water. The total payload of the 270 ships and 100 trawlers, excluding warships, came to 107,581 officers and men, 16,102 horses, 20,339 vehicles and 109,400 tons of supplies. In these operations 21 ships were lost.[23] The contribution of the Luftwaffe was highly significant, especially in the early days. In all, 582 transport planes, in 13,018 missions, carried 29,280 men and 2,376 tons of supplies to Norway.[24]

Norway was now an involuntary member of the Allies against Germany. Her forces were not fully mobilised, but the destruction of the *Blücher* and the delay in taking Oslo had enabled the monarch, King Haakon, and his government to escape northwards, during which flight they avoided capture by German parachute troops. Dr Curt Bräuer, the German minister in Oslo, met the King in Elverum, some 50 miles (80km) from the Swedish frontier, on 10 April by which time Quisling had proclaimed himself Prime Minister in Oslo. King Haakon declined to interfere with the decision-making powers of his existing government, but declared that he would abdicate if they agreed to surrender. They did not. Again they moved, to a village closer to the border called Nybergsund. On the evening of 11 April the Germans attempted to kill the King and his ministers with an air raid, and indeed thought for a while they had succeeded. Their intended victims watched the raid from the woods before moving on again, eventually to take up residence in Tromsö, in the far north. A difficult decision had been taken earlier on 11 April: Major-General Kristian Laake, the 65-year-old Commander-in-Chief of the Norwegian Army was replaced by Colonel Otto Ruge. He took control at 1100 hours and immediately moved his headquarters to Lillehammer, north of the capital on the road to Åndalsnes through the Gulbrandsdal valley, to command the battle to contain the Germans. The rest of the Allies met in conference at 1730 hours in London, the French having flown over for that purpose. The decision was taken to reinstate the Narvik expedition including French forces, and to consider the possibilities of landing to threaten Trondheim from Namsos and Åndalsnes.

The physical characteristics of Norway can be likened to a roughly-carved wooden spoon, bowl side down with the handle to the north. At the south the oval bowl rises to rugged mountains deeply cut by steep-sided glacial valleys. Oslo and Bergen are two-fifths of the way up from the southern tip, east and west respectively. Trondheim marks the join of bowl and handle, with Åndalsnes to the south-west at the head of a long fjord and Namsos on the coast to the north, west of the mountains that separate the main, inland road to the north, to Narvik, from the shore. There are two major routes coming up from Oslo, one along the Gudbrandsdal and the other, branching off to the east at Hamar, south of Lillehammer on Mjøsa lake, to head directly for Trondheim along the Østerdal valley. These were to become key routes for the German advance. The coast itself is a mass of islands, fjords and mountains. In April it is still winter in these latitudes and deep snow covered the terrain. It was a hostile theatre of war for both sides.

The Royal Navy acted swiftly against the German forces in Narvik, attacking on 10 April when two destroyers were sunk and three more damaged at the cost of the loss of two British destroyers. Three days later a more powerful force under Vice-Admiral Whitworth in the battleship HMS *Warspite* smashed the remaining German ships and left the German force under Major-General Eduard Dietl isolated. Hitler became very agitated about this and was in favour of giving Dietl permission to take his soldiers to Sweden and accept internment, but he was eventually dissuaded by his own high command. In Oslo the Germans had, perforce, been standing still as their supply lines recovered from the disastrous start of the operation and manpower built sufficiently to permit the next move. On 12 and 13 April General Falkenhorst gave orders for the occupation of the territory south-east of Oslo, which went smoothly, and the beginning of operations along the valleys north and north-west, Gudbrandsdal and Østerdal to the north, and Hallingdal and Numedal on the west. By the evening of 14 April the valley entrances and the whole of the south-east were secured; supply lines were safe and the essential jumping-off points for an advance were in German hands. Many of the Norwegians facing them had not yet been officially mobilised but were gathering for that purpose. In other cases, the men in a given unit had not trained together and did not even know one another as a result of the cessation of collective training in 1923. The forces north of Kristiansand collapsed in confusion and uncertainty, although a few determined individuals formed impromptu units in the mountains to the north. The Germans were even more flexible in their approach. With their basic plan severely disrupted, they improvised. The forces were carried in 'requisitioned' vehicles, and the depleted divisions (the 196th had two regiments in which losses to submarines had totalled nearly 900 men) made up units on an *ad hoc* basis as circumstances dictated and permitted. As tanks arrived from Denmark they were hurried forward where the danger of using them piecemeal was nullified by the Norwegians' complete lack of either tanks or anti-tank guns.

The problem facing Ruge, now promoted to Major-General, was that his 2nd Division, in the Oslo area, had been only partially mobilised and had already suffered at German hands. All he could do was to delay the enemy advance and wait for the Allies to land significant forces at Trondheim. The Norwegians, none the less, were stubborn in retreat. They held at Strandlykka, on the east shore of Mjøsa where the road enters a defile, from 14 April until, on 17 April, an enemy battalion outflanked them by coming over the ice of the lake from the west. A German parachute company was dropped at Dombås, about halfway between Lillehammer and Trondheim, on 13 April but it was not reinforced and it was obliged to surrender five days later. By 20 April the Germans had advanced some 120 miles (190km) to face Rena in the Østerdal, positions north of Hamar and Gjøvik east and west of Mjøsa and Dokka at the north of Randsfjord. Major-General Moulton observed:

The German advance over this distance in eight days was a feat of nerve, energy and resource, rather than of pitched battle. German disorganisation from sinkings and re-routings was less than that of the Norwegians caught unmobilised; nevertheless, by the ideas of the First World War when the

*machine-gun reigned supreme, it would have been easy for the German advance
to have foundered . . . . That it did not do so was largely due to the fact that the
Germans had room to manoeuvre, but also to the fact that they did manoeuvre
by bold, independent motorised advances, by mutual support of neighbours of a
column held up, and by the rapid deployment of artillery as few, if any, other
European armies would have done in 1940.*[25]

For the German army the easy part was now over. North of the lakes the
roads enter the challenging high country, pushing on up narrow valleys
flanked by snow-covered mountains. Here Norwegian resistance could be
better based, with road blocks covered by flanking fire from the heights. The
German answer was a change of tactics exploiting the lack of artillery on the
other side. Striking forces led by one or two tanks were launched head-on at
the obstructions while mountain troops, skiers, tried to work round the
flanks. The spearheads were organised with engineers immediately behind
the leading tanks, an infantry company with heavy weapons followed by a
platoon of artillery, and reinforcement companies of infantry, engineers and
artillery bringing up the rear. Where they ran into an exceptionally strong
line the Germans would attack the front at a number of points to break it
up and disorganise the defence.[26]

The eagerly-awaited British reinforcements were soon to arrive, but in a
manner and state of readiness for this conflict that was to leave much to be
desired. It had already begun badly with Admiral Pound's unilateral abroga-
tion of the original plans. Now his inability to liaise with the army was to
be matched by the actions of General Lord Ironside, Chief of the Imperial
General Staff. A Military Co-ordination Committee existed which was made
up of the three service ministers with their chiefs-of-staff. It was chaired by
the Prime Minister and six days before the German invasion the First Lord
of the Admiralty, Winston Churchill, had become vice-chairman. It was this
committee that took the decision, in the evening of 9 April, to make Narvik
the main objective and Trondheim the secondary one. Ironside assumed
Major-General P. J. Mackesy would command this new expedition and sent
him to embark with the Scots Guards from Scapa Flow to make a landing
near Narvik; the written orders were not shown to anyone else. Pound,
meanwhile, replaced Admiral Evans with Admiral the Earl of Cork and
Orrery who was given verbal orders by Churchill, Pound and by the committee, and was sent to sail from Rosyth. On 14 April he received a message
from Admiral Whitworth informing him of the vulnerability of the

Germans in Narvik now their ships had been destroyed, and saying, 'I am convinced that Narvik can be taken by direct assault without fear of meeting serious opposition on landing.'[27] Cork naturally decided to take action accordingly, but was over-ruled by the Admiralty. He then joined Mackesy at Harstad where he found the army in some confusion as they attempted to reunite men with their equipment and supplies. Cork favoured immediate action; Mackesy wanted to get his force properly organised first. In Churchill's words, 'A deadlock arose between the military and naval chiefs.'[28]

Meanwhile attention was switching to Trondheim. From the British Legation in Oslo, Mr Foley and a shorthand typist managed to join General Ruge at his headquarters at Øyer, just north of Lillehammer, on 13 April and two days later Lieutenant-Colonel King-Salter, fresh from his post as military attaché in Finland, joined them. They sent London all the information that could be desired about the real situation in Norway and Norwegian needs. In particular, that they were being pushed back along Gudbrandsdal and that, by way of Åndalsnes, a mechanised field regiment, a company of light tanks and three battalions of infantry should be sent. Ironside now came under pressure to change the emphasis of the army's efforts, but that would have been to ignore the fact that forces immediately available were disembarking on the Lofoten Islands.

The intrusion of Operation Hammer, the capture of Trondheim by a landing from Trondheimfjord, into Allied plans for Narvik was a confused business. Ironside recalled a visit by Churchill, together with Vice-Admiral Phillips, Deputy Chief of Naval Staff, at 0200 hours on 14 April. 'Tiny,' Churchill said, 'we are going to the wrong place.'[29] As a result of this and a meeting of the Chiefs of Staff the next morning, the 146th Brigade was diverted from Narvik to Namsos and a naval party was despatched to Åndalsnes. The rest of the plan for Hammer would have sent the 15th Brigade (brought from France) to land east of Trondheim, had the 147th in reserve, ordered the 146th and three battalions of Chasseurs Alpins to advance from Namsos and put the 148th in at Åndalsnes. This would be supported by naval artillery and by aircraft flying from *Ark Royal* and *Glorious*. An exciting scheme! It was never put into action. The Royal Navy had severe misgivings, for the area was well within striking range of the Luftwaffe, and the fates seemed to conspire to eliminate the military commanders appointed. The first, the robustly-named Major-General Hotblack, received his briefing in the Admiralty on 17 April, but was found in the early hours of the following morning unconscious, having suffered a stroke on the Duke of York's Steps. His successor, Brigadier Berney-Ficklin, was briefed, left for Scotland and was seriously injured when his aircraft crashed at Kirkwall on 19 April. The appointment of Major-General Paget coincided with the cancellation of the operation in favour of advances from the distant, flanking landing places. The decision was very much guided by the fear of enemy aircraft and the failure of the plan adopted was from just that cause.

Late on 16 April the heavy cruiser HMS *Suffolk* closed with the Norwegian coast at Stavanger and, as the next day dawned, she opened fire on the airfield at Sola. In some 45 minutes the fuel dumps had been set on fire and other damage had been done, though not enough to cause the Germans to record the incident as significant. As *Suffolk* turned away she received orders to pursue German destroyers reported to be in the area and as a result failed to make contact with the Blenheim fighters sent to provide air cover. At 0815 hours the first attack by the Luftwaffe began. At 1037 hours a Stuka dive-bomber scored a hit on X Turret which started fires and reduced the cruiser's speed from 30 to 18 knots as well as killing 33 of the crew. The attacks continued remorselessly. A third of the 33 missions flown against her in seven hours were by dive-bombers, the rest by high-level aircraft. The *Suffolk*, however, survived, reaching Scapa Flow with her quarter-deck awash on 18 April. Instead of taking this as a demonstration of the limitations of even unresisted bombing of a warship, the Royal Navy formed the view that their ships were dangerously vulnerable.[30]

The attempt against Trondheim therefore depended, initially, on forces landed at Namsos, a small port on the sea, north of the objective and the far side of a hilly peninsula defined on the east by Trondheimfjord, off which Beitstadfjord extends to the north, and Snåsavann lake. Between the last two bodies of water a neck of land at the town of Steinkjer offers access to the north–south road on the eastern side of the obstacle. In short, getting from Namsos to Trondheim is no easy business and the Germans defending their foothold were to be quick to push north to secure the approaches. Beginning on 16 April, the British landed part of the 146th Brigade (half each of 1st/4th Royal Lincolnshire and 1st/4th King's Own Yorkshire Light Infantry) together with, on 19 April, men of 5th Demi-Brigade Chasseurs Alpins at Namsos. They were brought in on destroyers for fear of air attack on their transports, and in the move from transport to warship and thence to shore supplies, ammunition and equipment were lost, forgotten or misdirected. The apparently sensible provision of ample arctic kit added to the confusion of men not trained in its use or familiar with its content. However, by 17 April they had secured Grong, a town on the railway north of Snåsavann and the isthmus at Steinkjer south of the lake. To advance further south without air cover or command of the fjords was unwise and here the Germans met them. They, however, possessed the powers the Allies lacked. On 20 April bombers destroyed Namsos, which was largely built of wood; houses, quays and wharves included. On 21 April a German destroyer succeeded in entering Beitstadfjord from Trondheimfjord, thus turning the Allied flank both with sea-borne fire power and by putting ashore a battalion of mountain troops with light artillery and mortars. The Luftwaffe then bombed Steinkjer. By means of remarkable and stubborn resistance, and by long night marches in thick snow, most of the Allied troops managed to pull back. By 28 April the order to evacuate had been given.

The force landed at Åndalsnes was intended to form the other half of a pincer to squeeze Trondheim, but events to the south changed that. Morgan's 148th Brigade arrived to relieve the vanguard of Navy and Royal Marines on 18 April in a state of disarray caused, like that of the 146th, by being embarked, disembarked and re-embarked as their chiefs in London changed their minds repeatedly. The equipment of 1st/5th Leicestershire and 1st/8th Sherwood Foresters was incomplete and mixed up. Brigadier Morgan sent a company of Sherwoods to Dombås in Gudbrandsdal, where the routes from the south branch, north for Trondheim and west for Åndalsnes, while he made contact with the Norwegians. The situation, they told him, was perilous and without immediate British support they would fail. The terrain was strange to the British and the morale of the Norwegians was low, so Morgan took the difficult decision to split his force and share it with his allies. They would also gain from use of Norwegian communications systems and other equipment they lacked. Unfortunately the decision on how these newcomers should be deployed also passed from Morgan's hands; they were scattered about amongst their allies. Then, as withdrawal again became necessary, reconstituting a coherent force proved to be impossible.

The now familiar story of confrontation and outflanking continued. The Balbergkamp height north of Lillehammer was outflanked while the defensive line formed at Tretten on 23 April was smashed by three tanks against which the British Boyes anti-tank rifles failed. Five tanks had reached Lillehammer the day before, one of which was a Mark IV, heavily armoured enough to be proof against the infantry weapon; perhaps this particular tank was involved.[31] In the confused withdrawal it was not possible, without killing their own men in great numbers, for the engineers to blow the bridge at Tretten. A significant number of British troops were cut off and made prisoner. That same day, in the Østerdal, the arrival of tanks and transport allowed Colonel Hermann Fischer to form a motorised detachment to spearhead the progress in the east. It was able to thrust onwards while the main body was delayed by bridges the German engineers were labouring to repair.[32]

The performance of the 15th Infantry Brigade in the Gudbrandsdal gave some indication of what might have been. The unit came from France, but consisted only of three infantry battalions and none of the divisional troops. That is, they were to leave behind field and anti-tank artillery, light tanks and engineers. They would also leave trucks and bren-gun carriers, the light, tracked vehicles that carried heavier equipment and radio sets. That they were allowed their own anti-tank company with its nine 25mm guns, supplied by the French, was small consolation. Then the paucity of transport obliged them to embark only two of the three battalions in Scotland. A final handicap was being landed in Molde, on the far side of the fjord from Åndalsnes, so that the Royal Navy could complete the operation by night. The newcomers arrived at Molde at 0400 hours on 24 April. At 0430 the next day they were at Kvam, halfway between Lillehammer and Dombås and digging in as best they could in the snow, ice and thawing fields. At 1130 hours the Germans arrived. A battalion commander of the King's Own Yorkshire Light Infantry, Major Cass, described them.

First came three tanks and about 50 lightly equipped infantry. Behind came more infantry on foot, motor-cyclists, machine-guns mounted in side-cars and towed guns. Behind again came motor vehicle after motor vehicle – lorries full of infantry, wireless trucks, tanks, tracked carriers, guns and many others. It was a target that gunners would dream about – three-quarters of a mile [1.2km] of confined road, crammed with troops and vehicles, all clearly visible from the observation post. Just one battery of 25-pounders could have blown the enemy off the road, but the nearest approach to artillery was the little anti-tank guns. All that could be done was to wait until the enemy came within rifle-shot.[33]

The 1st Battalion, Kings Own Yorkshire Light Infantry stayed there all that day and most of the next. They destroyed two enemy tanks and an armoured car before the German artillery took out the anti-tank gun responsible. Then they retreated to Kjørem where 1st York and Lancaster and a company of 1st Green Howards had established a position which held for most of 27 April until the woods caught fire from German shelling and a party of the enemy outflanked them over the mountains on the north, cutting the road behind them for a time. The British supply lines were now in jeopardy. On 26 April the Germans carried out air raids on Molde and Åndalsnes, seriously damaging them. At the same time Group Fischer was threatening their rear with its success in the Østerdal; it was held up by fierce Norwegian resistance at Naaverdalen but again the Luftwaffe intervened and bombed the defenders into withdrawal. At 2330 hours on 30 April the evacuation began at Åndalsnes. It was completed early on 2 May.

The British need for air support was not entirely neglected. On 23 April the aircraft carriers *Ark Royal* and *Glorious* sailed from Scapa Flow. The former had her two Skua squadrons, 800 and 801 while the latter had taken on board 18 Gloster Gladiators of 263 Squadron, Royal Air Force. A reconnaissance by Squadron-Leader Whitney Straight had located a frozen lake, Lesjaskogvann, between Åndalsnes and Dombås, which Norwegian civilians cleared of snow to serve as an airfield. The Gladiators landed there on the evening of 24 April. The support facilities were trivial. During 25 April ten aircraft were destroyed on the ground while the RAF claimed six German aircraft confirmed destroyed and eight others unconfirmed. That evening the surviving four aircraft flew to Åndalsnes where, fuel being exhausted, they were destroyed and their crews evacuated. From *Ark Royal* support was attempted for the 15th Brigade and her Skuas shot down four German aircraft for a loss of two of her own fighters, but, with no communication with the ground, coordination was impossible and the ship stood offshore so far that the usefulness of her obsolete aircraft was compromised.

All this time Major-General Dietl had held out at Narvik while the British commander stiffened his sinews in preparation for an eventual attack. Dietl had established a supply depot on the Swedish frontier, where he took Bjørnfjell on 16 April and a train from Germany arrived there ten days later with medical supplies and personnel, clothing and rations. The Swedes stood firmly against the supply of munitions of war. In addition Dietl had some 2500 German sailors who survived the destruction of the destroyers. The manoeuvres by the Allies and the Germans at Narvik prior to the attack in mid-May which gave the town, for a time, to the former, lie outside the remit of this work. What is significant is the German advance northwards from the Trondheim front and the Allies' attempts to counter it.

As the Allies withdrew from Namsos it had been the intention to leave the Chasseurs Alpins to fight a delaying action on the road northwards. The

French commander, General Audet, insisted that the route was impassable and they left by sea. The Norwegians knew better and both regular and irregular units remained to resist. The land from Trondheim northwards is the 'handle' of the metaphoric spoon, the summit of a range of mountains in the east forming the border with Sweden and the massively indented and island-strewn coast running only about 50 miles (80km) to the west of that. Only a single road of any size, the Arctic Highway, connects, at 100 mile (160km) intervals, Steinkjer with Mosjøen with Røsvik with Narvik with Tromsø. It squeezes past fjords and mountains, over hills and is broken by numerous ferry crossings. A small Chasseurs Alpins unit with a couple of light anti-aircraft guns manned by the British were landed at Mosjøen from a destroyer on 30 April and then replaced with the British 4th and 5th Independent Companies on 8 May.

The Independent Companies harked back to the light infantry of the Peninsular War and to the exploits of T. E. Lawrence in Arabia in the previous war. The idea was nurtured by an engineer, Major Holland, who had been appointed head of GS(R), the general staff research section, later Military Intelligence Research, in 1938. He was joined by Colin Gubbins who wrote of the units whose function they had been investigating that their actions would usually be fought 'at point-blank range as the result of ambush or raid'.[34] Immediately after the German invasion of Norway, in April 1940, the idea was rescued from the contempt in which it had been held for the previous decade and some 3000 volunteers were taken from Territorial regiments to be formed into ten companies to conduct irregular warfare. It was, of course, far too late to create units that would be able to operate efficiently in Norway, but the attempt to do so laid a foundation for the Commando and Chindit units that would follow eventually, and the Auxiliaries that would come into existence in England in the near future. For now they would be pitched against experienced mountain troops formed of men familiar with climbing, skiing and trekking in terrain similar to their own homelands.

Five independent companies forming Scissorforce under the command of Colonel Gubbins were sent to Norway. Their strength was 20 officers and 270 men each, made up of three platoons of three sections together with a fire support unit, an engineer unit and an HQ unit. They had backpacks, snowshoes, Arctic boots, leather jerkins and sheepskin coats. Each company had 30 days' rations and five days' pemmican (dried meat mixed with fat and dried fruit, an invention of the North American Cree tribe). They had

100,000 rounds of small-arms ammunition and £4000 of British and Norwegian currency with which to supplement their supplies.[35] They lacked land transport for their heavier equipment; indeed they had intended to slip ashore from the sea to carry out ambushes and raids, but now had to fight much like conventional infantry.

On 8 May Gubbins's men, 4 and 5 Independent Companies, found the Norwegians holding a position 25 miles (40km) south of Mosjøen but that was lost the next day and they fell back to the blown railway bridge just south of the town. Here 5 Independent Company stood with two companies of the Norwegian forces. They had the advice of Indian Army officers flown home and allocated to them on 4 May, and these men had served in the mountains of the North-West Frontier. The tactics adopted here were those of the Pathans the British had fought for so long. On 10 May, 60 cyclists heading the German advance were ambushed and most of them were killed or wounded. The next step, if the Pathan approach was to be maintained, would be to fall back to another ambush point and kill some more, but the Germans had already trumped the Allied ace. In Operation Wildente two Dornier flying boats landed 40 men near Hemnesberget, a town on the next major complex of fjords some 30 miles (48km) to the north. They were immediately reinforced by 138th Mountain Regiment transported by the Norwegian steamer *Nord Norge* which the Germans had captured at Trondheim. They were resisted by a platoon of 1 Independent Company which was soon forced to withdraw. Although the steamer was soon sunk by British warships the damage was done and the landing was supported by air supply. The front line was now at Mo; the Germans had covered half the ground between Steinkjer and Narvik and two of the Independent Companies were in danger of being cut off. Instead of ignoring this and pursuing guerrilla tactics, Gubbins pulled his Independents out by sea to Bodø, halfway between Hemnesberget and Narvik. Elsewhere, on 10 May 1940, yet greater events were unfolding. The German invasion of the Low Countries and the attack on France began.

The opportunity to wear the Germans down by harassment of their supply lines and the ambushing of their advance formations was not taken. Instead, the line at Mo was to be held. The Scots Guards and four 25-pounders and four anti-aircraft guns arrived by sea on 12 May and the 1st Irish Guards and the 2nd South Wales Borderers were sent to join them by road, once the voyage to Bodø was completed. The voyage was not a success. First, on 14 May, the *Chobry* was bombed and set on fire. Nearly 700 men of the Irish Guards were taken on board the destroyer HMS *Wolverine* in 16 minutes, but the equipment and three tanks of the 3rd Hussars, the only British armour to come near the action, went to the bottom of the sea. The Guards were taken back to Harstad to sort themselves out. Next, on 17 May, the *Effingham*, carrying the South Wales Borderers, ran aground and the troops had to be transferred to small vessels to complete their journey.

The rest of the German advance and Allied retreat followed a fixed pattern. The Allies selected a line between mountains and sea and the Germans outflanked it through the hills or, on occasion, with a water-crossing. The Germans exploited their air power and the Allies were fearful of risking their ships, leaving their soldiers unsupported. Gubbins, now a Brigadier, had been told on 20 May that the British were going to leave Norway, and during the next week he was obliged to sanction retreat again and again.

The details of the evacuation of northern Norway have no place here, except for the loss of *Glorious*. She had brought 46 Squadron, RAF, equipped with Hurricane fighters, on 28 May. The squadron was based at Bardufoss, north of Narvik, halfway to Tromsø. There it joined 263 Squadron, which had Gladiators. During the first week of June the embarkation from Narvik proceeded, with the only real threat, a German air attack, countered with air cover from *Ark Royal* and *Glorious*, the former flying fighter patrols while the latter was ready to take 46 and 263 Squadrons home. On 7 June they left Bardufoss and, the ten Hurricanes under the command of Kenneth Cross performing such a feat for the first time ever, landed on the carrier.[36] Unknown to them, a powerful German naval force was closing with them, though Admiral Wilhelm Marschall was by no means confident in his actions. He had been informed that the British force off Narvik consisted of two battleships, an aircraft carrier, four cruisers and 15 destroyers. In fact there were no battleships, two carriers, three cruisers and ten destroyers. Marschall had two battleships, *Scharnhorst* and *Gneisenau*, the cruiser *Hipper* and four destroyers. He decided to attack transport convoys on 8 June. A number of ships were seen and sunk, and the hospital ship *Atlantis* was left unmolested and, also in accordance with the laws of war, refraining from reporting the presence of German battleships. Scouting aircraft were launched but it was more by luck that, at 1636 hours, the *Scharnhorst's* look-out saw smoke above the horizon. In an action that lasted nearly two hours, *Glorious* and the two destroyers escorting her, *Ardent* and *Acasta* were lost. The destroyers fought doggedly to protect their charge and *Scharnhorst* was hit and crippled by a torpedo. There were 45 survivors of the British man-power of 1474 in those three ships.

The Germans felt entitled to congratulate themselves on their achievement. The supposed dominance of the Royal Navy had been exposed as a myth, the effect of air power had been demonstrated and the ability of their army to fight with speed and flexibility was now undoubted. Most important of all, for the future, was the success of their combined operations in making a seaborne invasion. Poland, after all, had been a relatively simple matter of driving over a frontier but Norway had required coordination of naval, air and land forces over a considerable distance. When the time came would not the English Channel appear trivial?

The invasion of France and the Low Countries

Just as the British were facing decisions that could spell defeat or victory in northern Norway, the Germans launched their great assault on France. It had the appearance of being a replay of 1914 with the major thrust being made in Belgium, but it was a much more brilliant campaign, based on the plan formed by Manstein. In October 1939 Colonel-General Gerd von Rundstedt, in command of Army Group A, had as his Chief-of-Staff Erich von Manstein, to whom he deferred in strategic planning. Neither of them were taken with the original *Fall Gelb* (Case Yellow) proposals which had, indeed, suggested a strike through Belgium, and they sought an alternative.

The Manstein plan – to cut the best mobile French and British troops off from their support and reserves by thrusting through to their south, and then to destroy them – was submitted to Oberkommando der Wehrmacht (OKW) (the Armed Forces High Command) in a memorandum counter-signed by Rundstedt and dated 31 October 1939. It did not mention Sedan or the Ardennes, but did offer the destruction of the enemy. It was not welcome. Oberkommando des Heeres (OKH) (the Army High Command) wanted time to increase the strength of the army after the Polish campaign and was mainly concerned with restraining Hitler from premature action. The meetings and arguments continued. In November Manstein summoned Guderian, now in command of XIX Panzer Corps, to discuss the possibility of passing a suitable force through the Ardennes to cross the river Meuse at Sedan and strike for Amiens. After careful consideration and study, Guderian assured Manstein that it was possible, provided the Panzers were present in sufficient strength; preferably the entire complement of Panzers in the German army.

The next memorandum, of early December, suggested that the principal use of the Germans' Panzer force should be on the Meuse. On 9 January 1940 an aircraft with Major Hellmuth Reinberger aboard blundered into Belgium at Mechelen and papers he was carrying detailing plans for the invasion of Belgium fell into Belgian hands. This confirmed Allied ideas about what would happen and the Dyle-Breda plan for a French and British advance into the Low Countries in case of German attack was adopted. Renewed foul weather delayed *Gelb* again and Hitler, appraised of the hornet's nest stirred up in Belgium and the Netherlands, cancelled *Gelb* for good. A new plan was demanded. The Allies' concept of likely German plans was clear from their troop movements after the Mechelen incident, and Manstein renewed his arguments for his plan. He was promptly posted to a new command as general of an infantry corps. Before he went a war game undertaken on 7 February tested the plan. It stood up well. A day or so later Colonel I. G. Schmundt, Hitler's chief adjutant, happened to visit Rundstedt's headquarters and Manstein had a chance to outline the plan to him. It was the first Hitler's staff had heard of it and the concept matched the Führer's own, but with added precision given by a trained military mind. A meeting between Hitler and Manstein was contrived, ostensibly to mark the occasion of his taking up his new command, and the morning of 17 February was spent in detailed discussion. Hitler then summoned the Commander-in-Chief of the army, Colonel-General Walter von Brauchitsch and Chief-of-Staff General Franz Halder to hear the astounding plan the Führer had devised. It could not, of course, be undertaken before late spring and an early summer campaign would follow. This suited OKH much better, and the army's recovery from the Polish campaign would also be nearly complete. A combination of chance and insight had given Germany a strategy that was to prove decisive.

In Halder's hands, Manstein's plan was taken to its logical conclusion. The operations of Army Group B under Colonel-General Fedor von Bock were to be a lure to draw the French and British north into Belgium. The action would have to be vigorous to be effective, but only three Panzer divisions, of which two would be transferred to Rundstedt as soon as possible, were left to him and his force was, overall, reduced by a third to 29 divisions. In the east, opposite the Maginot Line, Wilhelm Ritter von Leeb's Army Group C with 19 divisions was to make much of itself to keep the French there in force. Meanwhile the 45 divisions of Army Group A, which included seven Panzer divisions, would deliver the major blow. The 'sickle-cut', *sichelschnitt*, would slice the Allies in two.[37]

The attack on the Netherlands was in part conventional; a crossing of the River Maas (Meuse). The only unusual thing about it was the use of special forces, 'Brandenburgers', who by subterfuge took a train through the first and second defence lines as far as Zeeland, south-west of Nijmegen. The unconventional part was an attack behind the last of the Dutch defence lines into the heart of 'Fortress Holland' itself, the intended final redoubt. An airborne force under the command of Lieutenant-General Kurt Student was delivered along an axis from the Moerdijk bridges in the south to Rotterdam, Ockenburg and Ypenburg (south-west and east of The Hague respectively) to Valkenburg, south of Katwijk aan Zee. The Germans put 3500 men of 7th Airborne Division in place by parachute and followed that up with 12,000 men of 22nd Infantry Division in air transports. Their task was to secure the area, and the Dutch Royal Family, while 9th Panzer Division raced westwards to close the gap between the border and the coast. The airborne assault ran into considerable difficulties.

The parachutists were successful at Valkenburg but the Ju 52s bringing the reinforcements bogged down on the grass runway and only the first few could put down. Those following tried to land on the beach and of 26 that succeeded only six managed to take off again while the remainder were shot up by ground troops or by Fokker C-Xs of the Dutch Army Air Force. The parachute troops at Ypenburg and Ockenburg were scattered by anti-aircraft fire and, thus arrayed in small groups, were mopped up by Dutch forces without much trouble. Of the landings north of Rotterdam only the Valkenburg attack enjoyed any success, if being besieged can be so termed. In Rotterdam itself things went a little better in that the southern bank of the river was in German hands by the middle of the day, but attempts to advance across the bridges were bloodily repulsed. South of Rotterdam the landings around Dordrecht and to take the Moerdijk bridges were entirely successful.

Dutch efforts to exploit the river to dislodge Germans in Rotterdam failed entirely. A torpedo boat and a gunboat went into action but had to withdraw when their ammunition was exhausted. The destroyer *Van Galen* was hit by Stuka dive-bombers on the afternoon of 10 May and sank soon after. German efforts to envelop Fortress Holland on more than one front ran into trouble. In the north the attempted advance on Utrecht was checked at Renkum and then at the Grebbeberg where the 207th Division, reinforced by SS Stadarte 'Der Führer', would be held up for three full days.[38] The fortification known as Kornwerderzand at the Wons Position at the north-eastern end of the dyke across the IJsselmeer (or Zuider Zee) was to hold out until the final surrender.[39] It was in the south, where there had been the hope of flooding making the land impassable, that the invaders made ground. The flooding never took place.

The Dutch plans had been disrupted by the need to overcome the air-borne incursion behind their last line of defence, preventing reserves being sent forward to support the sagging front lines. The Grebbeburg, for example, was yielded simply because there were no reserves available to relieve the heroic but exhausted defenders.[40] From the second day onwards the issue became a race by the German tank units to reach Rotterdam in time. On the morning of 14 May the Dutch commander, General Henri G. Winkelman, received a message threatening the bombing of the city and of Utrecht if resistance continued. On the southern outskirts of Rotterdam tanks and infantry were gathering, having succeeded in crossing the Moerdijk by the captured bridges. Messengers went back and forth and Winkelman thought, as did his attackers, that the air raid had been called off. Half of the raiders, perhaps in ignorance of the counter-instruction, per-sisted and the city centre was severely damaged. The surrender was signed the next day.

The defences of Belgium were thought to be formidable. They included the massive fortress of Eban Emael, south of Maastricht near the junction of the Albert Canal and the Maas. Along the canal ran a line of fortifications, all precisely mapped by the Germans by November 1939. Three bridges and the fort were to be seized by glider-borne troops early on 10 May. One of the bridges was blown by the Belgians and another was taken but no further progress was made. However at Veldwezelt Sturmgruppe Stahl (Stormgroup Steel) succeeded and by evening 4 Panzer were able to pass. At the great fortress nine gliders landed, two having been lost on the way, and explosive charges were used against the steel gun turrets. Some defenders were stunned by the concussion and unable to prevent grenades being dropped through the embrasures. Other turrets were brought into effective defensive action which was suppressed by Stuka dive-bombers. Belgian forts further down the line covered the surface of Eban Emael with shelling, but the Germans held on against that and counter-attacks by the Belgian army. During the night, German infantry crossed the canal in rubber boats and brought their flame-throwers into action. The men within were at the end of their strength and the fort was surrendered shortly after noon on 11 May. The crossing of the Maas was secured for Germany.[41]

The Allied reaction was to put Plan D into action. The French rushed north, towards the Netherlands and Breda where they were destined to be halted and turned back, and east, towards Liège, to defend the Gembloux Gap. In the centre the British advanced to the River Dyle. The RAF and French aircraft attempted heroic but largely futile attacks on the German crossing points. On Sunday, 12 May, General René Prioux's Cavalry Corps, comprised of 2nd and 3rd Division Légère Méchanique, each with some 174 tanks at full strength, faced 3rd and 4th Panzer Divisions with, in theory, slightly greater strength. They had to fall back to some extent, but broadly speaking were holding their own on 15 May when news came of the developments to the south. The Germans were across the Meuse at Sedan on 13 May and at Dinant the next day. The order was given to pull out of Belgium.

To the troops of the BEF, who had seen some shelling but little else, the orders came as a shock and to the Belgians it was a thunderbolt. Major Lord Sysonby of 1st/5th The Queen's Royal Regiment, who was in reserve on the Escault near Audenarde, said in a letter:

The day before yesterday [Friday, 17 May] I was told at quarter to six p.m. to start a traffic control post at a crossroads five miles [8km] away ... By the time I got there portions of the Army had started pouring through. I can never describe to you the amazing scenes which took place. The inhabitants of the small village we were in were quite unprepared for this withdrawal and were completely stunned at the news that we were not advancing or even holding our ground ... these wretched people had to leave, carrying everything in one suitcase and leaving their life's work and possessions behind them. All that day, all the next day and all last night the traffic never ceased pouring through.

River by river, from the Dyle to the Senne, from the Senne to the Dendre and from the Dendre to the Escault the British fell back. The bridges were blown as they went. The artillery was in a constant state of redeployment as they, too, withdrew and took up positions to cover their comrades' withdrawal before moving to the rear again themselves. By Tuesday, 21 May the British had taken position on the Escault between Audenarde in the north, through Tournai to Maulde, halfway between Tournai and Valenciennes, there to stand against the Germans with the French First Army to their right and the Belgians to the north. Events elsewhere had already undermined this plan.

The idea that the Ardenne terrain would not permit the passage of armoured forces has been used as an excuse for the lack of foresight of General Maurice Gamelin and his colleagues in the French High Command. That they were taken by surprise by the German attack is certain, but that they believed the Ardennes to be impenetrable to an army is stretching credulity.

The description of the territory as 'impenetrable' has been attributed to Marshal Henri Pétain, who spoke of the Ardennes in March 1934, but went on to add 'provided we make some special dispositions'. In 1938 General G. Prételat was in command of manoeuvres that assumed an attack through the Ardennes of seven German divisions, four motorised infantry and with two tank brigades. The result was a defeat for the defenders of so comprehensive a nature that the wisdom of publishing it was questioned lest morale be damaged. As late as March 1940 a French Deputy (member of Parliament) reported to Gamelin that the defences of Sedan were entirely inadequate. An attempt to increase the fortifications had been started the previous autumn, but the severe winter prevented the pouring of concrete and the delivery of the necessary materials. On 11 April General Charles Huntzinger asked for another four divisions to work on the defences. He was refused. The history is thus not one of ignorance but of negligence.[42]

Through the southern Ardennes, Gruppe von Kleist, under the command of General Ewald von Kleist, had to clear roads and ran into some minor resistance before making impressive progress on the second day, 11 May, of their advance. Further north XV Panzer Corps also found trees felled across the roads, but as the Belgians intended, the area was lightly defended and was intentionally abandoned. Gruppe von Kleist, on the other hand, had a number of encounters with French units, but not enough to prevent General Guderian's XIX Panzer Corps being ready to assault the Meuse crossing point at Sedan on 13 May. On the morning of Monday, 13 May, General Pierre Grandsard, commander of X Corps, the left wing of Huntzinger's 2nd Army, asserted that nothing more would happen while the Germans brought up their heavy artillery and ammunition supplies; a few days' pause was, he thought, inevitable. At 11 a.m. the Luftwaffe started an immense air raid, pounding French fortifications with Stukas, Dorniers and Heinkels. Some 500 sorties were flown. Cowering under this torrent were the reservists of the 55th Infantry Division, one of France's weaker formations. The other division that made up X Corps, the 71st, had been ordered forward during the night but was not yet in position. French artillery fire was limited as there was a fear of running out of ammunition. The Germans were able to push tanks forward to the river and fire on the French pillboxes, many of them unfinished and not even equipped with doors. The 88mm anti-aircraft gun was also able to do substantial harm to French installations. Men crept forward with rubber boats, ready to attempt the crossing. The aerial bombardment culminated in precisely the concentrated dive-bomber attack Guderian wanted. The Germans crossed in assault boats and by the end of the day three pontoon bridges were in place carrying heavy vehicles over the Meuse and 1st and 2nd Panzer Divisions were rolling south.

Downstream, near Dinant, Major-General Erwin Rommel's tanks had advanced close enough to the Meuse to witness the destruction of the bridges by the Belgians. In the early hours of 13 May the 7th Motorcycle Battalion managed to cross the weir and lock at Houx, establishing a bridge-head on the western bank, while to the south assault boats worked under damaging fire to ferry troops over. By the following morning a pontoon bridge at Houx brought tanks over and Rommel was able to win a brisk action against French armour and infantry at Onhaye.

South of Sedan the French caused Guderian's force a few problems, but they opted to base their main defence on the ridge through Stonne. There the Germans fought them, but the principal thrust was turned through ninety degrees, westwards. On 15 May, 1st and 2nd Panzer crossed the Canal des Ardennes and, although held up for some hours by the gallant 3rd Brigade of Spahis, rolled away towards Montcornet. The progress was not unopposed by the Germans themselves. Friday, 17 May, brought a nasty surprise. An order arrived from Panzer Group ordering Guderian to stay where he was and await a visit from General von Kleist. They met at the Soize airstrip at 7 a.m. and Kleist delivered a tirade of condemnation for Guderian's excessive zeal.

The German High Command had always been worried about thrusting too far forward and exposing a vulnerable flank, but so far nothing had happened to reinforce their apprehension and Halder seemed to have joined the Manstein camp wholeheartedly. Hitler, however, was increasingly concerned about the southern flank and went to see Rundstedt, whose Army Group A War Diary reveals the view that:

The extended flank between La Fère and Rethel is too sensitive, especially in the Laon area . . . an open invitation for an enemy attack. . . .

Kleist also had been nervous throughout, and in this atmosphere his apprehensions had gained the upper hand. Guderian responded by offering his resignation. Kleist hestitated, startled, then nodded and told Guderian to hand over to the most senior of his subordinates. Guderian then signalled to Rundstedt his intention of going to Army Group headquarters, but was told to stay where he was and await Colonel-General List, commander of the 12th Army.

List conveyed the order to Guderian that he was not to resign and produced a masterly compromise. Guderian's Corps headquarters was to stay put while the Panzers were authorised to carry out a reconnaissance in force. Guderian wrote:

Then I set the 'reconnaissance in force' in motion. Corps headquarters remained at its old location in Soize; a wire was laid from there to my advanced headquarters, so that I need not communicate with my staff by wireless and my orders could therefore not be monitored by the wireless intercept units of the OKH and the OKW.

Without the knowledge of Kleist or Rundstedt the advance would proceed.

Fear of an attack on their flank was not misplaced, but the French managed to be sure it was mishandled. They put Colonel Charles de Gaulle in command of what was purported to be the 4th Armoured Division. The formation did not exist, and in two days de Gaulle had to cobble together what force he could: 24th and 46th Tank Battalions and 345th Tank Company. With this small strength he attacked Guderian's formation near Montcornet and, without air or artillery support, suffered at the hands of German gunners and Stuka pilots. More than 30 French machines were lost on 17 May, an event apparently too trivial for Guderian to note in his diary. Two days later, at Crécy-sur-Serre, de Gaulle tried again with no greater success. By then Guderian had reached St Quentin.

In the north Rommel was challenged by the French 1st Armoured at Flavion. Rommel wrote of this day:

My intention for the 15th May was to thrust straight through in one stride to our objective, with the 25th Panzer Regiment in the lead and with artillery and, if possible, dive-bomber support. The infantry was to follow up the tank attack, partly on foot and partly lorry-borne. The essential thing, to my mind, was that the artillery should curtain off both flanks of our attack. . . .

A better definition of a sickle-stroke is hard to imagine. When the French fired on Rommel's leading tanks, they took to the woods and kept going west, avoiding towns and villages which might slow the advance. Meanwhile his artillery and infantry engaged the French and kept them so busy that, by late afternoon, they were running out of fuel. By the end of the day the 1st Armoured had only 20 fully operational tanks left. Of the 500 or so German tanks they had faced, about 10 per cent had been knocked out. Rommel wrote:

After a brief engagement with enemy tanks near Flavion, the Panzer Regiment advanced in column through the woods to Philippeville, passing on the way numerous guns and vehicles belonging to a French unit, whose men had tumbled headlong into the woods at the approach of our tanks. . . .

They exchanged fire with the French some three miles north-west of Philippeville and Rommel then turned south to prevent the French getting away in that direction. Rushing around in a great anti-clockwise sweep, the Germans gathered up hundreds of prisoners with little resistance. The shock of their presence was enough. By the evening Rommel was some 7 miles (11km) south-west of Philippeville, on the hills west of Cerfontaine.

Looking back east from the summit of the hill, as night fell, endless pillars of dust could be seen rising as far as the eye could reach – comforting signs that the 7th Panzer Division's move into the conquered territory had begun.[43]

On 16 May Rommel smashed his way through the defences, such as they were, on the French frontier and did not stop even when darkness fell. The next day, Friday, saw him just outside Le Câteau, where the British had forced a check on the German advance in 1914. The last 24 hours had seen him advance more than 30 miles (50km) and he had outrun his supply lines. He busied himself with rounding up French units and bringing up supplies before rounding Cambrai and making for a position south of Arras on 20 May.

Guderian had continued his headlong progress, passing through Péronne and advancing north of the River Somme. The 7th Royal West Kents made Albert difficult to take, but Guderian let 2nd Panzer dispute that town and pressed on to Amiens where 7th Royal Sussex were on the hill south of the town and there 1st Panzer virtually wiped them out. The tanks refuelled from French road-side service stations and hurried on for Abbeville, which they reached by 5 p.m. During the night the Spitta Battalion of 2nd Panzer reached the sea near Noyelles. The Allies were cut in two. The next day, 21 May, there were no orders about which way they should go next, so Guderian

... spent the day visiting Abbeville and our crossings and bridgeheads over the Somme. On the way I asked the men how they had enjoyed the operations up to date. 'Not bad,' said an Austrian of the 2nd Panzer Division, 'but we wasted two whole days.' Unfortunately, he was right.

It was becoming evident to the British that the might of the French, on which so much reliance had been placed, was, if not a fiction, irrelevant given the mismanagement of the campaign by their commanders. The BEF fell back across the Belgian border, fighting as they went. The French, too, offered resistance as the briefly captured and then escaping Earl of Cardigan observed along the banks of the Escault. The presence of graves showed that there had been fighting and Cardigan could imagine small groups of Germans working forward through the bushes before springing a surprise attack.

To me the scattered French graves, encountered everywhere in groups of three or four or half a dozen, seem particularly tragic: here lie men who, making a stand in their own little sector, sacrificed everything to defend their country, while perhaps only a few miles away great gaps had been torn in the line of defence, allowing the tide of the German invasion to flow in behind and around them. They at least, whether aware of the threatening disaster or ignorant of it, held their ground to the last.[44]

As Rommel approached to circle Arras in a clockwise embrace, the British were advancing to protect the town. Major-General Harold Franklin's 'Frankforce' consisted of two tank battalions and three infantry battalions supported by two field artillery batteries and two anti-tank batteries. They ran into Rommel who fought them off but was badly mauled; he reported that five divisions had attacked him. The British, however, could not hold the town and fell back once more.

The possibility of linking up with forces south of the Somme was still entertained by the Allies until 25 May, when the Belgian line broke north-east of Lille and retreat to the coast for however much of an evacuation was possible became mandatory.

The Germans were not themselves as confident as they appeared. Rommel had excused his force's performance against the British tanks by exaggerating their strength. This confirmed German fears about their vulnerable flanks. Guderian wrote:

On 21st of May a noteworthy event occurred to the north of us: English tanks attempted to break through in the direction of Paris. . . . The English did not succeed in breaking through, but they did make a considerable impression on the staff of Panzer Group von Kleist, which suddenly became remarkably nervous.[45]

On Wednesday, 22 May Guderian was on the move again, to the north.

In the afternoon . . . there was fierce fighting at Desvres, Samer and to the south of Boulogne. Our opponents were mostly Frenchmen, but included a number of English and Belgian units and even an occasional Dutchman. Their resistance was broken. But the enemy airforce was very active, bombing us and firing their guns at us too, while we saw little of our Luftwaffe. The bases from which our planes were operating were now a long way away. . . .[46]

The British were also, from the other side of the Channel, flying within the outer area of their radar cover and out of secure airfields in England. In spite of their efforts Guderian's 2nd Panzer entered the outskirts of Boulogne that evening. Guderian now made fresh dispositions.

I decided to move 1st Panzer Division, which was already close to Calais, on to Dunkirk at once, while the 10th Panzer Division, advancing from Doullens through Samer, replaced it in front of Calais. There was no particular urgency about capturing this port.[47]

The danger of Guderian getting up along the Channel coast behind Gort was now severe.

On Friday, 24 May the Panzers were ordered to halt on the line of the River Aa and the Aa Canal. Rommel welcomed the opportunity to rest. Guderian was surprised and annoyed, but back at Army Group A headquarters the situation appeared in a light very different to that prevailing in the front line. On 29 February 1940 a collection of maps and manuals was published in Berlin for the use of the services only. Of this region, Volume I of *Militärgeographische Beschreibung von Frankreich* states that:

In wet weather wide areas become boggy and impassable on foot. Vehicles can in general only move on the roads available which are very numerous and mostly fortified. These and the little railways run throughout on dykes; these form with the numerous, in general not very wide, water ways, canals and ditches a dense mesh of sections suitable for rearguard defence.

The map that accompanies the manual, *Wehrgeologische Übersichtskarte,* comments on the terrain around Dunkirk:

Predominant soil type: peat, groundwater near surface. Passability by traffic and on foot: At all times passable with difficulty. Accessible to infantry in dry season. Obstacles: Soft ground, criss-crossed with many ditches, shallow ground water, can be dug out to form water obstacles. Artillery firing positions: wet, ground not able to take a load. . . . Artillery observation opportunites: flat, low lying, without rises in ground.[48]

The colour-coding matches that of the Nieuport/Dixmude area flooded by the Belgians in 1914 to frustrate the German attempt to envelop Ypres. The land not actually shown as being below sea-level gets a rating only marginally better. This was the official assessment and it was relied upon. To men who had seen the torn landscapes of the previous war the message was obvious and inescapable: this land would be death to tanks with the first drop of rain.

Guderian's memoirs record his anger and frustration, but when the order to move once more came through on Sunday, 26 May, his panzers did not roar forward. His unit's war diary records that he inspected the area on the following Tuesday, after rain had started, and declared that sending his tanks in would involve 'useless sacrifice of our best troops' and that holding their current positions to allow their 18 Army to attack from the east was the wise course of action. His report to Gruppe von Kleist said that the armoured divisions had only half their tanks left and that repairs were urgently needed for operations in the near future. Further he stated that a tank attack in the 'marshy country' recently soaked by rain would be pointless and that infantry were better suited to the terrain.[49] These observations evidently slipped his mind when writing his post-war recollections.

The evacuation of the Allied armies was very much more successful than anyone foresaw. The order to begin Operation Dynamo, as it was called, was given on the evening of 26 May, a week after Vice-Admiral Bertram Ramsay was appointed to make contingency plans for it. He was able to use vessels called in on 14 May to supplement the Royal Navy's Small Vessels Pool and, crucially, 39 additional destroyers to the 17 already under his Dover Command. These extra ships were taken from convoy escort work, and helped the destroyer force transport a third of the 366,162 men eventually brought back to England. The rest were evacuated by the 230 fishing vessels and 203 private boats involved. Calm weather with a good deal of poor visibility aided the operation, but the key factor was the professional ability of the immediate commanders involved. Ramsay was given the essential opportunity to rest by Vice-Admiral Sir James Sommerville's support, Rear-Admiral W. F. Wake-Walker commanded the beach operation and Captain William Tennant, appointed Senior Naval Officer, Dunkirk, at the outset made the vital decision to concentrate on evacuation from the port, rather than the beaches, of Dunkirk.[50]

German attempts to prevent evacuations both here and, in the coming weeks, further west, were poorly coordinated. There was excessive dependence on the Luftwaffe which was frustrated by overcast skies and damaged by RAF operations. During Dynamo 133 German aircraft were destroyed near, or adjacent to, the evacuation area for the loss of 106 RAF machines. German naval intervention was minimal. Nearly 200,000 British troops were brought home.

The fighting in France did not cease with Dunkirk. The majority of the 139,911 Allied forces evacuated, mostly French, shipped back to France by way of Le Havre and Cherbourg immediately to face the Germans south of the Somme.

Orders were given by Hitler on 28 May for the formation of a Panzer Group under the command of Guderian. On 1 June he established his headquarters at Signy-le-Petit, south-west of Charleville where he had been only a short while before, and set about assembling his new command. On Tuesday, 4 June Rommel and 7th Panzer were moving south towards the Somme to take part in the next phase of the conquest of France, *Fall Rot*, Operation Red. The orders for the destruction of the Allies south of the Somme and the Aisne were issued on Friday, 31 May. The west, from the Channel to Reims, would be taken by Army Group B while the east, from Reims to the Maginot Line, was the sector of Army Group A, leaving Army Group C in its former position facing the Maginot Line from the north. Only one fort of that line, at La Ferté, had been attacked and taken by the Germans. The rest would be left to surrender when all else had fallen. The new French Commander-in-Chief, General Maxime Weygand, had 60 divisions with which to face the 143 the Germans devoted to the operation. These had, in part, come from a thinning of the Maginot Line forces as well as what reserves were available, now 15 divisions, ten having been deployed in May, and there were elements of sound fighting forces rescued from Dunkirk.

The tactical approach was changed. Orders were given for selected strong-points to be defended with vigour and even to persist when surrounded. The troops would then break out when the main danger had passed, or the special shock troops being held in reserve would act to relieve them. Unfortunately the organisation of forces in the new formations necessary to realise the scheme demanded time, and that is what the Germans denied Weygand. In the west they were already in possession of bridgeheads at Abbeville, Amiens and Péronne. From the first two towns the two Panzer Divisions of Gruppe Hoth would strike towards the Seine while Gruppe von Kleist from Péronne would go for the Marne. East of Reims, Gruppe Guderian would spearhead the advance. As a preliminary Paris was bombed on 3 June.[51]

The Allied operations south of the Somme were woefully handled by the French commander and by 9 June Rommel's 7th Panzer were on the Seine at Rouen, leaving most of the British 51st (Highland) and 1st Armoured Divisions cut off. An attempt to evacuate them from St-Valery-en-Caux was largely unsuccessful. In the east Guderian's unit sliced through the French defences on 10 June, by-passing General Jean de Lattre de Tassigny's 14th Division's determined stand at Rethel. For the British, in the west, a final evacuation from France was the only course of action left.

General Sir John Dill, who became Chief of the Imperial General Staff in May, sent Lieutenant-General Alan Brooke to France. Brooke had returned from Dunkirk, where he had distinguished himself as the retreat took place, and was now to reconstruct the BEF from troops remaining across the Channel and two divisions from England, the 52nd (Lowland) and the 1st Canadian. He reached Cherbourg on 12 June, the day the 51st (Highland) surrendered to the Germans. He met Weygand two days later and, as part of the French 3rd Army Group, was instructed to retreat on Rennes as part of an admittedly unlikely scheme to set up a redoubt in Brittany. Brooke got in touch with London to say he thought the whole position untenable and that the British should pull out of France at once. Having just sent him there, his masters were not inclined to agree, so Brooke contrived to speak to Churchill himself. The outcome was what he wanted, release from French command and instructions to bring his men home.

From his headquarters at Le Mans, Brooke ordered the immediate re-embarkment of the Canadians from Brest and the 52nd Division were directed to Cherbourg leaving a rearguard at the foot of the Cotentin peninsula to cover their retreat. That left some 7000 Lines of Communication troops at Le Mans, 65,000 at Nantes and 20,000 at Rennes to be sent to appropriate embarkation points.

Then followed the difficult task of disentangling the British from the French without breaching the instruction to cooperate with them.

Fortunately General René Altmayer accepted gracefully that a parting of the ways had come. By the middle of Monday 17 June the British were moving up the Cotentin peninsula, 157th Brigade at Avranches and 3rd Armoured Brigade at St Lô. Lieutenant-General Marshall-Cornwall, whom Brooke had put in command of the troops formerly part of Altmayer's 10th Army, moved into Cherbourg to liaise with the French commander. It was Admiral Abrial, former commander at Dunkirk, once more presiding over a British departure. A defence line was set up through La Haye-du-Puits and Carentin, taking advantage of the marshy ground between them, the Marais de Gorges. The five battalions of French Marines were reinforced by the 5th King's Own Scottish Borderers, some anti-tank guns and scout cars, and a company of Royal Engineers.

Rommel's 7th Panzer was ordered forward once more that same Monday with orders to go for Cherbourg. They turned west near Sées and came across a French column on the march. After a while Rommel himself went forward to investigate.

The French captain declared that Marshal Pétain had made an armistice proposal to Germany and had instructed the French troops to lay down their arms. . . . I then requested the French captain to free the road for our advance and have his column moved off to the fields alongside it and ordered to lay down their arms and fall out. The French captain seemed to hesitate as to whether or not he should do this. Anyway, it took too long to get the French troops into their parking place and so I gave my column orders to move on. We now drove on past the French column, which stood on the road, with its guns and anti-tank guns still limbered up.[52]

The 7th Panzer Division drove on into the night and saw, far in front, the pyre of burning supplies at Lessay brightening the sky with its flames. At midnight they entered La-Haye-du-Puits. They drove on but, soon after, three vehicles went up in flames as they came under fire and, unwilling to put his men at risk, Rommel called a halt. They had, after all, advanced more than 140 miles (225km) that day. Next morning time was spent parleying with the defenders of the roadblock who refused to believe that Pétain had given an order to lay down arms. When Rommel moved in at 8 a.m. to bring the delay to an end the position had been abandoned. On they went, coming under fire a little further on as they made for Barneville. By 12.15 p.m. they were at Les Pieux, some 13 miles (22km) from Cherbourg.

The Kings Own Scottish Borderers (KOSB) had, in the process, been thoroughly outflanked and at 10.15 a.m. Marshall-Cornwall had ordered them to fall back. The Germans were getting too close too fast, and the instructions went out to destroy vehicles. The last of the troops and their commander were on board the SS *Manxman* and putting to sea by 4 p.m. Rommel was, at that moment, congratulating himself on how well things had gone. As soon as the last ship had sailed the French let loose with everything they had got. As his casualties began to mount Rommel pulled back to Sotteville where they discovered the abandoned headquarters of the Cherbourg command, complete with detailed plans of the defences. Thus briefed, the Germans were able to occupy a dominating position west of Cherbourg without firing a shot. On Wednesday, 19 June Cherbourg fell.

At St Nazaire and at Brest the departure of the British was close to panic-stricken. Assuming that the Germans were hard on their heels, orders were given for personnel only to be embarked and for all vehicles to be destroyed. In Brest the 1st Royal Canadian Horse Artillery protested mightily against the destruction of their guns and, as a result of a series of confusing messages, were already well on the way to completing the loading of their weapons when the order not to do so was confirmed. They lost their vehicles, but not the guns. The last ship sailed on Monday, 17 June and the last from St Nazaire the next day. W. Marett of the 1st Ambulance Car Company found himself caught up in the confusion at St Nazaire.

There were thousands of Frogs there, but our unit bypassed all of them (how or why we never found out) and we boarded a collier. With a full-to-overflowing number of troops aboard we pulled away from the dockside. The German fighters were overhead all the time: it was a very anxious period.

As we got into more open water, we were suddenly aware that the sea around us was full of British soldiers crying for help. This was a tragic sight but we could do nothing, and the ship kept sailing on. On reaching England we landed at Falmouth, and found out what had happened at St Nazaire. Just ahead of us the liner Lancastria, *a vessel of 20,000 tons with 5000 men on board, had been bombed and sunk. Upwards of 3000 men perished.*[53]

On 18 June Winston Churchill made a speech in the House of Commons which was later broadcast. He spoke of recent events only briefly, paying tribute to the forces that had resisted the German advance, but he gave his main attention to what he could foresee. He summarised the assets Britain could put in the field, giving, naturally, a somewhat rosy view. He drew attention to 'a very large and powerful military force' which the British had;

some million and a quarter men. He spoke of the Local Defence Volunteers (later named the Home Guard) which numbered another half million, but of whom, he admitted, only a portion were armed. He made encouraging remarks about armies from the Dominions. He made much of the protective ability of the Royal Navy and the high competence of the Royal Air Force, few though their numbers were. He wound up with a rousing, rallying call.

What General Weygand called the Battle of France is over. I expect that the Battle of Britain is about to begin. Upon this battle depends the survival of Christian civilisation. Upon it depends our own British life, and the long continuity of our institutions and our Empire. The whole fury and might of the enemy must very soon be turned upon us. Hitler knows that he will have to break us in this island or lose the war . . . if we fail, then the whole world, including the United States, including all we have known and cared for, will sink into the abyss of a new Dark Age made more sinister, and perhaps more protracted, by the lights of perverted science. Let us therefore brace ourselves to our duties, and so bear ourselves that, if the British Empire and its Commonwealth last for a thousand years, men will still say, "This was their finest hour."

The Battle of France was, indeed, over. On Friday, June 21 Adolf Hitler had the satisfaction of seeing the defeated French present themselves at the railway carriage at Compiègne to acknowledge their defeat.

The British losses were, in spite of Churchill's efforts to cheer his people, considerable. The total manpower loss, that is including people taken prisoner, wounded, dead of accident or disease, missing and killed in action, was some 68,700. Of the 2794 guns taken to France since September 1939, 322 had been brought back. The vehicles sent out numbered 68,618 of which 4739 were retrieved. Thirty per cent of the 109,000 tons of ammunition shipped over was repatriated. Twenty-two tanks were brought home.[54]

Churchill's observation that the Battle of Britain was about to begin was entirely accurate, but fortunately there was a delay. General Erhard Milch, having observed the abandoned equipment and munitions at Dunkirk, advocated an immediate airborne attack on England to secure fighter airfields from which dive-bombers could operate. Göring's response was to declare the idea nonsense.[55] He issued his general order for the campaign against England on 30 June and declared that the initial effort was to be directed against air force and air force support industry targets with weak defences and that civilian casualties were to be avoided. During this phase the facilities in France and the Low Countries would be developed to support more intensive activity. That done, the means of importing supplies and of manufacture were to be hit. The first detailed order from the Luftwaffe Operations Staff was issued on 11 July, the day after the first, exploratory attacks against shipping began. This order dealt only with anti-shipping operations and a small number of land targets in addition. On 20 July Führer Directive No. 16 created four Luftwaffe field marshals and Hermann Göring was given the newly invented rank of *Reichsmarschall*. The real planning then began, a full month after Churchill's speech anticipating the onslaught. The result was Führer Directive No. 17 issued on 1 August which confirmed Göring's original scheme to hit the RAF airfields and supply and support organisation. A further 11 days elapsed before the Luftwaffe went into action with a large-scale attack, what they called *Adlerangriff*, the attack of the eagles. In the meantime a continuous, lower-intensity air war was being fought in which the RAF learned vital lessons. The most important of these was that the V-shaped, close-formation unit of three aircraft doomed them to defeat and the more open four aircraft arrangement, working in pairs giving each other cover, was soon adopted. Another discovery was that the twin-engined German fighter, the Me 110, was too slow and vulnerable to be a danger to RAF Hurricanes or Spitfires.[56]

German plans were, in broad terms, known to the British. The Enigma machine code-breaking activities producing the intelligence known as ULTRA supplied the British commanders with Göring's order of 8 August sending all his Luftflotte, air fleets, into action; an order not immediately carried out because of the weather.

The weather forecast on 12 August indicated clear weather over England for the following day, and that became Eagle Day. Extensive softening-up attacks went ahead immediately and the radar installations at Ventnor on the Isle of Wight were destroyed; a German report stated that there were 'craters in the vicinity of the wireless station masts and the station quarters [were] on fire'.[57] The significance of the station as a long-range radar facility, and the fact that five others had also been hit but remained in operation, appears to have escaped German intelligence.

The weather did not clear as expected and the order to delay the operation was not fully communicated, so three German formations were over England in the morning, of which one, at Eastchurch on the Isle of Sheppy on the south of the Thames estuary, did real damage to a Coastal Command airfield. The main attack took place in the afternoon, when the weather was still not ideal, and Southampton suffered severely. The German claim was of 88 British aircraft destroyed; in fact 15 fighters were lost while the Luftwaffe suffered 39 machines destroyed.

Enigma decrypts provided warning of the attacks of 15 August and it was clear that the intention was to over-stretch the English and to smash the air-fields. The assault was based on the German 5th Airfleet's attempt to lure the RAF northwards by attacking the north-east, thought to be under-defended. It was a fine, warm day and Hawkinge and Lympne in Kent were hit first; Lympne was put out of action for the next two days. Then the massive for-mations were seen approaching the north-east. The radar gave the Operations Room of No. 13 Group a full hour to prepare, but even then the size of the forces facing 72 Squadron's Spitfires over the Farne Islands and 605 Squadron's Hurricanes over Tyneside was a surprise. The raiders lost 16 bombers and seven fighters before turning for home. The loss of so many fighters, about a fifth of its establishment, was to limit it to night operations in the future, for only the clumsy Me 110 fitted with drop tanks had the necessary range to attempt to provide cover for bombers flying from Norway. Its vulnerability was increased by the failure of the drop tank jet-tison mechanism which left them even more encumbered in fights against Spitfires.[58] In the afternoon Kent was again the target and as evening approached the scope of the battle widened to include Surrey and Hampshire. The Lufwaffe made 1786 sorties that day and claimed to have destroyed 99 British aircraft. That the true figure was only 35 is relevant to an objective assessment of the damage inflicted, but not to the German per-ception and thus German decisions. What was announced by Göring at a conference in Germany was that Stuka groups would, from now on, be covered by three fighter groups, one accompanying them into the attack, the second forming a vanguard and the third an umbrella to protect against attack from above.[59] The outcome of this day's fighting has been seen, in retrospect, as a turning point in the battle, but at the time uncertainty dogged all commanders. Air Chief Marshal Sir Hugh Dowding knew the reports reaching him were exaggerated. He later remarked that the successes were over-stated by about 25 per cent, but on 15 August the British claimed 180 victories when the true figure was only 75.[60] Both sides thought they were doing better than, in fact, they were. Given that the German estimate of serviceable British fighters made on 16 August allowed that there were 300, the events of subsequent days must have persuaded them they were close to achieving the domination they sought. In fact the number of fighters available to the British for operations never fell below 700 during August and actually increased by 50 that month.[61] The reserves, however, were fast becoming depleted as losses were made good and during the week of 17 August losses exceeded reserves for the first time; only energetic repair work kept numbers up.

Winston Churchill spoke in the House of Commons on 20 August to give an appraisal of the situation after almost a year of war and outlined the 'cataract of disaster' that had poured upon his country and its allies in the months past before offering words of encouragement and optimism. 'The British nation,' he declared, 'and the British Empire finding themselves alone, stood undismayed against disaster.' The Army had been rebuilt, he claimed, and more than two million men armed with rifles were at the ready. As for the navy, he hoped 'our friends across the ocean will send us a timely reinforcement to bridge the gap between the peace flotillas of 1939 and the war flotillas of 1941'. He then spoke of the war in the air and the work done in keeping machines, new and repaired, flowing to supply the losses, but most memorably he paid tribute to the airmen.

The gratitude of every home . . . goes out to the British airmen who, undaunted by odds, unwearied in their constant challenge and mortal danger, are turning the tide of the world war by their prowess and by their devotion. Never in the field of human conflict was so much owed by so many to so few. All hearts go out to the fighter pilots, whose brilliant actions we see with our own eyes day after day; but we must never forget that all the time, night after night, month after month, our bomber squadrons travel far into Germany. . . . On no part of the Royal Air Force does the weight of the war fall more heavily than on the daylight bombers who will play an invaluable part in the case of invasion . . . .

He then reviewed the contribution of the few allies left, paying tribute to Charles de Gaulle and the small Free French forces, but principally he offered a vision of American support in return for facilities in British bases world-wide. This would mean, he admitted, that the British Empire and the USA would have to be 'somewhat mixed up together in some of their affairs'. He concluded:

For my own part, looking out upon the future, I do not view the process with any misgivings. I could not stop it if I wished; no one can stop it. Like the Mississippi, it just keeps rolling along. Let it roll. Let it roll on full flood, inexorable, irresistible, benignant, to broader lands and better days.[62]

The underlying message was clear: hang on until the Americans come.

For a brief period from 19 to 23 August there was a lull. The weather was cloudy with showers and aircraft depending on the pilot's ability to see, rather than on instruments familiar today, could not operate efficiently. The Germans reassessed their tactics; in spite of their apparent success enough of the RAF survived to jeopardise the intended invasion. Göring ordered an intensification of the fight; ceaseless attacks were to lead to the weakening of the fighter forces and individual aircraft were to attack the aircraft industry and the RAF's ground organisation. In particular, the bases around London were targeted. In the south of England, Saturday, 24 August dawned fine and clear.

The effect of the raid on Manston, in north-eastern Kent, was so severe that it was abandoned except as an emergency landing field. North of the Thames, North Weald, south of Harlow, and Hornchurch, south of Romford, were hit. Portsmouth and Southampton were raided and, unable to navigate to bomb the oil installations at Rochester and Thameshaven, night raiders dropped their loads on the City and East End of London. On 26 August Biggin Hill and Kenley, south of London, were raided and the airfields north of the River Thames were hit again, as was Portsmouth. The decline in successful interceptions led Air Vice-Marshal Sir Keith Park, commanding 11 Group, to instruct formation leaders to radio details of the enemy back to base when they first saw them, thus permitting Operations Rooms to adjust their assessment of the situation. This was known as the 'Tally Ho!' procedure, the phrase being the call sign for the message.

The weather on 28 August was again fine and fair and the airfield raids continued. The stations alongside the Thames Estuary suffered and, that night, Liverpool endured the first of four nights of air raids. For the next week the airfield attacks continued relentlessly. On 30 August Biggin Hill was hit by 1000-pound bombs from low-flying aircraft. The damage was extensive. That night single aircraft struck at fields all round London and formation raids took place in the Midlands and South Wales. Fighter Command's heaviest losses were sustained the next day; 39 fighters shot down and 14 pilots killed, and again the airfields hit.[63] By the end of the first week of September the situation was desperate. While aircraft and pilots were still available, the airfields from which they had to operate were nearing destruction.

Notes and References

1 Guderian, Heinz, *Panzer Leader*, London & New York, Michael Joseph & Dutton, 1952, new edition Da Capo Press 1996, reprinted Penguin, 2000, pp. 73–4.

2 Guderian, Heinz, *Achtung – Panzer!*, London, Cassell, 1999, p. 205.

3 *Ibid.*, p. 206.

4 Maurois, André, *The Battle of France*, London, John Lane The Bodley Head, 1940, pp. 97, 98.

5 Reitz, Deneys, *No Outspan*, London, Faber & Faber, 1943, pp. 244–6.

6 *Ibid.*, p. 247.

7 *Ibid.*, p. 251.

8 *Ibid.*, p. 254.

9 *Ibid.*, pp. 255–6.

10 Moulton, J. L., *The Norwegian Campaign of 1940*, London, Eyre & Spottiswoode, 1966, pp. 52–4.

11 Ziemke, Earl F., *The German Northern Theater of Operations 1940–1945*, Washington, DC, Department of the Army Pamphlet No. 20–271, 1959, reprinted, Uckfield, Naval & Military Press, 2003, p. 36.

12 *The Rise and Fall of the German Air Force*, London, Air Ministry Pamphlet No. 248, 1948, p. 59.

13 Weal, John, *Messerschmitt Bf110* Zerstörer *Aces of World War 2*, Oxford, Osprey, 1999, p. 23.

14 Moulton, p. 66.

15 Churchill, Winston S., *The Second World War, Volume I*, London, Cassell, 1948, p. 446.

16 Ziemke, p. 43.

17 Moulton, p. 100, footnote citing Embry, Sir Basil, *Mission Completed*, London, Methuen, 1957, pp. 126–31.

18 Moulton, p. 101.

19 Churchill, p. 467.

20 Roskill, S. W., *The War at Sea 1939–1945, Volume I*, London, HMSO, 1954, p. 16

21 Ziemke, p. 52.

22 Mondey, David, *British Aircraft of World War II*, London, Hamlyn, 1982, p. 36.

23 Ziemke, p. 55.

24 *Ibid.*, p. 56.

25 Moulton, p. 145.

26 Ziemke, pp. 72–3.

27 Churchill, p. 483.

28 *Ibid.*, p. 484.

29 Macleod, R. and Kelly, D. (eds), *The Ironside Diaries 1937–1940*, London, Constable, 1962, pp. 253–8, cited in Moulton.

30 Moulton, p. 204.

31 *Ibid.*, p. 184.

32 Ziemke, p. 75.

33 Moulton, p. 195, quoting *History of the K.O.Y.L.I.* Vol. V, p. 84.

34 Ladd, James, *Commandos and Rangers of World War II*, London, Macdonald and Jane's, 1978, pp. 16–17.

35 Moulton, pp. 236–7.

36 *The Times*, 23 June 2003, Obituary of Air Chief Marshal Sir Kenneth Cross.

37 Marix Evans, Martin, *The Fall of France*, Oxford, Osprey, 2000, pp. 10–16.

38 Brongers, E. H., *The Battle of the Grebbeberg*, Battlefields Trust Conference paper, 2002.

39 Pallud, Jean Paul, *Blitzkrieg in the West, Then and Now*, London, Battle of Britain Prints International, 1991, pp. 132–3.

40 Doorman, P. L. G., *Military Operations in the Netherlands*, London, Netherlands Government Information Bureau and George Allen & Unwin, 1944, pp. 88–9.

41 Marix Evans, pp. 40–3.

42 *Ibid.*, pp. 48–9.

43 *Ibid.*, pp. 67–9.

44 Cardigan, the Earl of, *I Walked Alone*, London, Routledge & Kegan Paul, 1950.

45 Guderian, *Panzer Leader*, p. 114.

46 *Ibid.*, p. 114.

47 *Ibid.*, p. 116

48 *Militärgeographische Beschreibung von Frankreich, Teil I, Nordost-Frankreich*, Berlin, Generalstab des Heeres Abteilung für Kriegskarten und Vermessungswesen, 1940.

49 Ellis, L. F., *The War in France and Flanders 1939–1940*, London, HMSO, 1953, reprinted Imperial War Museum and Battery Press, Nashville, 1996, p. 208.

50 Brodhurst, Robin, 'The Royal Navy's Role in the Campaign' in Bond, Brian and Taylor, Michael D. (eds), *The Battle of France and Flanders 1940*, Barnsley, Pen & Sword, 2001.

51 Marix Evans, pp. 119–21.

52 Rommel, Erwin, ed. B. H. Liddell Hart, *The Rommel Papers*, London, Collins, 1953, p. 69.

53 Marix Evans, p. 156.

54 Ellis, p. 327.

55 Wood, Derek, with Dempster, Derek, *The Narrow Margin*, London, Hutchinson, 1961, p. 115.

56 Terraine, John, *The Right of the Line*, London, Hodder & Stoughton, 1985, p. 183.

57 Wood, p. 158.

58 Mondey, David, *Axis Aircraft of World War II*, London, Temple Press, 1984, pp. 175–6.

59 Wood, p. 169.

60 Terraine, p. 187.

61 Wood, p. 306.

62 Churchill, Winston S., compiled by Randolph S. Churchill, *Into Battle*, London, Cassell, 1941.

63 Wood, pp. 181–208.

chapter 2

The defence of Britain

Before the war, plans had been made and remade for the defence of Britain. The most significant change since the construction of the system of coastal gun emplacements, mobilisation points and London Defence Positions of the 1890s[1] was the advent of the aircraft. In the inter-war period there was a widespread belief, expressed publicly by the Prime Minister, Stanley Baldwin, that the bomber would always get through. Indeed, the RAF was so confident of this that the principal emphasis was on the development of its strategic bombing ability rather than ground support action in support of the Army which was one of the Lufwaffe's greatest strengths. Home defence was not, however, neglected. In 1936, after the formation of Fighter Command on 6 July under Air Marshall Sir Hugh Dowding, the Air Defence system was overhauled. The previous system had been rational, but demanded more than its component parts could deliver. Early warning had been reliant on sound mirrors, concrete dishes intended to reflect the distant noise of an enemy aircraft to be detected by a microphone. In ideal conditions, which were rare, they worked, picking up an incomer at a range of up to 24km (15 miles)[2] but the increasing speed of aircraft made what warning they could give insufficient.

In January 1935, H. T. Tizard's committee, charged with making a scientific survey of air defence within the Air Ministry, had its first meeting. A note from the Superintendent of the Radio Research Station of the National Physical Laboratory, Robert Watson-Watt, was considered. It proposed investigation of the use of radio wave reflections as a means of detecting aircraft and the committee approved the suggestion immediately. Watson-Watt had considered the matter from another angle in 1932; the way in which aircraft interfered with radio signals and upset broadcasts of radio programmes to the public. He submitted his paper, *Detection and Location of Aircraft by Radio Methods*, to the Ministry on 12 February. There was no equipment to do so as yet, but the short-wave, 10-kilowatt transmitter at Daventry used by the BBC for overseas broadcasts could be used and an improvised receiver could be connected to a cathode ray oscillograph. The experiment to see if it worked took place on 26 February. In a Northamptonshire field west of the A5, Watling Street, south of Weedon on the side-road to Litchborough, a Morris car parked the caravan it was towing and four men made ready to make their observations. A Handley Page Heyford biplane bomber from Farnborough flew up and down a pre-determined course and the signal they hoped for appeared.[3] On 13 May 1935 the 'Ionospheric Research Station' opened at Orfordness in Suffolk and work began on the development of the new system. It was called radio direction finding (RDF) which summoned up the familiar idea of an aircraft navigating by means of detecting a radio beam and explained the eventual building of radio towers. It was in fact a radio detection and ranging, or radar, system.

By August 1940 the radar system in Britain consisted of 51 fixed instal-lations and a number of mobile units as well. The original experiment had used a widespread signal which now was the basis of the 21 Chain Home (CH) stations which were able to detect aircraft at distances of up to 120 miles. Coastal defence research had led to a system that was converted to locate low-flying aircraft. This was installed in 30 locations as Chain Home Low (CHL) which had a range of 50 miles. The Mobile Base (MB) radar, intended to cover damaged CH and for overseas use, had a range of 90 miles. The coverage had gaps only in part of Wales, the Bristol Channel and north-west Scotland. Otherwise radar encircled the island, ready to detect raiders approaching Britain.

Once they had arrived the task passed to the Observer Corps, an organ-isation established in 1925. They were equipped with relatively primitive apparatus: binoculars, a telephone and a pantograph mounted on a circular map table in order to establish the bearing of an aircraft. The observer esti-mated the height of the aircraft, set the reading on the height bar, and then a reading could be taken from the map table (as a numbered square) and the result reported to the plotting room at the observer group centre. Some observer posts used sound plotting which yielded a bearing and direction of flight for the aircraft. From the hundreds of uncomfortable posts, exposed to all weathers, the information flowed through the centres to the RAF, up to a million reports a day, each arriving within 40 seconds of the observation being made.[4]

The communication with, and location of, friendly fighter aircraft was by means of radio modified to transmit signals to permit direction finding (DF). The signal given out could be picked up and the direction from which it was coming determined by listening stations so that the bearings set out on a board crossed at the point of origin. The radio in the aircraft was fitted with a device known as 'Pip-Squeak' which switched on the high frequency (HF) transmitter for 14 seconds in every minute and then the radio reverted to its normal send-and-receive mode. It was possible to switch off Pip-Squeak when necessary.[5]

Fighter Command itself was organised in four groups. The north of England, Scotland and Northern Ireland was covered by 13 Group; central England and East Anglia by 12 Group under the command of Air Vice-Marshal Sir Trafford Leigh-Mallory; the south west by 10 Group; and the south-east, including London and Essex, by 11 Group commanded by Air Vice-Marshal Sir Keith Park from headquarters at RAF Hillingdon at Uxbridge. A group was responsible for the defence of its own area and had its own operations room. Each group was sub-divided into lesser units called sectors based at a main fighter station with its own operations room to which direction-finding stations were linked. From there a number of satellite airfields were controlled. Over them all was the Fighter Command operations room at Bentley Priory near Stanmore in Middlesex. Data were received by operations rooms and displayed on large, horizontal or slightly sloped maps on which markers could be moved about to indicate the presence of enemy and defending aircraft formations. This was supplemented by wall displays constantly updated to provide other, crucial information about the status of the fighter squadrons, the weather, the time and so on. Operations rooms also handled liaison with anti-aircraft and other defence forces.[6] The effective performance of these sophisticated arrangements lay at the heart of the air defence of Britain.

The ground defences became the business of the Home Defence Executive, set up under General Sir Edmund Ironside, Commander-in-Chief Home Forces on 10 May 1940; the day on which the German campaign in the Low Countries and the Ardennes began. The fear was that a combined airborne and seaborne attack would be mounted by Germany and that 5000 paratroops and 20,000 armoured and infantry troops could be landed either in East Anglia, the favourite guess, or on the south coast.[7] As the bulk of the army's transport and armour was in France, a mobile defence was not considered practical and a system of linear defences was devised. On 25 June the plan was approved by the Chiefs of Staff. The essentials were these. Along the coast a defensive crust was to oppose enemy landings while reinforcements were hurried up. Inland the Home Guard, as the Local Defence Volunteers were known from July, was to man road blocks sited at 'nodal points', often semi-fortified villages also known as anti-tank islands, and at favourable locations in the terrain that were hard to by-pass. The heart of the country was protected by the GHQ Line, based on rivers and canals as anti-tank defences and with a great number of concrete defence works, in the process of construction. In July 1940 it ran from Middlesbrough to York and then to the western shores of the Wash, continuing from the south of the Wash through Cambridge to pass east of London towards Maidstone and thence west to Basingstoke before turning north. At Tilehurst, west of Reading, it turned west to run towards Bristol.[8]

The coastal defences included Emergency Coastal Batteries to protect the ports and landing places armed with any sort of gun that could be found. In the main the weapons came from naval vessels scrapped after the previous war; 6 inch (152mm), 5.5 inch (140mm), 4.7 inch (120mm) and 4 inch (102mm) guns. Very little ammunition was available. At Dover, to counter the huge artillery pieces being installed by the Germans near Calais, two 14 inch (356mm) naval guns, named Winnie and Pooh, were brought out of retirement. The beaches were defended with anti-tank obstacles, large concrete blocks, wedge-shaped scaffolding fences twice a man's height and with barbed wire and mines. Pillboxes, small concrete fortlets, provided shelter for small arms and light artillery weapons to cover the landing areas. Behind the beaches, roads were furnished with road blocking apparatus which was sometimes as primitive as a couple of concrete blocks into which a length of rail track could be mounted. Little conical or pyramid-shaped concrete blocks 2 feet (0.6m) high, called pimples, were part of the armoury. Anti-tank devices, walls of concrete with an overhang or steep-sided ditches, were built or dug. The work was done in a great hurry, and even more urgency was brought to bear after the evacuation of Dunkirk, but it was not all systematic or tactically sound. The *War Office Manual of Coast Defence (Provisional)* of 1930 had recommended organising them in groups to create

Figure 2 On the hillside near the Shere to East Clandon road, the track to Hollister Farm is guarded by a pillbox and an anti-tank block which was designed to take one end of an RSJ (rolled steel joist) which would block the advance of a vehicle; part of the GHQ Line

Figure 3 A map showing the principle lengths of coastline protected by 'Emergency Batteries', the main 'GHQ' defence line and local 'stop lines'. (after Andrew Saunders, *Fortress Britain*, p. 216)

Figure 4 A line of anti-tank pimples on the edge of the wood west of Port Lympne Wildlife Park

'defended localities', in 1940 spoken of as nodal points, but local contractors and amateur defenders of England, lacking professional supervision, tended to linear arrangements of defensive works.[9]

In addition to light arms, the Home Guard inland was equipped with other, curious weapons sited to support the intermediate stop-lines and delay any enemy advance. The Petroleum Warfare Department was formed on 9 July and, after the idea of creating walls of fire offshore had foundered on the rock of practicality, it devised the Flame Fougasse. This was a type of mine (the French word *fougasse* means a buried explosive device) made of a mixture of tar, lime and petrol or gasoline. It was contained in a 40-gallon drum and ignited by a small charge which blew steel filings into the cocktail. The mine blew up, spraying a burning, adhesive liquid over anything in its path, tank, truck or person. The mines were usually deployed in groups of four alongside roads passing through cuttings or between high banks. A more complicated idea was to flood a section of road in a defile with petroleum released from pipes and set it on fire with a Molotov Cocktail, a petrol bomb.[10]

Another anti-tank weapon was the Spigot Mortar or Blacker Bombard. This fired an oval bomb 29mm in diameter from a launching tube the rearward extension of which consisted of handles for aiming and a firing

Figure 5 The admirably preserved Spigot Mortar base and pit partly concealed by a garden fence alongside the A3100 north-east of Godalming. The weapon was mounted on the stainless steel pin. The recess in the brickwork served as a magazine for the ammunition

Figure 6 Second World War additions to the Norman castle at Pevensey: above, an observation post and below, two machine-gun emplacements, their embrasures now stopped up

mechanism. The weapon was mounted on a steel pin fixed into the top of a concrete cylinder some 4 feet (1.22m) high and 3 feet (0.9m) in diameter set in a pit. It had a range of about 400 yards (365m).[11]

The most familiar surviving defence structure is the pillbox, an invention of the Russians in the Russo-Japanese War of 1904–5 taken up by the Germans in the First World War and copied by the British. In June, the Directorate of Fortifications and Works at the War Office published designs for about a dozen different sorts of pillbox from which local builders deviated with enterprising individuality, stimulated by local conditions, available materials and whim. Some were disguised as commonplace features of the countryside and representations of things such as shop-fronts were painted on them. They were low masses of thick concrete with walls pierced with loop-holes for rifle, machine-gun or anti-tank gun fire. Ordinary field and garden walls were also prepared as defensive positions by making loop-holes in them.[12] Even the walls of the Norman castle at Pevensey, close to William the Conqueror's landing place, were modified for twentieth-century purposes by building in an observation post and light machine-gun emplacements while the castle itself became a military headquarters once again.

In order to make navigation difficult for an invader the order was given, on 31 May, for all signposts to be taken down, milestones to be removed and street names, village name signs and railway station signs to be taken down or obscured. Steps were also taken to reduce the availability of fuel for vehicles by removing pumps from service stations in all coastal areas and detailed orders were given for the destruction of those that were left, should the occasion arise. For the protection of citizens a Protected Area was delineated and all civilians, save those in essential services, were evacuated. By mid-July some 80,000 people in Kent, about 40 per cent of the population, had left the coastal towns and those who stayed were told that, should an invasion take place, they would have to stay where they were to allow the Army to move freely. Local commanders would have the powers to permit them to go. In East Anglia, still considered a likely landing place, the evacuees numbered 127,000; about 50 per cent of the inhabitants.[13]

The fall of France and the departure for England of the last of the BEF from Marseilles on 20 June[14] changed the circumstances for the defence of Britain. It also brought home General Sir Alan Brooke with first-hand experience of the campaigns before Dunkirk and, afterwards, in Normandy. His return did not bring the unalloyed welcome to which he was entitled, for on reporting at the War Office in London on 20 June he ran into complaints about the stores left behind in Brest. Somewhat testily he wrote in his diaries that the adherence to London's orders would have added to the stores the loss of the Canadian Division, the 52nd Division and all Lines of Communications manpower.[15] Within a week he had been appointed to his old post as Commander-in-Chief of Southern Command. He found a peace-time atmosphere still prevailed and, while he had V Corps, which included a division of the Australian Imperial Force, the 4th, 50th and 48th Divisions and various other units, there was a great deal to be done to put them on a war footing. The Australians, for example, would need a month in Brooke's estimation to get up to combat readiness, which was scarcely surprising given that they were the equivalent to the British Territorial forces in training and experience. At that time, as in the previous war, the Australian regular army was not permitted to serve overseas which is some explanation of the early losses its Imperial Force suffered in both wars.[16] As Brooke toured his command he became more and more angry at the situation he found; although there were men enough, if not in plenty, they were, after ten months of war, virtually untrained. Certain senior officers were found wanting and replaced. The next three weeks passed, for Brooke, in feverish activity making his force ready for the invasion he was certain was coming.

None of the Matilda A12 tanks, the type that had caused Rommel such problems, were brought back from France and for a while the only such tanks in England were those of the 8th Royal Tank Regiment. Of the 50 tanks the battalion had, approximately one third were A12s, the rest being A11s which had exposed tracks and machine-gun armament. Production of more A12s was not swift, in part because the War Office chose this critical moment to insist on design modifications. The 4th Royal Tank Regiment was re-equipped with A12s and was one of the units with a special railway train allocated to it to rush it close to impending action.[17] What could be achieved to increase tank provision was limited by the mismanagement of two decades. As David Fletcher has observed:

By the summer of 1939 there were two types of light tank, five types of cruiser tank and three models of infantry tank either in production or development, not counting designs that would be aborted. These various tanks used six different types of suspension, seven different makes of engine and four different systems of transmission, not to mention tracks and other detail features, all of which demanded different spare parts, different repair skills and even driving techniques. About all they had in common was the two-pounder gun mounted in eight of them, yet not one of them was capable of being improved in this vital respect without taking serious liberties with the basic design ...[18]

The Prime Minister was also on the move. On 2 July he went to look at coastal defences, meeting the commander of the 3rd Division, General Bernard Montgomery. The energetic, waspish general showed Churchill everything he could think of, including an exercise simulating the ejection of Germans from Shoreham airfield. At dinner in Brighton that evening, Montgomery complained that his division, the only fully equipped division in England, he claimed, was allotted a static role. There were, he pointed out, thousands of buses in England. In his memoirs Montgomery wrote: 'I do not know what the War Office thought, but I got my buses.'[19] Unknown to Montgomery, the day after the visit a memorandum from Churchill to Anthony Eden read:

I was disturbed to find the 3rd Division spread along 30 miles of coast, instead of being, as I had imagined, held back concentrated in reserve, ready to move against any serious invasion... the infantry of this division, which is otherwise fully mobile, are not provided with the buses necessary to move them to the point of action.... Considering the great masses of transport, both buses and lorries, which there are in this country, and the large number of drivers brought back from the BEF, it should be possible to remedy these deficiencies at once.[20]

On 19 July, while visiting the Isle of Wight, Brooke received a message to meet the Secretary of State, Anthony Eden, in London that evening. There he was told he was to succeed Ironside the next day. On the afternoon of 20 July he found Ironside had already left, with no handover of the demanding and complicated task; just a note to wish him well and tell him that the Rolls-Royce lent for the use of the C-in-C Home Forces was at his disposal.

In the next two days he made an intensive study of the situation as seen from this new eminence and came to a revised conclusion on the conduct of the island's defence. He wrote:

... much work and energy was being expended on an extensive system of rear defence, comprising anti-tank ditches and pillboxes, running roughly parallel to the coast and situated well inland. This static rear defence did not fall in with my conception of the defence of the country.... To my mind our defence should be of a far more mobile and offensive nature. I visualised a light defence along the beaches, to hamper and delay landings to the maximum, and in the rear highly mobile forces trained to immediate aggressive action intended to concentrate and attack any landings before they had time to become too well established. I was

*also relying on heavy air attacks on the points of landing, and had every
intention of using sprayed mustard gas on the beaches.*[21]

Brooke maintained his high work-rate and energetic travelling. A week after
his promotion he was in Scotland, where he found the 46th and 9th Divisions
woefully untrained but he was cheered by the standard reached by the 5th
Division's 152nd Brigade. In the second week of August he toured Kent and
Sussex where he found matters somewhat more to his liking as well as wit-
nessing experiments in mining roads and in setting them afire with petrol.
As a result of the visit home of General Archibald Wavell from Egypt, three
regiments of tanks left for North Africa, thus weakening Brooke's forces.
Meanwhile Lord Beaverbrook, Minister of Aircraft Production, was creating
a private armoured force to protect his factories. An encouragement was a
meeting on 17 August with a member of the Air Staff, Air Vice-Marshal
William Sholto Douglas, with whom Brooke worked out the details of how
Bomber Command would cooperate in the case of invasion.[22]

The Royal Navy

The relevance of the Royal Navy was limited by the obligation to protect
convoys of merchant ships importing vital supplies, both foodstuffs and
munitions, to Britain. Overall, policy had not changed much since 1914
when the Admiralty declared:

*. . . the principal function of the Grand Fleet appears to be to ensure that the
outer sea communications are unmolested to such a degree as to obviate any risk
of starvation. . . . If this is so we have no right to risk the Grand Fleet in
operations where there are two other lines of defence. . . the whole question of
resisting invasion rests with obtaining the earliest information of the actual
embarkation of the troops.*[23]

The threat to merchant shipping had been much increased, first with the
loss of Norway and the consequently improved access to the North Sea and
the North Atlantic for German surface ships and submarines and, second,
with the loss of France where the availability of Brest and St Nazaire prom-
ised haven for the very largest of German ships. The Royal Navy's concern
was not unfounded. So, just as it had during the Dunkirk evacuation, the
disposition of forces became a painful balancing act. The convoys were as

important for the defence of the country as for the feeding of it. On 3 July, for example, the SS *Britannic* left New York for Liverpool with ten million rounds of rifle ammunition, 50,000 Enfield rifles and 100 75mm field guns.[24] On 10 July Colonel Ian Jacob reported that 250,000 rifles, 77 million rounds of ammunition and more than 300 75mm guns with nearly half a million high explosive (HE) shells had arrived. Three days later the *Western Prince* sailed with another 50,000 rifles, not in convoy but relying on her speed to evade German U-boats.

On 1 July Western Approaches Command had one cruiser and 23 destroyers to protect the vital merchant fleets. Another five destroyers were at Portsmouth and five again at Dover. The Nore Command had three cruisers and seven destroyers at the Humber, nine destroyers at Harwich and a cruiser and three destroyers at Sheerness on the southern side of the Thames. On the Tyne were a cruiser and 12 destroyers of which ten were of the Escort Force. The rest of the Home Fleet, five battleships, three cruisers and nine destroyers, was at Scapa Flow with another two cruisers at Rosyth and the aircraft carrier *Argus* on Iceland escort duties.[25]

Against the Royal Navy three forces had to be evaluated in determining what could be done to protect Britain against invasion. First, in the Dover Straits, the Germans had installed heavy guns which would provide formidable cover for an invasion force. Second, the experience of the Norwegian campaign had illustrated all too graphically, in naval eyes, the power of aircraft; the loss of HMS *Gurkha*, the lucky escape of HMS *Rodney* and the image of HMS *Suffolk* limping homeward, her decks awash, remained bright and terrible. Third, the German navy's strength, both above and below the waves, had to be taken into account. In this last, estimates were quite wrong.[26] It was thought that *Scharnhorst* and *Gneisenau* were fit for sea, though the former was still being repaired after damage suffered off Norway on 8 June, of which the British were unaware, and the latter after damage inflicted by a torpedo from the submarine *Clyde* on 20 June. Both ships were discovered to be in Kiel on 1 August. The two old battleships were also assumed to be serviceable and up to four cruisers as well. In short, there was an erroneous belief that British capital ships could not risk entering the North Sea although the threat of two battleships and five cruisers demanded a countervailing force. A good deal of argument ensued.

To oppose the invasion fleet itself, four destroyer flotillas with cruiser support were proposed. They would be stationed at the Humber, Harwich, Sheerness and either Dover or Portsmouth, indicating the enduring conviction that East Anglia would be a target. On 26 May the Chiefs of Staff stated their conviction that the Navy and Air Force together could prevent an invasion, but went on to say that the crux of the matter was air superiority. On 10 July the Admiralty was pressed on its readiness and gave Mr Churchill to understand that over a thousand small vessels were able to guarantee that some 300 little ships would be on patrol at any one time, though it was later admitted to the Cabinet that as many as 100,000 Germans might be landed in England all the same.[27] The Navy's own estimation of its effectiveness seems to have been fairly low and the disagreement between Admiral of the Fleet Sir Charles Forbes, Commander-in-Chief of the Home Fleet, and the Admiralty over the deployment and use of His Majesty's ships was serious. Forbes's views were not shared by everyone. Admiral the Hon. Sir R. Plunkett-Ernle-Erle-Drax who commanded at the Nore was vigorous in arguments to retain his cruiser force, saying 'to destroy an invading force we need gunfire and plenty of it.'[28] These internal arguments aside, the extent of the cooperation between the Royal Navy and Home Forces was, apparently, woefully limited.

Reinforcement of the forces facing the Low Countries and France took place to the detriment of the cover given to convoys. By 29 July three more destroyers were at Sheerness, nine more at Harwich with another six on their way, and five corvettes as well. The effect was clear to see. The already heavy loss of 288,461 tons of shipping in May rose in the next three months to 585,496 tons, 386,913 tons and 397,229 tons. Forbes was deeply worried and implored the Admiralty to release ships for convoy protection; he was denied.[29] He suggested diverting German strength to Norway by mounting raids on that coast. He was denied again. He warned that a new factor was to be taken into account, the battleship *Bismarck*. She was not, in fact, ready for sea, but Forbes moved a large part of the fleet from Scapa Flow to Rosyth on 13 September to be ready.[30]

Intelligence

As in all warfare, the acquisition of information about the enemy's strength, dispositions and intentions received considerable attention. There had already been some outstanding failures such as the surprise attack on Norway and the complete failure to anticipate German strategy in France. In addition to traditional sources such as individual spies, the ability to read enemy messages, to crack constantly changing codes, was, for most of the time, an asset of British intelligence. In 1919 a Dutch inventor, Mr H. A. Koch, patented a cipher machine, known today as Enigma, which was then marketed by a Berlin engineer, one Arthur Scherbius. The enterprise failed as a commercial undertaking but was acquired by the German Army and Navy in the late 1920s. Their confidence in the security of the codes generated by a machine that was capable of generating hundreds of millions of combinations was misplaced; the limitation of the paucity of letters in the alphabet and the need to spell out numerals were the crucial weaknesses. Polish intelligence obtained machines and was reading some messages as early as 1932, the French six years later and the British, thanks to the Poles who presented them with a machine in July 1939, were placed to decode German signal traffic and develop that ability at the Code and Cypher School at Bletchley Park, near Milton Keynes. The 'product', the intelligence produced, was code-named ULTRA.[31]

On 17 May 1940 the Chiefs of Staff issued a directive ordering the Joint Intelligence Committee (JIC) to take the initiative in telling the Prime Minister, the War Cabinet and the Chiefs of Staff of any new, significant information that came to it. The distribution of this intelligence was refined and more precisely targeted in the following weeks. Intelligence from other sources acquired during the campaign in France demonstrated that ULTRA was reliable. The British could now plan their defence with confidence using the product of the Enigma machines. The Luftwaffe's codes were soon broken, in part because of slipshod signallers who failed to observe the Luftwaffe's own regulations, and the Army codes followed. The German Navy messages remained secret for only a few more weeks.[32]

In spite of this advantage, the British understanding of where the Germans intended to strike remained poor until the end of the summer; at all times it was assumed that sophisticated plans had already been prepared for the conquest of Britain. What the JIC did do was to tighten up the inter-service pooling of intelligence by forming a sub-committee, the Combined Intelligence Committee (CIC), in late May specifically to consider everything bearing on an invasion and, significantly, to mastermind the aerial reconnaissance undertaken by the RAF Coastal Command. By late June the Luftwaffe's build-up and refitting in France and the Low Countries was known and the installation of the heavy guns opposite Dover had been observed, but the possibility of the build-up of an invasion fleet beyond the reach of British reconnaissance in the Baltic Sea was ever-present in the thoughts of the CIC. Consequently, when it considered the report from

Turkey of a conversation in which the German Military Attaché outlined something later recognisable as the actual invasion plan, it merely took note that the Channel might be the place it could happen.[33]

It was at the end of July that information began to build indicating that the south coast, and not the east where the bulk of British forces were still deployed or in reserve, was the German target. On 29 July ULTRA yielded an order to German pilots to abstain from bombing British Channel ports. On 11 August they learned that a number of Luftwaffe units had been placed under a commander prominent in close support of the army in the French campaign. The next day the same commander was allocated 30 men with a perfect knowledge of English. In early September the stationing of dive-bombers near the Straits of Dover and the transfer of level bombers from Norway to France was detected. Reports from the Photographic Reconnaissance Unit from 1 September onwards indicated the increase of barges near Ostend from the 18 seen on 31 August; by 7 September there were 270 of them. Similar increases at Flushing (Vlissingen), Dunkirk and Calais were seen. The work on the gun batteries facing the Straits was speeding up, but still the JIC hesitated; maybe this was for support to an east coast invasion. What was clear was that the danger level was becoming high, an impression reinforced by the capture of four Germans on the south-east coast who admitted that their task was to report on troop formations in the area Oxford/Ipswich/London/Reading, the location of reserves that could oppose landings both in the east and in the south.[34]

Alan Brooke had spent the previous night at the Prime Minister's residence, Chequers and at dinner had defended the British Isles against an invasion masterminded by Churchill. Brooke's diary does not reveal who won. The next entry, for 7 September, includes the words:

All reports look like invasion getting nearer. Ships collecting, dive bombers being concentrated, parachutists captured, also four Dutchmen on the coast. . . . On arriving in office was sent for to attend COS meeting to discuss latest intercepted message concerning plans for putting down fog [smoke-screen]. . . .

At 2007 hours on 7 September the Chiefs of Staff and GHQ Home Forces sent out orders for 'Cromwell', the state of readiness order, 'invasion imminent', for Eastern and Southern Commands. It was widely interpreted as a signal that the invasion had actually begun; church bells were rung and the Home Guard turned out. As a result the action to be taken on this order was clarified, but the incident did no harm in stirring people up and bringing the possibilities more graphically to mind.

The Auxiliary Units

Invisible when the Home Guard responded to Cromwell were the formations created to operate behind enemy lines. Brigadier Colin Gubbins had come back from Norway to find that his Independent Companies were to be reformed into larger units called Commandos. He was given a new job, the creation of an underground army. He came under the control of Military Intelligence (Research) which was the vague title given to the department run by Colonel John Holland who had devised the scheme. Recruiting began at once amongst military units and they sought out men familiar with irregular warfare and those who could operate independently. Civilians were sought as well: teenage Boy Scouts, gamekeepers and the like. In Gubbins's words, men 'who know the forests, the woods, the mines, the old closed shafts, the hills, the moors, the glens – people who know their local stuff'.[35] The range in the end was very wide, both in terms of their calling in civilian life and also in age. Farm labourers and tin miners rubbed shoulders with parsons and doctors while the youngest were still teenagers and the oldest past retirement. They had the appearance of members of the Home Guard, but they never went on the official roll.

The Auxiliaries were trained at a country house near Swindon in Wiltshire where they learned all manner of methods for killing people, with and without armament. For explosives they were among the first to be issued with plastic and they were taught to use sophisticated time pencil detonators. Their weapons were many and unconventional. When American 'Tommy' guns became available, the Auxiliaries were the first to get them. The newly delivered American-manufactured rifles were also issued to them. At Churchill's insistence, every man received a revolver. Care had to be taken in the deployment of these men, for some were averse to destroying features of their home landscape such as ancient bridges. The men of Kent, in particular, were found to be unsuited to serving in their own county and outsiders were brought in. It had been the lack of sufficient ruthlessness that had prevented the sluices being opened in the Netherlands to frustrate the German advance.

There were already a number of 'stay-behind-the-lines' formations in being as a result of local initiatives taken by army commanders. One such was that of Captain Peter Fleming, brother of intelligence officer and later the James Bond author Ian Fleming, reporting to General Andrew Thorne of XII Corps in Kent.[36] He had established himself at 'The Garth' at Bilting close to the main road between Ashford and Canterbury and began laying in supplies of weapons such as bows and steel arrows. With this as his head-quarters and training centre, Fleming set about building a number of hideouts in the region. In these, a small group would be able to survive without any other support. 'Observation units' of this kind were amalga-mated with the Auxiliary forces but by the time this occurred a good deal had already been done. Fleming and his number two, Captain Michael Calvert, distributed explosive-filled milk churns to various trusted people. Buildings attractive as headquarters for the invaders, bridges and other targets were made ready for demolition. Caches of food and medical sup-plies were set up. Weapon stores were established.[37] In this way, small groups of a dozen or so men with one officer, perhaps 20 such units in all, were organised during the summer of 1940.

The functions of the Auxiliary Units were not confined to sabotage and assassination but included gathering information and passing it back to the regular forces. This involved setting up dead-letter drops so that observers could send their messages to their controllers, still behind enemy lines. From there, radio had to be used and the need to improve on amateur oper-ators with detectable transmitting equipment was obvious, but impossible to satisfy in short order. Messages were coded and a 24-hour watch was kept to receive them at the Divisional headquarters. A very few sets were specially created for experimental use in Kent during the summer by the Secret Intelligence Service, but they required special receiving equipment which was likely to be a problem.[38] In essence, the Auxiliary Units would be on their own, out of touch and expendable.

The final days

The evidence that the invasion was near was mounting as the second week of September passed. On 13 September the Royal Navy moved the battle-ships HMS *Nelson* and HMS *Hood* to Rosyth near Edinburgh to secure the North Sea while HMS *Revenge* was sent to Plymouth. Nineteen squadrons of Coastal Command were now patrolling offshore to observe the first signs of the Germans, but the bulk of their activity was off the east coast. The English Channel was patrolled at dusk with 'Moon 1' operating mid-channel north of Le Havre and Dieppe, 'Moon 2' north of Cherbourg and 'Moon 3' south of Plymouth. The coast between Dieppe and Dunkirk was overflown by 'Dundee' once every 24 hours as was the Normandy coast by 'Hatch' and above the Belgian and Dutch coasts 'Hookos' flew after dusk and before dawn, but continuously in moonlight.[39] Aggressive action against the gathering fleets of barges could now begin. During the nights of 5 and 6 September Blenheim medium bombers began the campaign and by 13 September 91 sorties were flown by Bomber Command against the ports in which the invasion force was gathering. Eighty-four barges were claimed sunk at Dunkirk on 17 September and two nights later the total destroyed since the previous fortnight reached the 200 mark. The Royal Navy joined in with an attack by the 2nd Cruiser Squadron on 8 September, but reported no ships at Calais and the next night the 21st Flotilla's destroyers confirmed this, adding that very few were to be seen at Boulogne either.[40]

General Alan Brooke was maintaining his touring programme and, though still deeply concerned that he lacked sufficient strength to throw the Germans back into the sea, was becoming a little more approving of what he saw. On 12 September he joined the Prime Minister on a visit to Shorncliffe, near Folkestone, to inspect the defence of the Narrows, the Straits of Dover. They examined 9.2 inch railway guns, coast guns and the defences as far as Dungeness before turning back to Dover and going north to Ramsgate. Brooke's customary criticisms are absent from his diary entry and, instead, he comments on the enthusiasm with which Churchill was received. His apprehensions are expressed openly on 14 September.

A quieter night on the whole, but plenty of AA fire. Went to see the 3rd Independent Brigade commanded by Smyth. Got back to the Office about 5pm. Ominous quiet! German shipping reserves greatly reduced and air action too. Have the Germans completed their preparations for invasion? Are they giving their air force a last brush and wash up? Will he start tomorrow, or is it all a bluff to pin troops down in this country while he prepares to help Italy to invade Egypt etc??

The next day he wrote:

The suspense of waiting is very trying especially when one is familiar with the weakness of our defence! Our exposed coastline is just twice the length of the front the French were holding in France with about 80 divisions and a Maginot Line! Here we have 22 divisions of which only about half can be looked upon as in any way fit for any form of mobile operation! Thank God the spirit is now good. . . .

Invasion!

On 16 September the Germans, apparently, sprang a surprise. A great strike was mounted against the north-east coast, far from the forces tense with anticipation in Kent and Sussex. The German Operation *Herbstreise*, Autumn Journey, was, in fact, a plan with twin objectives. In the main it was a fake invasion of the British east coast between Edinburgh and Scarborough, but a secondary purpose was to release German surface vessels into the North Atlantic. It had been preceded by two other feints, manifested in radio traffic of increased density and observable gatherings of troops, in the Netherlands and intended to reinforce the idea of an attack on East Anglia. Autumn Journey went a great deal further. The German heavy cruiser *Hipper* with a light cruiser and two destroyers had surprised the British Northern Patrol in the Denmark Straits, the area between Iceland and the Faroes, north-west of the Shetland Islands. At the same time the fake invasion fleet set sail from Norway.

The fleet was composed of four convoys. Convoy I was made up of the steamers *Stettiner Greif, Dr Heinrich Wiegand* and *Pommern* escorted by two vessels from 17th Anti-submarine Flotilla, two from 11th Minesweeper Flotilla and two other vessels. The steamers had actually taken on board troops of the 69th Infantry Division in Bergen. Convoy II from Stavanger embarked the 24th Infantry Division on the *Steinburg, Bugsee, Ilse LM Russ* and the *Flottbeck*. They were escorted by eight ships from 17th Anti-submarine, 11th Minesweeper, 11th patrol and 7th Torpedo Flotillas. Convoy III was to carry 214th Infantry Division in *Iller, Sabine, Howaldt* and *Lumme* guarded by two boats of 17th Anti-submarine Flotilla and four superannuated torpedo boats. The most impressive of all was Convoy IV with the four, fast steamers *Europa, Bremen, Potsdam* and *Gneisenau* of which the last two were actually loaded with troops at Hamburg. These groups put to sea in the early evening of 16 September. Within a few hours they had disembarked all the troops, Convoy I at sea into six boats of 55th Flotilla, Convoy II at Haugesund, Convoy III at Kristiansand and Convoy IV at Cuxhaven.

Preceding these four flotillas was a cruiser group comprised of the cruiser *Nürnberg*, the light cruiser *Köln*, the gunnery training ship *Bremse*, three fleet escorts and two torpedo boats. The morning of 17 September saw these forces sailing west and south-west as if for north-east England and southern Scotland and further north three trawlers were reporting the movements of large troopships. A captured British aircraft transmitter was also pressed into service to send fictitious reports of a massive fleet.

Although in great doubt about the reality of this threat, the Royal Navy had no alternative but to react. The action in the Denmark Straits was real enough and ships were sent from Scapa Flow to reinforce the patrols in place. From Rosyth the Royal Navy sent, at Admiral Forbes's orders, a task force to attack the oncoming convoys. This was more to his taste than sitting and waiting. He expressed himself strongly:

. . . the Navy should be freed to carry out its proper function – offensively against the enemy and in defence of our trade – and not tied down to provide passive defence to our country. . . .[41]

At the same time, it was feared that the action in the Denmark Straits was an indication of a breakout by a substantial force into the North Atlantic, additionally fuelled by German disinformation about a possible strike, perhaps by *Bismarck*, against Madeira, the Canary Islands or the Azores and Cap Verde.[42] The Northern Patrol was reinforced and the capital ships were made ready for the defence of the Mediterranean approaches. Forbes was not to be dissuaded from his view that the defence of the kingdom was a matter for the Army and the Air Force; the destroyers already deployed at Harwich, Sheerness, Portsmouth and Plymouth were more than enough. The Dover Flotilla had been sent westwards on the entirely reasonable grounds that they were excessively exposed to air attack in port.

As Tuesday, 17 September drew on the opposing forces closed in the North Sea. The RAF and the Fleet Air Arm attacked the Germans, the former with Blenheims with fighter cover and also giving fighter escorts to the few remaining Blackburn Skua dive-bombers of 800 and 803 Squadrons. They claimed three ships were hit. Then it grew dark and, abruptly, at about 2100 hours, the German convoys scattered and ran for Norway, there to merge with coastal shipping. The entire activity had been a deception.

Keeping cool

With the withdrawal of *Herbstreise* came no lessening of tension. Among the population of Britain the mood was less of apprehension that the enemy might come than of a wish that the waiting would be over and done with. It was assumed that England would be next on Hitler's list of targets. Among the senior command the question was more precise. If the Germans did not launch their attack in the next four weeks or so the weather would prevent the attempt being made in 1940. Brooke was keeping a careful eye on the weather. On 18 September he remarked, 'Wind has dropped and weather unfortunately finer.' On 20 September, 'weather is improving!'

Brooke's forces waited and trained, watching and listening for the German attack and sheltering meanwhile from the Luftwaffe, while cheering on the RAF. At Dover the 1st (London) Division stood. To their right, on the Medway, were the New Zealanders and south of them, covering the coast, the 45th Division. The 29th Brigade was north of Eastbourne and 1st Independent Brigade north of Worthing. The 4th Division was north of Chichester Harbour and to the rear of these, around Guildford, the reserves consisting of the 1st Canadian Division, 1st Armoured Division and 1st Army Tank Brigade, all these of VII Corps. To the west, V Corps had the Australians and the 42nd Division, part of GHQ Reserve, south-west of London with the 3rd Division and 21st Tank Brigade further west. North of the capital the 43rd Division, 2nd Armoured Division and 21st Brigade were in reserve. There were, as Brooke said, more, but these were to be the forces with which he would meet and defeat Operation Sealion.[43]

Notes and References

1 Saunders, Andrew, *Fortress Britain*, Liphook, Beaufort Publishing, 1989, p. 190 *et seq.*

2 Lowry, Bernard (ed.), *20th Century Defences in Britain*, York, British Council for Archaeology, 1995, p. 36.

3 Wood, Derek, with Dempster, Derek, *The Narrow Margin*, London, Hutchinson, 1961, p. 56.

4 Wood, pp. 69–71.

5 *Ibid.*, p. 82.

6 For detailed information see Wood, Chapters 6 to 10.

7 Collier, Basil, *The Defence of the United Kingdom*, London, HMSO, 1957, p. 123.

8 Wills, Henry, *Pillboxes: A Study of UK Defences 1940*, London, Leo Cooper, 1985, p. 11.

9 Saunders, p. 216.

10 Fleming, Peter, *Invasion 1940*, London, Rupert Hart-Davis, 1957, pp. 208–9.

11 Lowry, pp. 87–91.

12 *Ibid.*, pp. 79–84.

13 Collier, p. 144.

14 Marix Evans, Martin, *The Fall of France*, Oxford, Osprey, 2000, pp. 155–6.

15 Alanbrooke, Field Marshal Lord, *War Diaries 1939–1945*, London, Weidenfeld & Nicolson, 2001, p. 88.

16 Cape, Major-General T. F., in conversation with author, Canberra, July 2002.

17 Fletcher, David, *Matilda Infantry Tank 1938–1945*, London, Osprey, 1991, pp. 9–14.

18 Fletcher, David, *Mechanised Force*, London, HMSO, 1991, p. 127.

19 Gilbert, Martin, *Finest Hour*, London, Heinemann, 1983, p. 625.

20 *Ibid.*, p. 624.

21 Alanbrooke, p. 94.

22 *Ibid.*, p. 100.

23 Roskill, S. W., *The War at Sea 1939–1945*, London, HMSO, 1954, p. 248.

24 Gilbert, p. 626.

25 Collier, p. 440.

26 Roskill, p. 249.

27 *Ibid.*, p. 251.

28 *Ibid.*, p. 258.

29 *Ibid.*, p. 253.

30 *Ibid.*, p. 257.

31 Dear, I. C. B. and Foot, M. R. D. (eds), *The Oxford Companion to World War II*, Oxford, OUP, 2001, pp. 265, 910.

32 Hinsley, F. H., *et al.*, *British Intelligence in the Second World War*, *Vol. I*, London, HMSO, 1979, pp. 160–4.

33 Fleming, p. 172.

34 Hinsley, pp. 183–4.

35 Lampe, David, *The Last Ditch*, London, Cassell, 1968, p. 68.

36 Warwicker, John (ed.), *With Britain in Mortal Danger*, Bristol, Cerebus, 2002, p. 1.

37 Lampe, p. 83.

38 Warwicker, p. 180.

39 Collier, Map 19, facing p. 223.

40 Collier, pp. 224–6.

41 Actually written 28 September. Roskill, S. W., *The War at Sea 1939–1945*, London, HMSO, 1954, p. 257.

42 Warlimont, Walter, *Inside Hitler's Headquarters 1939–45*, London, Weidenfeld & Nicolson, 1964, p. 110.

43 Collier, Map 17, p. 217.

chapter 3

Planning Sealion

The British were under the impression that the Germans had created a master plan for the conquest of Western Europe, including the British Isles, before September 1939 and the invasion of Poland. Nothing could be further from the truth. The campaign in the Low Countries and in France that unfolded from 10 May 1940 onwards was intended to conclude with the defeat of the Allies at the Channel when, sliced in two by the Panzer Divisions, they would submit. France eventually did so, but the British scurried away to their island and plans for what to do next were vague.

Thought had been given to the possibilities after a victory on the mainland of Europe as long ago as November 1939, but it was not the OKW, the supreme command of the armed forces, the Army or Adolf Hitler himself that initiated the process, but the German Navy. One possibility was blockade, a denial of necessary supplies to Britain. If the Führer selected this option the duty would fall on the Navy, but if the alternative of invading Britain was picked no less a task would be visited on the Navy. Grand Admiral Erich Raeder wanted to be prepared, and on 15 November he set up a unit under Chief of Staff Vice Admiral Otto Schniewind to examine the problem. Rear Admiral Kurt Fricke and Captain Hans Jurgen Reinicke then spent five days on the task.[1] The result was 'Study Red', a paper of just over a dozen pages which looked at a landing on a 60-mile (100km) front west of the Isle of Wight. The area was selected because of the port facilities that could be acquired and the practical aspects of transporting the invasion force received little consideration. They concentrated on the dangers attending a voyage from German ports to the objective; the needs to suppress both Royal Navy and Royal Air Force intervention. Four requirements thus emerged:

- that the Royal Navy be kept at a distance or that it should be destroyed if it approached;
- the Royal Air Force had to be destroyed;
- the British coast defences had to be destroyed;
- British submarines had to be kept away.

If all this could be achieved, an invasion seemed possible. It was scarcely a profound analysis of the idea; indeed, it is surprising that something so trivial was accorded any respect at all. The Channel ports were rejected as starting points on the grounds of being too vulnerable to attack by the British and the whole strategy was for a long-distance armada emanating from German home waters. It was clearly a work conceived to support the favoured approach of economic blockade to be set out in a paper that was to become the Führer Directive No. 9 of 29 November.[2] It was, nevertheless, circulated to OKW and to the Army High Command, OKH.

To those who recall the outstanding achievement of Operation Overlord, the invasion of Normandy in 1944, or the yet more amazing Falklands War when a seaborne force operated successfully in a theatre thousands of miles from home, the challenge facing the German staff may be difficult to picture. In 1940 only two opposed invasions had taken place in living memory: Norway and Gallipoli. The former had been against a weak adversary close to the mainland while the latter had not been a success. The new element in the equation was air power. In the case of Study Red the air power of the defenders was given pride of place. By the summer of 1940 the view taken by the Army was different; it saw the Norwegian campaign as being similar to a large-scale river crossing and it had just carried out another crossing, at Sedan, admittedly on a smaller scale but with signal success in terms of the use of air power.

In December 1939 Colonel Heinrich von Stülpnagel, head of Army Operations Section in OKH had circulated a memorandum requesting assistance in an examination of landing possibilities in England. The study was called *Nordwest* and Major Helmuth Steiff was to coordinate it. Steiff was the most junior officer to whom such a task could be given and the whole process, in the opinion of the American scholar Rear Admiral Walter Ansel, demonstrated that the Army was attempting to evade the serious examination of the idea.[3] The document that emanated from the Army proposed landing on the east coast, and when the Navy had closed the Straits of Dover, held off the Royal Navy, cleared the mines and provided landing craft, it would then give covering fire for the landings themselves. The Navy responded by sending a copy of Study Red with covering comments pointing out that it would take a year to get a landing fleet together and emphasising the vastly superior power of the Royal Navy. The Navy's memorandum listed ports for which detailed data had to be obtained and went on to say:

Apart from the possibilities for landing at the ports named [above], a landing on the open coast has to be considered. . . . The problems are chiefly of a nautical nature, since wind and swell make unloading difficult or impossible. Furthermore, the depth of water makes it necessary to unload troops and equipment, including motorised weapons, in special boats or barges which have to be . . . brought with the fleet. Even in good weather, this kind of transshipment would prove very time-consuming. This in turn will reduce the element of surprise and involve a higher threat to the fleet lying at anchor for a lengthy period. Furthermore this section of the English coast is poorly provided with protected bays and the depth of water is so shallow that transport vessels of any great draught will have to anchor some distance offshore.

Amongst the conclusions were that the creation of a bridgehead by paratroops seemed indispensable, that cutting off supplies to Britain and attacking her ports to that end was more important than preserving ports for an invasion and that, should the western front come to a stalemate, an invasion might offer a route to forcing Britain to sue for peace.[4] The Luftwaffe commander, Field Marshal Hermann Göring, threw the idea out in a single-page letter, finishing with the observation that landings could only take place if England was already defeated. This mass of conflicting material was afterwards called Study *Nordwest*, though it was not in fact a single, coherent document. For the time being the matter rested there and the Germans concentrated on preparing for conquest on the mainland of Europe.

With the fall of France and the presence of the Germans all along the Channel coast, two courses of action were possible against the British: to starve them out or to invade them. Admiral Raeder feared that the second of these options would be revived and met Hitler on 21 May 1940 to explain why the difficulties were so great. The Channel was, he argued, bedevilled with currents and sandbanks and the coast beyond bastioned with great cliffs. The Royal Navy was immensely strong and, finally, the RAF would have to be entirely suppressed if an invasion fleet was to avoid being cut to ribbons. Hitler made no comment and Raeder continued to worry. Admiral Fricke made a fresh examination of the matter in *Studie England* which took account of such matters as tides and weather and the new circumstances of their presence on the Channel. The south coast of England was designated their target and plans sketched for blocking the Channel with minefields and establishing air supremacy. On 31 May investigations of requirements for a landing fleet were put in hand and practical considerations of how to close the Straits of Dover were initiated; all without directives from higher command. The Navy was not alone in thinking about England. Colonel Walter Warlimont, deputy chief of the Armed Forces (*Wehrmacht*) operations staff heading Section L (*Landesverteidgung*, National Defence), recalled that as the siege option was being followed, orders had been drafted in June to reduce the German Army's strength to 120 divisions, freeing men for the work against England by the other services.[5] Regarding this as unsatisfactory, Warlimont and his colleagues of Section L decided to take the initiative and put forward an alternative future strategy. The draft proposals that resulted for attacking England did not find favour with General Alfried Jodl, Chief of Staff of the Armed Forces High Command; it emerged that feelers had been put out to the British offering peace terms and the time was not right. None the less an order of 28 June was issued to information media to spread the misleading word that Ireland was the place the Germans would go for next. Jodl privately pressed his own views on Hitler suggesting that, as Britain was clearly on her last legs, the Luftwaffe should strive for air superiority and also carry out terror strikes on towns, the seaborne supplies should be cut off and invasion should be the final act when resistance had become impossible; maybe as soon as late August.

The crucial development in the planning took place in a remarkable exchange of information between the Army and the Navy. At the end of June General Franz Halder, Chief of the Army General Staff, was in Berlin for private, family reasons and took the opportunity to meet Admiral Schniewind, his opposite number in the Navy. The soldier had the land forces needed waiting on the French coast and the sailor was open-handed in supplying the product of his own studies of how to deliver Halder's forces to their objective. They shared information on the best ports of departure and the most favoured landing places. Sea conditions, beach conformations and the state of moon and tide were examined. It became clear to Halder that the opportunities for landings fell either in mid-August, in later September or, and this was very close to the end of the suitable weather, mid-October. The Army plans, hitherto omitting the naval view, were now much enhanced.[6] Admiral Raeder maintained his opposition and at a meeting on 11 July he rehearsed his arguments yet again. Hitler appeared to agree, which is why his next decision was a shock.

Meanwhile, Jodl's thinking was summarised in his memorandum of 12 July.

1) General

   The landing is difficult.

   Reasons:

   a) *Britain has command of the sea. Therefore a landing is only possible on the south Channel coast, where we can make up for a lack of sea-power by domination in the air, and where the sea-crossing is short.*

   b) *Recognising this situation Britain has grouped the bulk of its land forces in such a way that they can be thrown against the German troops in a short time.*

   c) *The preparation of shipping capacity in northern French ports is visible to the enemy. Therefore a strategic surprise will not be achieved.*

   Therefore the landing must take the form of an opposed river-crossing on a broad front, with the Luftwaffe taking the role of artillery. The first wave of troops must be very strong and, instead of building a bridge, a fully secured sea transport lane must be created in the Straits of Dover.

2) Organisation of command and preparations.

   Overall command is in the hands of the Führer.

   Army, Navy and Luftwaffe under their C-in-Cs. The C-in-C Army will presumably assign one army group to the complete operation on the British mainland, and in conjunction with C-in-C Navy will arrange for further units to be brought over and supplied, as required.

3) Preparations

   ... It will be necessary to land fighting troops of seven divisions at seven different points between Dover and Bournemouth, along with the necessary flak artillery, to protect the beaches, as well as initial supplies of ammunition, food and fuel....

*It is essential that the Navy is in a position to lay and guard a dense barrier
of mines on the left flank between Portland and Alderney (100km) and on
the right flank between Calais and Ramsgate (50km). Regardless of this
barrier on the right flank, it will be possible, if need be, to exploit Dunkirk
and Ostend as ports of embarkation as well....[7]*

Jodl was clearly substantially behind Halder in his appreciation of what was
required.

On 13 July Halder and his commanding officer Field Marshal Walter von
Brauchitsch arrived to meet Hitler equipped with detailed invasion plans.
They had to listen to a long, wide-ranging talk from Hitler before they could
get a word in, but the theme kept reverting to England; why was she
unwilling to make peace? Halder noted that the fall of the British Empire
was not what the Führer wanted, for the ruins would be occupied by Japan
and the USA without benefit to Germany. Finally the latest Army plan was
presented and, surprising casually, accepted. On 16 July Führer Directive No.
16 was signed, ordering preparations to commence for the operation, now
called Sealion. The text included the explanation that, as England was not
prepared to make peace, she had to be eliminated as a base for operations
against Germany and the preparation was to be completed by mid-August.

The reactions in Army and Navy High Commands were very different. In
the former all was positive bustle, in the latter dismay. The order was clearly
based on the Army's draft and remained a massive river crossing in concept;
considerable work had to be done to realise the Führer's plan.

Intelligence

The plans for invasion depended, naturally, on the information available to
the Germans. Certain examples of their knowledge survive in the shape of
maps and handbooks and there are records of the assessments they made of
the British order of battle. It is clear, however, that they lacked any significant network of spies or agents, contrary to popular British belief at the
time.

A significant source of information was the British press from which
photographs had been chosen, supplemented by British maps and picture
postcards. On 15 August 1940 the German Army's Berlin-based publishing
operation issued *Militärgeographishche Angaben über England: Südküste*, a
volume of maps and photographs describing the south coast from the Scilly

Figure 7 A photograph of the seafront at Hastings in the holiday season was among the illustrations of the German handbook to the South Coast of England

Isles to Margate, to be followed on 20 August by *Ostküste*, Margate to the Humber. The book also contained a geological map with a classification of land characteristics, such as suitability for tracked vehicles, aircraft landings, providing building materials and yielding drinking water. The local maps were reprinted from Ordnance Survey mapping and overprinted to show the location of the accompanying photographs. While it is amusing to see a beach illustrated covered with deckchairs and fashionably clad holiday-makers, the pictures also give an excellent impression of the physical conditions in which the Army might find itself in conflict. The volumes are also equipped with profiles of the land as seen from the water to assist a landing craft find its destination.

Sheet maps of the various regions of Britain were published to give information on particular subjects such as the electricity supply network and the water distribution system. A useful map showed the major water obstacles. More detailed mapping was made available at a scale of 1:25,000. This included information on defensive installations such as pillboxes, anti-tank ditches, gun emplacements and anti-aircraft guns, presumably compiled both from pre-war observations by tourists and wartime aerial observation. A map of scale 1:100,000 was similarly marked, but included extensive hatching to show where the British had rendered potential landing fields unsuitable for aircraft by digging ditches, erecting poles or parking cars and trucks scavenged from breakers' yards. The mapping and study of the terrain is discussed in greater detail in Chapter 6.

The social and political landscape of Britain was another subject treated in a detailed publication, *Informationsheft GrossBritannien*, for the creation of which both SS General Walter Schellenberg and Major Walter zu Christian have been credited or blamed, depending on the commentator's viewpoint. The handbook purports to give German invaders information on the structure of British society and its major institutions. The coverage of the Secret Intelligence Service (SIS) was remarkably accurate, a characteristic for which two captured British operatives, Major Richard Stevens and Captain Sigismund Payne Best, endured largely undeserved condemnation, for most of the data had been furnished by a paid agent, Colonel C. H. Ellis who had been working for the Germans since 1923. The description of the SIS and the listings of its people, complete with addresses, were of higher quality than the analysis of the other organisations with the exception of the police. The handbook ordered the immediate arrest of the individuals about whom it gave this information, but included a number of other people who

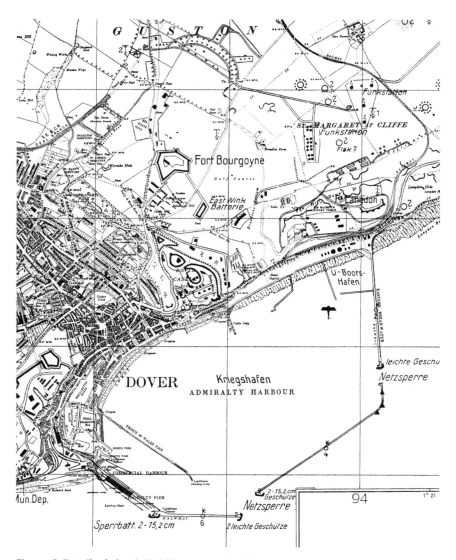

Figure 8 Detail of the 1:25,000 map updated to 8 August 1940 showing the area around Dover. The map is based on Ordnance Survey 6-inch map. Symbols are defined in the appendix, p. 261. (*Stellungskarte Grossbritannien*, Berlin, 1940, Bodleian Library C16[16])

happened to have their details on German files, bringing the total to 2820 names. In a second list the institutions with which they were associated were given. The publication, for all its faults, was a chilling indication of the intention to eliminate all resistance in the soon-to-be-conquered country.[8]

In the most important area of all, the appreciation of the strength and disposition of the British land forces, the German intelligence was seriously deficient. The *Abwehr*, the intelligence department of the German Armed Forces High Command, was headed by Admiral Wilhelm Canaris. His organisation had failed to assemble accurate information and had no network of agents in place to supply it. The opinions of German commanders reflected the conjectural basis of their assessments. Jodl remarked at an OKW meeting on 31 July that the invaders would face a poor British army which had, as yet, been unable to adjust to modern warfare. Hitler, on the other hand, spoke of a 'defensively prepared and utterly determined enemy ...'.[9] The number of divisions the British had in the field was over-estimated in total and underestimated in operational status. On 17 September Canaris's department stated that there were 34½ divisions, of which 20 were on coastal defence duties and of those 14 were fully operational and the balance were in reserve, but only four of those were operational. There were, in fact, 29 divisions and eight independent brigades, all below strength. On the map showing British forces as at 20 September, five divisions are correctly identified and located and another ten are placed within 10 miles of their true positions, but nine are in the wrong place, five admitted to be in some unknown place and eight fictional divisions are listed. In the broadest of considerations the errors balanced out, but for operational purposes on the English mainland the mistakes were serious, exposing the German forces to tactical disadvantage.[10]

The *Abwehr* attempted to rectify this situation by sending spies to Britain, but they were incompetent and quickly caught. Peter Fleming tells[11] of four agents who were sent by fishing boat from Le Touquet on 2 September. Two, Dutchmen, Charles van der Knieboom and Sjord Pons, who later claimed to have been blackmailed into the mission, landed near Hythe early the next morning and by 0530 hours were in the custody of the Somersetshire Light Infantry. Neither spoke English with any fluency and they appear to have been untrained. The other pair landed at Dungeness. One was a German, Rudolf Waldberg, who could speak French, but no English. The other, another Dutchman, or so he said, one Carl Meier, used his English to order a glass of cider at the Rising Sun in Lydd at breakfast time and was arrested when he later returned, as suggested by the alert land-lady, at a time at which licensing laws allowed the purchase. His companion was arrested the next day. A party of two men and one woman were later sent ashore in Scotland from a seaplane and were arrested within a few hours. Even when information did make its way back to Germany, interpret-ation of facts could lead to misinformation. A report of 2 September described defences between Tunbridge Wells and Beachy Head, among the sand-hills and bathing places. Tunbridge Wells is, however, in the very centre of the south-eastern landmass, and Fleming speculates that the name of Mr Tunbridge, the owner, displayed above the door of the village stores at Camber-on-Sea was the cause of the confusion. The report itself was trivial and the fact it was mulled over with care is indicative of its rarity. In his diaries the Italian Foreign Minister Count Galeazzo Ciano di Cortellazzo deplored his country's lack of intelligence sources in Britain and contrasted it with German good fortune. The entry for 11 September has the remark:

It seems incredible, but we do not have a single informant in Great Britain. On the other hand, the Germans have many. In London itself there is a German agent who makes radio transmissions up to 29 times a day. At least it is so stated by Admiral Canaris.[12]

Clearly Canaris was at pains to give the impression of having an effective organisation under his command.

In one area the Germans enjoyed a brief success. Their navy's *Beobachtungs-Dienst* or B-Dienst as it was abbreviated, was the cryptanalysis or code-breaking department. Before the war it had unravelled the Royal Navy Administrative Code, used for less secret communications, and it went on to crack the Naval Cypher which was used for higher security messages. It did not, however, manage to read the signals of Flag Officers or the Commanders-in-Chief. None the less, in April 1940 B-Dienst was reading between a third and a half of all Royal Navy signal traffic. This changed in August when the Administrative Code was replaced with Naval Code No. 1 and the Naval Cypher with Naval Cypher No. 2 and it was not until September 1941 that the Germans regained access to Royal Navy messages when Cypher No. 3 came in. The loss of this stream of information in August was keenly felt, a German Navy staff officer observing that many a surprise encounter with the British had been avoided in the past and that the availability of this knowledge had become a part of German operational planning. Although it bears not at all on the invasion plans, it is interesting to note that the British Merchant Navy Code, used to communicate with merchant ships and introduced in January 1940, was captured at Bergen in May and read thoroughly until the end of 1943.[13]

Planning in detail

With Hitler's issue of Führer Directive No. 16 the armed forces were obliged to get down to planning in earnest. Hitler followed his order up with a speech to the German people given at Kroll Opera House in Berlin on 19 July in which he voiced an appeal to Britain to cease the struggle. It was a clever move to prepare his followers for renewed conflict.

The Army went to work on Sealion with enthusiasm. One of their number, General Georg Hans Reinhardt, grasped the crucial problem: this was a seaborne assault on a defended shore. The requirement was to land tanks, trucks, men and horses from shallow-draft vessels and, so far, it had not even been tried. Moreover, the vessels themselves were not available in sufficient numbers; the assembly of the means to invade was a massive task in itself and the augmenting of existing machines and vessels with new devices yet greater.[14] The result was a limitation on the size of the initial landing force. At the same time the Army and the Navy were at odds over the extent of the front on which landings were to take place. The Army feared a narrow front which the British might contain and pinch out while the Navy feared having to secure a great extent of the Channel against the Royal Navy. The Army's plan was for Army Group A, under the newly-promoted Field Marshal Gerd von Rundstedt, to land with the 16th Army on the right from Margate to Hastings and 9th Army between Beachy Head and Portsmouth, while Army Group B under Colonel-General Fedor von Bock would be on the left from Lyme Bay to Weymouth. The front was 237 miles (380km) long involving 30 infantry, six armoured and four motorised divisions. A meeting of the Army and Navy commanders took place with Hitler on 21 July at which Hitler rehearsed the naval misgivings and then threw the problem back in Raeder's lap; when would the Navy have the answers? The Luftwaffe, in the shape of Göring or anyone else, was not represented at all and Raeder's query about the final achievement of air supremacy hung in the air without response. Halder noted that the decision to proceed in 1940 depended on the Navy's response.

The Army proceeded with its plans, regardless of Reinhardt's comments,

and on 23 July at its headquarters in Fontainbleau a table-top exercise confirmed, in its own eyes, the virtues of its schemes. Then, on 28 July, the
Navy's plans arrived. A smaller operation over a longer time was the best
that was offered. Further consultation revealed even more pessimistic comments. First, the need for a dawn landing and some moonlight for the
crossing meant that the operation would have to be carried out, at the
earliest, in late September when the weather would be less certain. The task
of holding the Channel open for invasion craft from Lyme Bay to the
Thames was just too great. Finally, the lack of landing craft meant that the
second landing wave could not start until 48 hours after the first and,
further, that wave would take between eight and ten days to cross.[15] The
next meeting with Hitler was scheduled for 31 July.

Before that word came of Josef Stalin's meeting with the British envoy Sir
Stafford Cripps in Moscow to reinforce Hitler's growing desire to tackle the
threat of Bolshevism. On 29 July Jodl called a meeting of the senior staff of
Section L which took place in its special railway train *Atlas* in Bad
Reichenhall station. Warlimont wrote:

*Four of us were present sitting at individual tables in the restaurant-car. Instead
of what we expected, Jodl went round ensuring that all doors and windows were
closed and then, without any preamble, disclosed to us that Hitler had decided to
rid the world 'once and for all' of the danger of Bolshevism by a surprise attack
on Soviet Russia to be carried out at the earliest possible moment, i.e. in May
1941.[16]*

There was a confusion of queries. Jodl told them the problem would arise
anyway and was best dealt with sooner rather than later. As to the dangers
of aerial attack on the Fatherland's cities, the Luftwaffe would, its skills
honed against Russia, have no difficulty in dealing with the British should
Sealion take place in 1941. At Armed Forces High Command clarity of
purpose was clouded.[17] Further objections to the Russian venture were
voiced and fear of that new scheme strengthened their support for Sealion.
Get the more mature initiative over before embarking on the next, was the
sum of the advice.

The Führer conference of 31 July then took place. Raeder made the
Navy's presentation. First, he pointed out that 15 September was the first
suitable date for the operation and that the weather usually improved at the
back end of that month. He then expanded on the dangers attendant on the
Channel crossing, the difficulty in satisfying the perfectly reasonable

requirements of his Army colleagues and finished by suggesting the whole thing be delayed until the following year. The meeting decided to continue preparations with a view to making a final decision in a week or ten days' time. Halder noted the focus was to be on 15 September as a target date.[18]

Arguments between Army and Navy were stilled in the first week of August because much energy was being put in to the testing of the landing craft developed by General Reinhardt and the Navy's *Fregattenkapitän* Heinrich Bartels and the top brass went off to see the results. Then hostilities resumed at a conference on the Channel coast. The broad front needs were expressed by Halder, the narrow by Schniewind. The extremes of the front were severely questioned by the Navy. In the east the invasion of the east coast of Kent, centred on Deal, was deemed doomed. The off-shore shoals and on-shore cliffs spelled disaster. On the extreme west the Lyme Bay venture was also potentially fatal, this time because of exposure to the Royal Navy. The Army eventually summed up its case in a memorandum to the Armed Forces High Command.

OKH 10.8.40

From Army High Command to the Chief of the Wehrmacht High Command
Re Operation "Sealion"

SECRET

Despite the binding instructions of the OKW to both the army and the navy, a confidential exchange of ideas between OKM (Naval High Command) and OKH (Army High Command) has so far failed to reach a common basis upon which the two arms of the Wehrmacht can carry forward the practical preparatory work with the required uniformity and with the mutual trust that is particularly important for this operation. Time is pressing. The differences of opinion which still stand in the way of uniformity in our preparations are therefore presented in the following document with the request that the Wehrmacht command send us their definitive opinion in the near future.

I   OKM:

(a) *The OKM considers the landing operation is only feasible in the area that is roughly bounded by the lines Dunkirk–Folkestone and Boulogne–Beachy Head. Only in this narrow area does the OKM believe it is able to provide some security for the continuous transport of elements of the Army to the English coast, but points out that even here the weather situation hardly guarantees the passage of strings of barges over several days.*

    A landing in the area to either side of Deal, which would significantly improve the beaching conditions, is rejected because, for navigational reasons (the Downs banks) the transport fleet must make its approach parallel to the coast and only appears feasible if no further enemy response is to be expected from the coast.

(b) *The OKM is in a position to put in readiness, in the harbours between Ostende and Boulogne, the shipping capacity necessary for carrying across the first echelons of some six divisions. In addition, further capacity is to be made ready in the harbours of Rotterdam and Le Havre and brought into use for transporting the second echelons of these divisions. A further increase in transport capacity is thought to be impossible due to the limited number of usable ships (given as 150) and especially tugs; it is also to be noted that no significant increase in the number of barges can be expected. The duration of the passage carrying six landing divisions for the first encounter including certain army troops is jointly calculated by the OKH and OKM at approximately six days.*

(c) *The OKM considers it impossible to carry out a landing in the western area of the Channel and therefore rejects a launch from the Le Havre area aimed at the coast between Eastbourne and Portsmouth, and also a launch from Cherbourg towards the Lyme Bay coast.*

    In the Navy's view, the action of the British fleet that is certain to be expected against the transport operations across the breadth of the Channel, can neither be blocked passively (mines) nor can it be paralysed or removed by the Luftwaffe. The transport fleet will be largely exposed and defenceless against destruction by the enemy, who in this event will ruthlessly deploy all resources at his disposal at sea. Because of the shelving of the Atlantic bottom, and the swell and surf that this creates on the English coast, a crossing of the wider section of the Channel using loaded barges, is out of the question. It would therefore have to be carried out using sea-going ships. However, the Navy tells us that this would necessitate an unloading period of 36 hours. Employing this method must be ruled out in view of the coastal defences and the likelihood of the British fleet attacking either from the Atlantic or from Portsmouth.

(d) *The OKM does not believe it is possible to achieve either operational or tactical surprise over the enemy. Their knowledge of the coastal area and the need to carry out the loading on the French mainland to a large extent on the previous day, will leave the British in little doubt as to the location and approximate time of our landing, even if their Air Force were to have been largely driven out of the skies by then.*

II OKH:

In view of this position taken by the OKM, the OKH must specify the following *requirements* for a potentially successful execution of the landing operation:

(a) *A landing on the English coast* only *between Folkestone and Eastbourne is not sustainable.*

In the above sector we must even today reckon on fully operational coastal defences with a strength of about four divisions (not counting those manning the coastal forts). In the adjacent coastal sector Margate–Folkestone we must assume there are two further divisions, and in the sector between Eastbourne and Portsmouth again two divisions – not counting the crews of the coastal forts. If not attacked themselves, these reserves can be thrown in to defend the Folkestone–Eastbourne sector when it comes under attack. Behind these, the British command certainly has five combat-ready divisions at its disposal between London and Salisbury, including one armoured division; in emergency even one more each outside Chatham and in London. The disruption of the formations of the landing forces, due to the unpredictability of the crossing and the landing, will leave us facing enemy superiority, which can only be mitigated by simultaneous landings on as broad a front as possible. Compensating for this weakness by deploying the Luftwaffe will be limited by the capability of the Luftwaffe over the sea and by the confusing nature of the terrain, which diminishes the effectiveness of our pilots.

The terrain in the relatively narrow sector is extraordinarily unfavourable for all arms, especially for the deployment of highly mobile units. Both the promontory between Dungeness and the Military Canal, and the coastal area between Bexhill and Eastbourne are marshland criss-crossed with countless ditches and watercourses – ideal for defending by the enemy, impossible for deploying our own tanks. The crucial high ground surrounds the entire landing front in a semicircle and provides the British with a natural defensive position. From this narrow and unfavourably situated beachhead, a swift breakthrough, either by taking out Dover or rolling up the coastal defences near Deal, could only be expected in unforeseeably favourable circumstances.

The duration of the crossing is far too long. Even if we succeed in throwing the first echelons of six divisions ashore and forming narrow beachheads with them, the outcome of the first battles, which still have to be fought against considerable superiority, is questionable, especially if the second echelon of these divisions and the most essential infantry units are only ready for combat after six days. On the assumption – an optimistic one

given the likelihood of disruption by bad weather and British naval forces –
that even this mission can be completed, it would still be necessary to wait
for at least a further six divisions but more importantly further supporting
troops and anti-aircraft artillery, before being able to break out from the
narrow beachheads and advance on our first operational objective, the line
from the lower Thames to Southampton. Accordingly, this operation could
scarcely begin before the 14th day after the landing. However, this gives the
enemy the opportunity, even if he chooses not to defend himself by attacking
during the period of our numerical inferiority, to build up and deploy
adequate forces for an effective defence on a general line from Chatham to
Brighton, in such a way that there would appear to be no prospect of rapidly
breaking through this defensive line. This in turn removes an important
factor for our swift success in Britain.

A landing in this sector alone accordingly presents itself as a frontal attack
against a defensive front, without any certain prospect of surprise, with
inadequate forces, mounted on too small a scale and only capable of
reinforcement in a piecemeal fashion.

(b) OKH must therefore request that a simultaneous landing be launched from
Le Havre and carried out west of Brighton.

Only by broadening the landing-base will it be possible to surprise the
British forces at a point where they are less likely to expect us, to confuse the
enemy by achieving local successes and thus significantly improve the
prospects of overall success.

If the British defend by attacking, as our latest intelligence tells us we
should expect, the enemy forces will be fragmented.

In the event of a purely defensive strategy by the British, it will from the
outset be impossible for them to build up a defensive front along the
Chatham–Brighton line and pressure will be put on them which could lead
to them rapidly abandoning the whole region south and south-east of
London. The prospects of an early opportunity to land near Deal thus
become greater.

The terrain around Brighton is particularly suitable for deploying more
mobile units.

Only if sufficiently strong forces can be landed and supplied with
sufficient speed, does there seem a prospect of achieving the first operational
objective (Thames Estuary/Southampton) at an early date, thus creating the
conditions for a further swift and successful operation.

(c) The OKH is very unwilling to abandon the idea of a landing in Lyme Bay, *because it is precisely such a landing, far removed from the others, which would be particularly effective in fragmenting the British forces. It is also the case that an advance from Lyme Bay, roughly in the direction of Bristol, must have a very considerable effect on any defensive front planned by the enemy in southern England. The landing in Lyme Bay, which can only be carried out by ocean-going ships and therefore makes it necessary to effect the unloading offshore in lighters, would have to be made possible through the use of airborne troops. In view of the weak and apparently negligible coastal defensives in this area, the chances of such an operation succeeding are good. The forces would also be supplied by air.*

III   Result:

OKH must therefore conclude:

1)   *From the Army's point of view, we cannot be responsible for a landing between Folkestone and Eastbourne alone. Even with the best preparation, the chances of success are extremely low.*

2)   *A simultaneous landing near and to the west of Brighton is essential. An early landing at Deal is necessary for the swift capture of the heights north of Dover.*

3)   *Sufficient shipping capacity must be made ready to enable us to land the first and second echelons of a total of ten divisions with appropriate supplies, within four days, on the English from Ramsgate to west of Brighton. Further troops and supplies must follow at a faster rate than previously planned.*

4)   *The idea of a landing in Lyme Bay should, if at all possible, be retained. The shipping capacity necessary for this must be made ready separately.*

(signed) von Brauchitsch[19]

In fact the Army had recognised the irrelevance of the Lyme Bay objective weeks earlier, but they kept it in play to put pressure on the Navy to grant what was really important. The Deal landing idea was more serious as it gave access to the broad, chalk uplands of the North Downs, good tank-bearing country. Jodl now made his comments and cast doubt on the future of Sealion.

13 August 1940
Situation assessment by General Jodl (Chief of Wehrmacht Operations)
about a landing in England

Berlin 13.8.1940

SECRET COMMAND MATERIAL
ONLY TO BE READ BY OFFICERS

Assessment of the situation arising from the views of the Army and Navy on a landing in England

1) *The landing operation must under no circumstances fail. A failure could have* political *consequences, which would go far beyond the military ones.*

2) *If a failure is to be ruled out, as far as it is possible to judge, I agree with the Army in my view that it is necessary:*

a) *to get a simultaneous foothold from Folkestone as far as Brighton Bay*

b) *to be able to get ten divisions ashore in this sector within four days*

c) *to follow up with three more fully equipped divisions across the Straits of Dover, even if the sea conditions rule out the use of barges, while the troops landed further west would be reinforced with airborne troops*

d) *to ensure that there are no British military vehicles left on the south coast of England, especially not in Portsmouth,*

e) *to know that the British air force has been or can be deprived of any ability to retaliate*

I believe the Luftwaffe will achieve the preconditions for (d) and (e). The next eight days will bring clarity to this situation.

However, should the Navy not be in a position to fulfil the requirements (a), (b) and (c) – and this now has to be precisely clarified *– then I consider the landing to be an act of desperation, which would have to be risked in a desperate situation, but which we have no reason whatsoever to undertake at this moment.*

3) *There are other ways of forcing Britain to its knees. For this purpose I consider a much closer* military *co-operation by the Axis Powers to be necessary, than has been the case hitherto.*

This objective can be achieved through:

a) *The continuation of the air war until* all defence installations and materials in southern England have been destroyed. *All Italian combat aircraft not currently deployed must be called in for this purpose.*

b) *The intensification of the U-boat war from our bases in France, by calling in half of all Italian submarines.*

c) *The denial of Egypt to the British, with German help if necessary.*

d) *The denial of Gibraltar to the British in cooperation with the Spanish and Italians.*

e) *The avoidance of operations which are not necessary to the* defeat of Britain, *but which only represent desirable war aims that can be achieved without difficulty after our victory over Britain (Yugoslavia).*

We should not be operating with war aims in view, but fighting for victory. Britain's will to resist must be broken by next spring. If this cannot be done with a landing, then it must be done by other means. All other tasks must take second place to this most important of missions.

We are now entering the decisive battle against Britain. In doing so we must bring the basic rules of war into play, within our coalition too; we must concentrate all our forces at the critical place, namely the air and U-boat war against the mother country of Britain.

The Italians have shown a certain willingness to join with us in the battle against the British mother-land, if for no other reason than that they realise they can only make effective use of a proportion of their forces in their own theatre of war. This correct notion must be converted into action with all available energy. I believe that in discussion with the Duce, we will be able to persuade him that we should fight the final battle of this war, not merely side by side but hand in hand. A decisive outcome will be wrested from the enemy all the more speedily.

(signed) Jodl

[handwritten note]

Agreed!
[P] K[eitel] 13/8

The broad content of this has been presented to the Führer by the head of OKW.
20

Admiral Fricke saw this as a chance to persuade Jodl to advise against Sealion but the General avoid committing himself, so the enterprise remained a possibility and, on 16 August, Hitler ordered the continuation of preparations with 15 September in view as S-Day, the Lyme Bay landing officially cancelled and the Deal landing simply ignored. The westernmost landing area was now Brighton and here the Navy was willing to concede assistance. They agreed to protect the deployment of 500 motor boats to carry two regiments, 2100 men, with howitzer and anti-tank guns, assuming that a similar number of paratroops were landed on the Downs to the north of the objective and that the Luftwaffe would protect the western flank. On 22 August the proposal was modified with the Navy cutting the motor boat content and substituting 100 coastal motor-sailers and 25 steamers. The Army and Navy haggled on for some days over this issue with Warlimont acting as mediator. On 26 August Hitler came down on the Navy's side.[21] What was now called 'Blue Move', from the northern ports from Ostend to

Boulogne, would carry troops to the Folkestone to Hastings beaches while 'Green Move' carrying the 9th Army would be in two parts, half in the east sailing from Le Havre along the coast to Boulogne and then crossing under the cover provided for Blue to Beach D (Bexhill-on-Sea/Newhaven) while the other half would head direct for Brighton and Beach E.

Issuing orders

With the meeting of 26 August the arguments were at an end and final orders for Sealion could be issued. The Navy's documents comprised a mass of paper, the accumulation of drafts and redrafts made as the discussions swayed from one scheme to the next. They were the result of an amazing effort to create an operation the like of which the world had never seen. The Army's orders, by contrast, were relatively brief.

OKH, 30.8.40

Nr 26

30 August 1940
Instruction from the Commander-in-Chief of the Army (OKH)
for the preparation of Operation "Sealion"

1) Mission:
The Supreme Commander has ordered the three armed services to prepare for a
forced landing in England. *The purpose of this invasion is to eliminate the*
home territory of Britain as a base for continuing the war against Germany and,
should it become necessary, to occupy it to the full extent.

The order for putting the invasion into effect depends on the political
situation. The preparations are to be made in such a way that execution can take
place starting on 15.9.

It will be the Army's task, *while continuing to fulfil its occupation*
assignments in France and to guard the other fronts, to land with strong forces in
southern England, to defeat the British army, and to occupy the capital and
further regions of England if the situation requires it.
2) Codeword:
The operation bears the code-name: 'Sealion'.
3) *The evolution of the operation is dependent on a larger number of*
   circumstances which cannot be determined in advance. Therefore the

*preparations for the embarkation, crossing and first landing must be made
so flexible that the commanders can handle any unforeseen changes in the
situation without wasting time. Officers and men must be aware that the
nature of transport by sea makes it inevitable that units lose their cohesion
and that unfamiliar situations can arise, which can only be kept under
control through the highest degree of initiative by all officers.*

4)   Planned execution:

(a)   *The* Luftwaffe *knocks out the British air force and its service bases and
gains air superiority. The [German] Navy creates mine-free channels and,
supported by the* Luftwaffe, *interdicts the flanks of the crossing zone.*

(b)   *The landing forces of the Army, with specially equipped leading echelons
of the divisions of the first wave, initially gain local beachheads. Without
delay they broaden out these isolated beachheads to form a single cohesive
landing-zone, the occupation of which covers the disembarkation of the
subsequent troops and ensures the early establishment of a unified command
on the English side of the Channel. As soon as sufficient forces are
available, the assault begins against the first operational objective: the line
from the Thames Estuary, over the high ground south of London, to
Portsmouth. We can expect British counter-attacks against the first German
troops to land, and resistance using all resources against the expansion of
initial German gains. This will entail bitter fighting. The leadership and
deployment of our troops must be appropriate for these first decisive
engagements.*

(c)   *After achieving the first operational objective, the* next task of the Army
*will be to defeat all enemy forces remaining in southern England, to occupy
London, to clear southern England of the enemy and to secure the general
line from Maldon (NE of London) to the Severn Estuary.*

Orders about further assignments will be issued at the appropriate time.

(d)   *The enemy dispositions will, as hitherto, be continuously reported to the
army groups and armies*

5)   Chain of command and disposition of forces:

*Responsibility for executing the tasks assigned to the Army will initially lie
with Army Group A (with 16th and 9th Armies). Whether, at a later point,
elements of Army Group B will also be deployed, depends on how the
situation evolves.*

*For the battle-order of forces assigned to Operation 'Sealion', see Appendix
1 [not reproduced in this work].*

The tasks of the Army Groups hitherto (coastal defence, occupation duties, securing the demarcation-line) remain as before.

6) Assignments for the Army Groups and Armies:

a) Assignment for Army Gp A:

Proceeding on the orders of the OKH the Army Gp forces a landing on the English coast between Folkestone and Worthing and initially takes possession of a coastal strip, from which the landing of further forces can be secured – including by the use of seaward facing artillery – and the conditions necessary for continuing the invasion can be created. It will be desirable to render harbour facilities on the English coast usable at an early stage, in order to enable subsequent forces to be disembarked rapidly.

Following the arrival of sufficient forces on English soil, the Army Gp proceeds with the invasion and occupies the line Thames Estuary–heights south of London–Portsmouth. As soon as the situation permits it, mobile units are to press on into the area west of London, with the objective of sealing London off from the south and west, and capturing the Thames crossings for the advance towards the line Watford–Swindon.

b) First assignments for the Armies:

16th Army will embark in the selected harbours between and including Rotterdam and Calais. Landing on a broad front between and including Folkestone and Hastings, it will take possession of the territory at least as far as the line: hills midway between Canterbury and Folkestone–Ashford–hills 20km N of Hastings. It is important rapidly to deny the enemy access to the port facilities at Dover. The coastal area Ramsgate–Deal, which for navigational reasons can only be approached once the coastal defences have been knocked out, must as quickly as possible be captured from the landward side.

It is anticipated that paratroopers will be deployed simultaneously with the landing to take rapid possession of the heights N of Dover.

9th Army, landing simultaneously with 16th Army between Bexhill and Worthing, takes possession of the coastal zone as least as far inland as a line from the hills 20km N of Bexhill to the hills 10km N of Worthing. It has to be prepared for the fact that only the 1st echelon of three divisions of the first wave can be sent directly across the Channel from Le Havre, while the 4th division, as well as the later echelons and waves, launched from Boulogne, must make the crossing relying on the better secured crossing-zone of the 16th Army, and depending on circumstances will be disembarked either E or W of Eastbourne.

The use of paratroops is anticipated for the capture of Brighton.

Separation-line *between 16th and 9th Armies: Boulogne (9)–Hastings (9)–Reigate (16).*

The timing *of the landing on the English coast will be the subject of separate orders. It is anticipated that the landing will be at daybreak. However, dependence on the weather and tides may compel a landing in broad daylight. In this case the large-scale use of smoke-screens (from aircraft, vessels and artillery) will be necessary.*

c)   Assignment for Army Gp B

Army Gp B does not take part in the first assault wave. If sea conditions prove favourable, consideration will be given at a later juncture for Army Gp B, starting out by air and sea from the Cherbourg area, to force a landing at Lyme Bay. Initially it would occupy Weymouth and the hills running from 20km N of Weymouth to 15km N of Lyme Regis, in order to advance, on orders from OKH, in the direction of Bristol. Later on the occupation of the counties of Devon Cornwall by elements of Army Gp B, may be considered.

Army Gp B, in conjunction with naval staff will decide on the ports of embarkation and their capacities, and will prepare its landing forces in such a way that, on orders from OKH, they can be brought up for embarkation within five days. The following orders for the preparation and disposition of forces relate principally to Army Gp A, but also apply in general terms to Army Gp B.

7)   Disposition of forces:

The detailed disposition is a matter for the Army groups or Armies according to the variation in embarkation facilities and the initial tasks on English soil.

In addition to the individual instructions already given in this respect, the following points should be noted:

a)   *The composition of the 1st echelon of the 1st wave, given on 20.7 in OKH GenStdH [army general staff] Org. Abt. [organisation dept.] Nr 1084/40 g.Kdos, is only intended for general guidance. The faster and more copiously combat troops and weapons can be brought over, the better – even without undue concern for organisational cohesion! What matters is the assembling of combat groups suitable for the tasks to be performed.*

b)   *Units of the armoured and/or fast mobile formations, especially armoured cars (U) [underwater], are to be integrated into the landing echelons at an early juncture.*

c)   *Heavy batteries for use as coastal batteries on the far shore must be brought in so that the Calais–Deal and Boulogne–Hastings crossings can be covered by artillery from both shores as quickly as possible. (Group Art.Kdr 106, later also Art, Abt. 1/84) For the integration of flak artillery, see Appendix 3 [omitted in this work].*

d) Tasks of the pioneers [engineers]:

   aa) Support for troops at embarkation, especially where this takes place away from harbours.

   bb) Support for the first beaching on a broad front (assault-craft, motor-boats, float-bags).

   cc) Support for the disembarkation of men, vehicles and horses from the transport vessels, especially on open coasts.

   dd) Support for the first troops ashore, in removing obstacles, especially mines, on the beach; support for the infantry in the subsequent invasion.

   ee) Holding forces and defensive equipment in readiness to support the defence of the beachheads gained.

   The forces deployed for tasks (aa) and (cc) will in general remain firmly in place, so that, under the command of special staff, they can carry out the embarkation and disembarkation of the later waves.

e) *The temporary measures for providing covering fire against shore targets during the landings are to be employed with special rigour by all departments, in accordance with the leaflets, etc. issued.*

f) *Every landing unit in the leading echelons must be composed in such a way that even on the smallest scale it is capable of performing independent combat tasks, once the landing has taken place. The officers of the units will form part of their leading sections.*

g) *The loading of the ships for the second and subsequent waves cannot be rigidly scheduled in advance. Close organisational cooperation is required between the naval and army departments to make it possible to organise the loading of the ships quickly and flexibly, as the situation dictates. For this purpose, a reliably operating intelligence network is indispensable.*

h) *The requirements of the O.Qu. [senior quarter-master] England must, as soon as the transport situation allows it, be taken into account by the A.O.K [Army Command] in the order of march (see Appendix 4) [omitted in this work].*

7) [sic] Preparation of forces:

a) 1st wave:

   The forces envisaged for the 1st wave are to be put in readiness close to the operational harbours prepared by the Navy.

   The 'operational harbours' are, for the 16th Army:

   Rotterdam

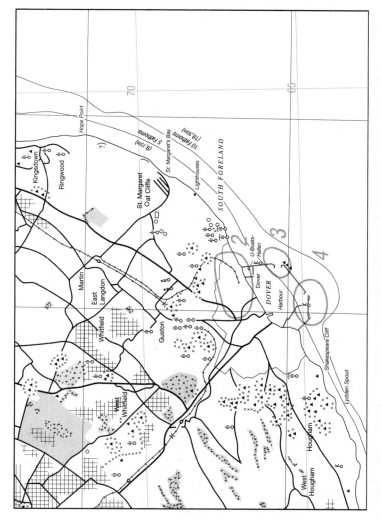

Figure 9 Detail of defences map of 3 September 1940 showing Watling Street north-west of Dover with pillboxes (black triangles) surrounded with barbed wire (crosses) and fields blocked with obstacles to prevent aircraft landing (cross-hatching). A key to symbols is given in the appendix. (After *Befestigungskarte Grossbritannien*, Berlin 1940, Bodleian Library, C17[42L])

Antwerp

Ostend

Dunkirk

Calais

For the 9th Army:

Boulogne

Le Havre (the latter only for the 1st echelons of three divisions)

The following are designated as "auxiliary harbours" (not to be used for embarkation purposes):

Nieuwport

Gravelines

Further embarkation on the open beach, in river estuaries or small harbours will only be possible to a limited extent.

Details of the location, method and sequence of the first embarkation are immediately to be worked out by the armies (liaison officers) with the relevant naval departments, who have received instructions. The principle must be that as much of the equipment and supplies as possible is to be loaded beforehand, so that the final loading of troops and horses can be limited to the shortest time possible.

The acquisition, equipping and readying of transport capacity is the job of the Navy and is controlled through special powers by the naval commanders.

The installation of weapons of all kinds on the barges – in so far as it has not already been carried out by naval departments, including on the tugs – is the responsibility of the troops and is to be implemented to the largest extent possible in accordance with the leaflets issued. Covering fire for the landing troops, provided from seaward, will be supplemented by armed naval vessels (minesweepers, etc.).

b) 2nd wave:

The mobile units to be brought across in conjunction with the first wave are to be called in by the Army for the inland advance at the appropriate time, and should be placed in readiness close to the operational harbours. The locations for embarkation are:

For the 16th Army: Rotterdam and Antwerp

For the 9th Army: Boulogne

The bringing up of these forces is to be prepared in such a way that from 15.9 onward it can be carried out in three days. The general HQs, divisions and regiments of the mobile units assigned to the 16th and 9th Armies will, *for these preparatory operations, be immediately placed under the command of the two AOKs [Army Commands].*

c) 3rd wave:

The formations of the 3rd wave not scheduled for transport by rail are to be brought up to the coast by the Army groups not later than the morning of 15.9. Where and when sea transport will be possible, it is not possible to assess at the moment. They will therefore have to be grouped in such a way that their leading elements can reach the Army's most suitable harbours in three days' march.

In the case of the formations to be brought up by rail by the OKH (see Appendix 1) [omitted in this work], Army Gp A must report the required arrival time and unloading area.

d) 4th wave:

The OKH reserves will remain for the time being in their present locations and will be called up by OKH as required.

In the arrival and preparation of the forces of all waves care must be taken to avoid any unnecessary bunching, and to ensure the necessary air cover in discussion with the relevant air-fleet command.

8) Luftwaffe activity:

a) Operational Luftwaffe

See Appendix 3 [omitted in this work].

b) Army air formations

See Appendix 3 [omitted in this work].

9) Secrecy:

The preparations for the planned landing require the maintenance of particular secrecy. The fact that a landing in England is being prepared, is not something that can be concealed. So it is all the more important to do everything possible to keep secret the timing of the proposed landing as well as the crossing areas.

10) Deception measures:

Measures designed falsely to indicate intentions to land on the east coast of England and in Ireland, have been put into effect. Details about this have been sent to the departments concerned.

11) Reports:

The following are required from Army Gp A by 3.9:

a) *Plan for launching the first wave, preparation of forces (map!). Use of paratroops, etc.*

b) *Planned preparation of the 2nd wave (map!).*

c) *Planned command-posts from General HQ downwards.*

d) Calculation of the anticipated time required for bringing across the individual echelons and waves (in consultation with naval departments).

e) Request concerning arrival-time and unloading area of the divisions of the 3rd wave, being brought up by rail.

f) Proposal for time of day for the landing.

g) Proposals and suggestions

[signed] von Brauchitsch

Appendices:

Appendix 1:   Survey of formations involved
Appendix 2:   Orders for intelligence links
Appendix 3:   Orders for Luiftwaffe formations
Appendix 4:   Orders for supply
Appendix 5:   Distribution of shipping between the ports of departure[22]
  [Appendix material omitted from this work]

Nothing if not stubborn, the orders preserve, at 6c, the plan for a landing at Lyme Bay, but leave room for it to be aborted. The confusion likely to attend the landings is anticipated at 7a and the use of U-designated armour, underwater machines, is indicated in 7b. The encouragement of initiative at junior levels of command is strongly made at 7f. In all this careful specification, the orders then have a second section 7! It is also informative to see, in this state-of-the-art operation, provision for the transportation of horses.

The preparations continued as quickly as possible, but the Navy was obliged to admit that 15 September could not be held as S-Day and they suggested 24 September instead. The delay was vital to lay mines, deploy submarines and launch the diversionary activity in the northern North Sea. A marginally smaller delay was conceded.

3rd September 1940
Instruction from the Wehrmacht High Command (OKW)
concerning the timetable for Operation 'Sealion'

TOP LEVEL – OFFICERS ONLY

SECRET COMMAND MATERIAL!

Re: Operation "Sealion"
In the preparations for Operation "Sealion" the following deadlines are currently applicable:

1) *Earliest time for:*
   a) *Departure of transport fleets is 20.9.40*
   b) *S-Day (day of the landing) is 21.9.40*
2) *The order for the launch of the operation will be given on S-Day minus ten, so it is forecast for 11.9.40.*
3) *The final commitment to the S-Day and S-Time (start of first beach landing), will be made not later than noon on S-Day minus three.*
4) *All steps must be taken in such a way that 24 hours before S-Time the operation can still be stopped.*

Chief of the Wehrmacht High Command

(signed) Keitel[23]

The orders for the air support were issued on Göring's behalf two days later.

Nr 28
5th September 1940
Order from the Commander-in-Chief of the Luftwaffe
concerning the deployment of the Luftwaffe in Operation "Sealion"

TOP LEVEL – RECIPIENTS ONLY
SECRET COMMAND MATTERS   10 copies

1) Change to the intentions of the Army High Command
   Crossing by the 16th Army from Rotterdam–Calais to the coastal sector Folkestone–Hastings.
   Crossing by the 9th Army – 1st echelon of 1st wave departing from Le Havre, later elements from Boulogne – for the coastal strip between Bexhill and Worthing.
   1st operational objective:
   To reach the general line Thames Estuary–hills S of London–Portsmouth.
   To achieve this, the first assault objective is to occupy the territory at least as far as the line:
   Hills midway between Canterbury/Folkestone–Ashford–hills 20km N of Hastings, and the coastal strip at least as far as the line: hills 20km N of Bexhill–hills 10km N of Worthing.
   Army Grp B:
   Does not take part in the 1st assault. Provided the sea conditions remain favourable a crossing can be considered at a later juncture from the Cherbourg area to the Lyme Bay coastal sector.

2) *The direct support of the landing operations and advance of the army is in the hands of Luftflotte 2 (VIII Flieger-Korps) and of Lfl. 3 (I Fl.Korps), as ordered by C-in-C Luftwaffe, Staff Ia Nr 5925/40 of 27.8.40 fig 3b. The direct support of the possible landing by Army Grp B is the task of Lfl. 3.*

3) *The deployment of the Flak-Korps is the subject of Ob.d.L. Staff Ia Nr 5929/40 (op 2) of 28.8.40. However, we must be prepared for the likelihood that Flak regiments posted to Berlin and central Germany will not be able to be brought back. Assuming replacements for these will be necessary, they will come from the area of Luftflotten 2 and 3. Orders will follow concerning the allocation and provision of special vessels (pontoons) to the Flak corps.*

4) *The separation-line between Lfl. 2 and 3 for reconnaissance and combat (incl. Flak-Korps) is to be changed as follows: St Quentin (3)–Boulogne (3)–Hastings (2)–Reigate (2)–Hendon (3)–Elstree (2)–Banbury (3)–old separation line.*

5) *The new subordinate relationship of VIII Fl.Korps under Lfl. 2 takes effect with Ob.d.L. Staff Ia Nr 8342/40 of 26.8.40. The new subordinate relationship of I Fl.Korps under Lfl. 3 takes effect from a special order from the Ob.d.L. after completion of the 'Loge' attack.*
   The I Fl.Korps is to be left in its former operational area.

6) *The separation line for air defence between Lfl. 2 and 3 remains unchanged. Flak cover for the I Fl. Korps also remains* unchanged *and is provided by Lg. Belgium/Northern France, in the same strength as hitherto.*

7) *Lfl. 2 will immediately put the western part of Lg. Belgium/Northern France at the disposal of Lfl. 3. Responsibility for supplying it lies with the L.Dv.g.90 of Lfl. 2.*

8) Subordination of fighter and heavy fighter units [Jagd- und Zerstörerverbände]
   After completion of the "Loge" assault, it is expected that the former subordinate relationships will come into force again.

9) Reconnaissance:

a) *Lfl. 2 and 3, with the subordinated reconnaissance units, will take over the long-range reconnaissance for Army Gp A and for AOK 16 and AOK 9. Gen. Der Lw. with the Army High Command is instructed to deploy the reconnaissance formations placed under the command of the Army High Command only in agreement with Lfl. 2 and 3.*

b) *Before the start of Operation Sealion and during it, uninterrupted reconnaissance against enemy naval forces is to be guaranteed as follows: Lfl. 2: In sea area Square 05 East 4761–Middlesbrough–along the English coast as far as Sheerness–Furnes–along the Belgian/Dutch coast to Den Helder.*

Lfl. 3: In sea area Carnsore Point (S coast of Ireland)–along S coast of Ireland as far as Bantry Bay–Square 24 West 1949–Square 14 West 9989–Brest–Cherbourg–Brighton.

For this purpose it is intended that the reconnaissance formations of the Gen. Der Lw. with the Army High Command should be subordinated to the Luftflotten.

10) *To protect our flanks in the short-term combating of enemy naval forces at the eastern and western approaches to the Channel, strong combat forces must be placed in readiness close to the Channel. Close cooperation must be assured between these forces and reconnaissance, in accordance with 9b. This shall not affect the tasks of direct support of the army and the continuous combating of the enemy air force.*

11) *As ordered in Ob. d L. staff Ia Nr 5925/40 of 27.8.40, Lfl. 2 and 3 must immediately establish contact with the relevant army and navy departments and in close conjunction with them bring preparations to a conclusion. Conclusion of preparations must be reported to Ob.d L.by 15.9.40*

(signed) Jeschonnek[24]

This brought the Luftwaffe into line with the final, agreed plans for Sealion. All that remained was to give orders for the operation to proceed.

Notes and References

1 Kieser, Egbert, *Operation Sea Lion*, London, Arms and Armour, 1997, p. 83.

2 Ansel, Walter, *Hitler Confronts England*, Durham, NC and London, Duke University Press and Cambridge University Press, 1960, p. 45.

3 *Ibid.*, p. 47.

4 Klee, Karl, *Das Unternehmen Seelöwe, Vol. 2*, 1958, trans. A. McGeoch.

5 Warlimont, Walter, *Inside Hitler's Headquarters 1939–45*, London, Weidenfeld and Nicolson, 1964, p. 104.

6 Kieser, pp. 93–4.

7 Klee, trans A. McGeoch.

8 Erickson, John, in *Invasion 1940*, London, St Ermin's Press, 2000, p. vi *et seq.*

9 Fleming, Peter, *Invasion 1940*, London, Rupert Hart-Davis, 1957, p. 179.

10 *Ibid.*, pp. 179–81.

11 *Ibid.*, p. 184 *et seq.*

12 *Ibid.*, p. 190, footnote.

13 Dear, I. C. B. and Foot, M. R. D. (eds), *The Oxford Companion to World War II*, Oxford, Oxford University Press, 1995, pp. 91–2.

14 Ansel, pp. 159–60.

15 *Ibid.*, pp. 168–9.

16 Warlimont, p. 111.

17 *Ibid.*, pp. 111–12.

18 Ansel, pp. 182–6.

19 Klee, pp. 345–50, trans. A. McGeoch.

20 *Ibid.*, pp. 353–5.

21 Ansel, pp. 232–3.

22 Klee, pp. 360–7, trans. A. McGeoch.

23 *Ibid.*, p. 369.

24 *Ibid.*, pp. 370–2.

chapter 4

The gathering force

While the high commands were engaged in the drawing up of plans and the negotiations and arguments resulting from them, practical activity was needed to create what was intended as the greatest invasion fleet ever seen and assembling it for action. The problems included ferrying the forces across the Channel, getting them and their equipment ashore, and ensuring that sufficient shipping was then available for the second and third waves of troops and for supplies.

The early plans called for landings of forces originating from the Calais, the Le Havre and the Cherbourg base areas. It had to be assumed that, unlike the Norway operation, landings would be on open beaches rather than through ports and that steamers or warships could not be used to get men ashore. The inshore operations would be by barge or other shallow-draft vessels and while the short Calais-to-Folkestone journey might be made towing barges filled with troops, the longer Le Havre-to-Sussex crossing would require transfer of men from ship to barge near the English coast. The number of ships needed to deliver the First Wave, 13 divisions, could not be provided so the plan was to take over a first wave, two regiments from each division, and follow that with a shipment of the third regiment and the divisional troops. The projections for the first echelon of the first wave were that the fleet required would be, for the Kent coast landings, 550 barges towed by 185 tugs and then, inshore, by 370 motorboats. The Sussex coast operation would need 25 steamers, 250 barges, 90 tugs and 180 motorboats and the Lyme Bay attack, which was still contemplated at this time, would need 18 steamers, 180 barges, 60 tugs and 120 motorboats. In sum, the Navy had to provide 43 steamers, 980 barges, 335 tugs and 670 motorboats; a formidable fleet to find.[1]

The fleet

The discussions between the Navy and the Army, mediated by Colonel Warlimont, led to the abandonment of the Lyme Bay expedition, save as a mention in the Army's orders, and the reduction of the left flank to a single division supported by paratroops to be landed on the hills north of Brighton, giving a new total of nine divisions to be ferried over. With this plan in place for the September landings, the transport fleet took on its final specification. Each part of the fleet had an alphabetic designation matching that of the target beach. Beach A, the Deal landing, had been abandoned as had Beach H, the Lyme Bay destination. Beach B, between Dungeness and Folkestone would be the destination of Transport Fleet B consisting of Tow Formation 1 from Dunkirk (75 tows), Tow Formation 2 from Ostend (25 tows), Convoy 1 from Ostend (eight transport ships) and Convoy 2 from Rotterdam (49 transports and 98 barges). Transport Fleet C, bound for the Hastings to Dungeness sector, was of one Tow Formation (100 tows) and Convoy 3 from Antwerp (57 transports, 114 barges and 14 pusher boats). Fleet D, heading for the Eastbourne to Bexhill-on-Sea sector, consisted of 165 tows from Boulogne. The longest crossing would be made from Le Havre by Transport Fleet E and the troops had to go ashore from small motor vessels, so the fleet was made up of 100 coasters and 200 fishing boats to ferry ashore the troops from Convoys 4 and 5, each of 25 steamers.[2]

Making plans was one thing, finding the ships and assembling them was another. It would have been hard enough in time of peace, but in war they had to be concealed if possible and protected from attack by the British. At the same time, they had to be available before the invasion so that loading and unloading could be practised by the Army. Further, the peculiar purpose for which they were required called for modifications. Landing craft, as they became known by the end of the war, had not yet been developed and the concept had to be built from first principles. The meeting between General Reinhardt and Admiral Schniewind on 10 July 1940 led to the immediate establishment of a testing centre to conduct trials. The first of these was at Westerland on the island of Sylt on the north Friesland coast where mounting field artillery on small vessels was tried out and experiments were made with submersible tanks. They also looked into the problem of launching assault boats from transport vessels and the use of the new landing barges which, based on a pre-war design, had been hurried into production. A mere five weeks after it was set up the Westerland Trials Command was superseded by a new centre at Emden, near the north Netherlands border. Here the Army's Engineer Training Battalion 1, the Trials Command of the Merchant Shipping Division of the Navy and a special Luftwaffe unit under Major Fritz Siebel formed an inter-service group. A wide range of craft was tested here from heavy duty barges to assault boats. Between 25 July and 5 September some 1000 assault boat coxswains were trained here.[3]

Figure 10 Testing an assault boat launching system. This used a box frame to lower a cradle into the sea. The alternative was to slide the boat down a ramp into the water. (Coll. Peter Schenk)

The ships

The transport fleet of 164 ships was supplied by commandeering their number, plus ten extras, from the ordinary merchant fleet with the addition of a number from French and Dutch sources. A speed of 12 knots was desired, but to make up the numbers it was necessary to settle for 8 knots. The ships had to have deep through decks and large hatches though some were passenger vessels. They were all called steamers rather than transports so the Army would understand. Some of them had been used in Norway and there were even a few that had seen service in the Spanish Civil War, but almost all had to be converted to take men and horses, with all the drinking and sanitary installations that implies. Emergency and rescue equipment went on board, as well as communications installations. Guns were mounted, many of them 75mm field guns on wooden platforms. Six ships were allocated to the Chief Quartermaster for resupply work.

In order to get in close to the coast near Brighton, the Navy planned to take over about 200 fishing boats and 100 other small craft, all of which were termed motorboats in the documents. They were meant to be capable of 7 knots but that was at the upper limit of their power for many of them. They were to be crewed by civilians who were said to be very keen in spite of, or maybe because of, the fact that most of them were about 16 or 17 years old. The ships could not be beached as they did not have flat bottoms, so troops were to be ferried ashore in assault craft launched from wooden ramps lowered from the sides of the motorboat or from metal cradles lowered to water level.

Another type of vessel classified as a motorboat was the motor fishing vessel, of which 1600 were requisitioned and put to service as infantry transports, pushers for barges and, the swifter of them, light command boats that could move fast to marshal towed formations. Tow groups were made up of six tows, that is, a tug, an unpowered barge and a powered barge, and a naval officer had the task of keeping this flotilla in good order. The slowest of the motorboats were to be towed across the Channel before making their final run in under their own power. They were fitted with light machine-guns.

As the powered barges did not have the speed required to cross and keep station in convoy, they were to become part of a 'tow', that is, a three-vessel group as given above. Tugs with at least 250hp engines were needed and it soon became apparent that not enough of them could be found. The numbers were made up with fishing trawlers and by allocating some barges to be towed by, or more accurately, lashed alongside, transport steamers. The tugs also served as troop carriers with small groups of shock troops aboard and so they took assault boats and dinghies as well.

The boats

The assault boat, *Pioniersturmboot 39*, had been approved for use by the Army in 1936. The design was for a boat 5.98m (19.3ft) long and 1.58m (5.2ft) in the beam powered by a 30hp Otto outboard engine with the propeller at the end of a shaft some 2.5m (8.2ft) long so that a small depression of the motor by the coxswain could lift the propeller blades clear of the water and of any obstacle over which the boat was passing. The top speed was about 25km/h (15mph) and the boats had been photographed making spectacular leaps over ramps set in the water. There was a light machine-gun mounting forward. They had a crew of two and could carry six infantry soldiers, fully equipped. The tests at Sylt went well and 1300 boats were ordered. By mid-September only 400 or so had arrived. The assault boats were supplemented with rubber dinghies of which there were two main types. The *Grosser Flosssack 34* which was 5.5m (18ft) long and the *Kleiner Flosssack 34* which was 3m (10ft) long. The larger weighed 150kg (330lb) and the smaller a third of that, so they were quite easily launched but both

Figure 11 A *Pioniersturmboot* in action, clearing an obstacle at speed. (Coll. Peter Schenk)

were very hard to paddle and they were used with outboard motors or sand-
wiched between assault boats. The assault boats were launched 1000m (0.62
miles) off-shore, the small rubber dinghy 500m (547yds) out and the large
dinghy only 300m (328yds) away from the beach.[4]

Figure 12 Training for landing in England. Camouflaged motor boats steady a barge
while a primitive ramp is put together. A motor-powered inflatable dinghy is in
attendance and a motor transport vessel lies off-shore. (Coll. Peter Schenk)

The barges

Two types of barge were available for the invasion force. One, the *Prähme*, was
a river freight vessel while the others were coastal barges. The *Seeleichter*, a flat-
bottomed, coastal barge, was used for taking loads between sea-going ships
and the shore and the *Schuten* to store goods temporarily, acting as a floating
warehouse. The river-going vessels were frequently powered by 1940. Most of
the 2318 Prahms came from the Rhine, and a number of different types
existed. The smaller, termed Type A1, were 38.5m (126ft) in length while the
larger, Type A2, were 50m (164ft) overall. There were 1336 A1s and 982 A2s
in Operation Sealion. These barges were converted to carry tanks by having
cross-bracings fitted and the bow rebuilt with a ramp within, a removable
wooden bulkhead and a ramp of track supports without. The external ramp
was never entirely satisfactory for it depended on the barge being solidly

beached if it was to hold steady. Further, it delivered the exiting machine into the water if it was afloat and on to a dry beach only after the tide had dropped and it was beached. The water was something tanks could deal with, but trucks could not. The problem was not solved before mid-September.

The need for cross-Channel transport was felt early on by such units as Engineer Battalion 47, from which an officer went to the captured French aircraft factory near Albert on the First World War battlefield of the Somme. There he asked the commander of the Luftwaffe formation which was getting the place back into production if he could take some of the disused fuel tanks (according to Ansel[5]) or aircraft floats (according to Schenk[6]). Siebel was an aircraft manufacturer who had given employment to Göring after the First World War and whom the commander of the Luftwaffe had now engaged to help in aircraft production. When he discovered what the engineer wanted the materials for, to make cross-Channel rafts, he turned his mind to the problem himself. He suggested using bridging pontoons as floats and redundant, water-cooled aircraft engines for propulsion, a powering system that was also applied to barges. The AF barge was a modified unpowered vessel to which two BMW 6U (600hp) aircraft engines were fitted at the stern on a specially constructed gantry. They were clumsy, noisy, slow and only capable of forward motion unaided and only about a hundred were available for Sealion, but move they could, at about 6 knots.

Figure 13 Barges assembled at Rotterdam Meerhaven. A gantry with aircraft engines is fitted to the vessel on the right. (Coll. Peter Schenk)

The Type AS barge was an armoured, powered infantry vessel, strengthened against enemy fire by reinforcing its sides with concrete. They carried ten assault boats which used slides for launching. Eighteen were ready for Sealion. None of the vessels discussed so far were capable of putting armour ashore fast. The ramps in Type A craft took time to erect and the tanks emerging were in danger of being targeted by the enemy before they got into action. The problem had been addressed in part with the invention of both submersible and floating tanks, but these still had to be delivered and disembarked effectively. For this purpose the Type B barge was developed from the Type A to launch the armour into water some 4m (13ft) deep. A limiting factor was the slope of the ramp which could not exceed 30° and therefore had to be 11m (36ft) long. The unpowered barge was towed to the required depth where it dropped an anchor from the stern and two from the bows either side of the launch area into which the ramp was thrust, floating on a rubber dinghy until weighted down by an emerging submersible tank. After unloading the Type Bs were to go back for a conventional load to land on the beach. The initial order for 60 such barges was subsequently increased to 70. The floating tanks were very wide because they had their flotation tanks fixed on either side and a new barge, the Type C, had to be built to take them. To avoid the dangers of having a large exit opening in the bow which would have endangered the vessel at sea, the door was made in the stern and the ramp was fixed in position permanently; the barge moored stern shorewards, the stern opened and out drove the tanks into the sea.

The tanks

In service at the time were two tanks that satisfied General Guderian's specification in guns, the Panzer (PzKpfw) III Ausf E, with a 5cm gun where the earlier model had a 3.7cm gun and the Panzer IV with a 7.5cm weapon. The former weighed 19.5 tonnes and the latter, depending on the precise model, between 17 and 21 tonnes; neither suited for flotation devices. To obtain the necessary firepower ashore these tanks were fitted with deep wading equipment which allowed them to operate in water up to 3.96m (13ft) deep.[7] At the end of June a tank was delivered to the Naval Shipyard at Wilhelmshaven for testing under the supervision of the Director of Equipment, Captain Paul Zieb. They took it to Schilling for the purpose. It was fitted with a schnorkel which had an extension tube attached to a float which also carried a radio antenna. Extensive safety precautions were taken and they experimented with an emergency lift. A diver attached the hook of a crane and the machine was lifted out of the water in 'only a few minutes' which they decided gave enough opportunity to resuscitate the men inside. The tank performed well, except that, if it halted, it tended to sink into the seabed and was in danger of becoming stuck.[8]

Although the first, experimental tank had done well, the task of making tanks waterproof in large numbers was a considerable undertaking. Rubber coverings that could be blown off with explosive cables were fitted over every opening. The difficult joint between the turret and the hull was sealed with an inflated hose. The exhausts were fitted with special valves to keep seawater out and the engines cooled by letting seawater into the cooling system. The steering was either by gyro compass or by instructions received by radio. Various accidents occurred, one fatal when exhaust gas got into the tank, and the lesson learned was that underwater obstacles could not be seen and avoided. Otherwise the machines, once the water sealing problems had been overcome, did well. By late August 160 Panzer III(U) tanks with 3.7cm guns, but only eight with Guderian's choice of 5cm guns, were ready, as were 42 Panzer IVs.

The lighter Panzer II was, at 8.9 tonnes, suited to surface operation when equipped with floats. These took some time to manufacture. As the gun was only a 2cm weapon, the vehicle was more of an armoured scouting machine than a combat tank. There were 52 of these finished by the end of August, giving a theoretical strength of over 260 machines for Sealion: the equivalent of an armoured division.

Floating fortresses

The Army did not rest content while the Navy laid on the transport, as the search for flotation devices at the aircraft works in Albert showed. In July *Pionierbataillon 47* had been ordered to use any auxiliary and bridging equipment to create sea-going rafts. All sorts of materials were pressed into service. Bridge pontoons and sections looked promising, but a sea test between the mainland and Jersey revealed their vulnerability to flooding and demonstrated that another device, a kapok-filled sack, soon became dangerously water-logged. Major Siebel designed a ferry using Engineer Pontoon Bridge B pontoons with a timber superstructure and splashboards powered by airscrews, but that also was found wanting. Inspiration came with the discovery of closed-in pontoons abandoned by the British in their retreat and the closed pontoon floats of the Austrian Herbert bridge were brought into service as well as the massive pontoons of the 1938 heavy bridge. A catamaran was created by making a timber deck between the nine-section floats. Siebel offered 750hp BMW propeller engines and it was also found that 75hp Ford V8 truck engines could be mounted on them, giving a combination of steady Ford power for cruising and a boost of BMW for attack. After a number of men had been finely and thoroughly sliced up by the propellers, someone thought it wise to put protective grilles around the airscrews. About 20 Herbert ferries were made.[9] With multiple engines they were challenging things to control as engine minders and machines had to be working in perfect harmony to keep the craft running straight and true. Best of all were the heavy pontoon ferries which were much more stable and could carry an entire anti-aircraft or *flak* unit of one 8.8cm and two 2cm guns. These floating batteries were to be deployed on the flanks of the advancing fleet. About 25 were ready for Sealion.[10]

Figure 14 A heavy bridge pontoon ferry with two 8.8cm flak guns undergoing trials. (Coll. Peter Schenk)

The gunboats, land tows and hospital ships

The regular Navy was going to be fully occupied with flank cover duties and with the diversionary operation in the North Sea, while the Luftwaffe could not fly continuously, so provision had to be made for artillery support from the sea. This was discussed with Admiral Schniewind on 17 August and it was decided that 20 barges would be made into floating 15cm gun batteries. This gave problems of stability at sea and there were not enough tugs to tow them, so it was decided to use the coasters instead. Only five ships were found for this purpose, four of which were armed with 15cm guns and another with two 10.5cm guns. All had 2cm Oerlikons as anti-aircraft weapons. Twenty-seven lighter vessels were also converted by mounting 7.5cm field guns, but these proved less satisfactory as everything was crammed in without enough room to work the guns and the 3.7cm anti-aircraft guns properly. However, they were capable of giving some support to the infantry when landing.

There was no time to develop elaborate jetties or piers that would convert the open beach to a seaport but thought was given to movement on the newly captured beach. The engineers and gunners already used tracked vehicles in their work but in addition to their needs there would be the extra work of getting bogged-down trucks and other vehicles off the beaches or out of mud. The forces already equipped were formed into land-tow groups and additional tracked machines were brought into service from the numbers of captured or redundant vehicles the Germans had acquired.

The Army asked for 1000 beds in 20 hospital ships but the Navy was unable to comply in full. The beds were provided, but in 15 vessels which were converted for the purpose in ten days. The tasks included not only the treatment of the wounded but also the rescue of wrecked units and the evacuation of casualties over the whole width of the front. An attempt was made to register the ships with the Red Cross but the British objected, saying that they were too small to be able to give treatment to the wounded.[11]

The build-up

The challenge of gathering the invasion fleet together involved more than engineering work to convert them to their new use, though that was demanding enough. First, the barges had to be found and requisitioned. The

Naval Bases in Germany were responsible for this and the Bremen base set up an office in Koblenz to have easy access to German inland waterways. The barges had then to be moved to the yards responsible for the conversion work and the harbours from which they were destined to sail made ready for them and for those who were to sail in them, involving commands in the Netherlands and in France. Those who used to sail in them had also to be dealt with, for while the skippers were retained to man them in war, their families, who had lived aboard, had to be housed elsewhere.

In a paper given at the Führer meeting of 26 July the Naval High Command had gone into the matter thoroughly. The impact on domestic commerce and manufactures was pointed out before the raw material requirements were listed:

- 30,000 tons of steel;
- 40,000 cubic metres of wood;
- 75,000 cubic metres of concrete.

The diversion of resources from naval construction would delay the building of the battleship *Tirpitz* by a month. The cable industry, making submarine nets, mine cables and so forth, would lose three weeks' production. Sealion must, therefore, be given overall priority. Hitler agreed to this and work went ahead, but the speed with which barge conversion could be done was disappointing. On 8 August delivery of vessels to German yards for work to begin stood at 331 instead of 436. In Belgium and the Netherlands things were going a little better and the shortfall was made up by the discovery of more barges in France. However, by 26 August it became clear that, in France, fewer than 175 vessels would be ready by 1 September instead of the 224 planned. The supervisor of shipyards reported on 30 August:

. . . the search encompassed the area from Le Havre up the Seine to 150km [90 miles] above Paris. The barges were widely scattered and were hidden, to some extent, in the Seine tributaries. At the beginning the daily intake was 15, which rose to 50 barges. In about 14 days 450 barges were seized. These barges had to be unloaded by the Transport Chief with the assistance of the Wehrmacht Transport Directorate and distributed to the various shipyards. The daily target was 30–49 barges.

The report continues to explain the delay in doing the conversion work, some six days, occasioned by the shortage of qualified workers and appropriate tools. To that was added the dearth of materials and the lack of cooperation shown by the French. However, with output running at 20–25 barges a day, 300 were forecast to be available by 10 September. In the event, the first 200 were ready three days later and the final 100 on 21 September.[12]

Work on barges once they got to the yards was better organised in Germany where some 7000 civilians joined the engineer troops to do the job. Most productive of all were the Belgian and Dutch yards where Amsterdam turned out 390 barges, Rotterdam 649 and Antwerp 100.

The steamers needed were gathered in from the conquered territories to supplement those supplied from Germany. About 130 were found as far south as the Gironde, but in sum 111 came from Germany, 31 from France and 26 from the Low Countries. The conversion of transports to take men, horses and vehicles proved to be as demanding as the modification of barges. The report from the depot at Stettin (Szczecin on the River Oder) gives an indication of the problems. First, manpower; they had been allocated only 75 Polish workers to convert 38 ships. Then there was not enough room to berth the ships alongside the warehouses so materials had to be ferried out to remote moorings. They were short of stores to the tune of 50,000 lifejackets, 2000 iron rafts, 200 wooden rafts, 4000 paddles, 10,000 vehicle chocks, 100 boathooks, 100 assault ladders, 150 horse boxes, 4000 horse stalls, 200 wash stands, 100 cranes for loading motor vehicles, 50 cargo nets, 10 gangways, 350 hatchways, 100 WC cabins, 100 lifebelts and 1000 fenders. The response was enterprising and vigorous. The workforces of various companies were pooled and reorganised to concentrate on specific tasks. The carpenters were gathered together to make the wooden rafts, for example, while an improvised legion of sailmakers got to work turning out lifejackets.

Getting hold of the number of tugs proved difficult. By 15 August the 39 Navy tugs had been augmented by 59 requisitioned and 100 privately owned. It was thought that Belgium and the Netherlands would yield about 80, but none had come from France and so fishing trawlers were found: 90 collected at Wesermünde and 47 at Cuxhaven. Rotterdam gathered 65 locally and got another 20 from Koblenz. Eventually the rest were squeezed out of France.[13]

Moving the vessels from the yards to the embarkation ports was the next problem. The small boats could take an inland route through the canal system or by river; the Rhine, for example, debouches into the river systems of the Netherlands. There the Schelde near Antwerp gives access to canals to Ghent, Bruges, Ostend, Dunkirk and Calais. On 30 August, for example, it was reported that Convoy 506 left Emden for Le Havre by the inland route. The sea routes were more hazardous. From the north ships made their way in peril of mines or of attack from air or sea through the West Frisian Islands to the Netherlands and the Channel ports. Even inland things did not go all that smoothly. On the Seine a weir was in need of repair but the French company given the contract made slow progress and the water level went on falling until tugs could not move. The German Army Engineers took over.

The build-up at the embarkation ports was quickened in September, although the reported figures are difficult to interpret as they appear to have been compiled on varying criteria and probably include some vessels which then moved on westwards. Ostend, for example, reported 196 barges on 12 September but only 76 a week later. By 19 September there were, perhaps, 24 barges in Nieuport, 136 in Dunkirk, 40 in Gravelines, 204 in Calais, 236 in Boulogne and 47 in Le Havre. The 19 September figures for motorboats run Dunkirk 15, Calais 38, Boulogne 151, while motor fishing vessels read Calais 92, Boulogne 125 and Le Havre 100 as against zero for Dunkirk, Calais and Le Havre a week earlier.[14]

The Army prepares

With the arrival of the first of the barges and ships in the embarkation area the Army was able to start training its troops in their use. Before landing in England the Army had to be loaded aboard their ships and it was not until early September that this problem could be tackled. The large ships presented the least problem. With four hatches open 854 men, 62 horses, 88 motorcycles, 21 cars, 34 trucks, five anti-tank guns, eight field kitchens, six wagons, 28 carts and 30 bicycles could be loaded in seven hours. The fewer the hatches, the greater the loading difficulty. Horses were a severe challenge as they slipped about on metal decks making a fearful clatter which scared them even more. However, they were a crucial element of the transport system, vital for pulling field kitchens, supply carts and wagons and even some of the guns, for the combat troops may have been motorised but the bulk of the Army still depended on horse-drawn vehicles. Getting tanks and other vehicles aboard demanded cranes which were standard for dockside work, but off-loading onto rafts when the machines had been transported by ship instead of barge required strengthened cranes for lifting them onto rafts to be towed ashore. By contrast, the Army found a barge taking 150 men took only an hour and a half to load and they had been able to begin training on these smaller vessels in mid-August. The beach at Paris Plage, near Le Touquet was chosen, although it was rather gentle and welcoming sloping sand instead of the shingle and steep beaches to be encountered in England. On 17 August a demonstration was laid on for the Army High Command and the 16th Army sailed from Boulogne to land there in brilliant, peaceful sunshine. In spite of these perfect conditions things did not go smoothly. Some barges ran aground too far out to unload their troops, others had trouble with the unloading ramps and everything moved too slowly. The Engineers, it was agreed, had done well, but much more practice was ordered by General Halder.[15]

Once loaded, a proportion of the vessels would have to wait for hours while the flotilla was assembled for departure.[16] In some ports, Dunkirk, for example, the time available to clear the port would be as short as an hour and a half; delay meant waiting for the next tide. The needs of the second and subsequent sailings were also considered as darkness could be the vital contributor to survival under air or sea attack. Loading in the dark was thus another skill to be mastered. It was necessary to use lights to load heavy equipment onto transport ships which risked air attack so it was decided this should only take place when the operation was actually taking place. The time taken was between 25 and 50 per cent longer than daytime working.[17]

The landings and handling of the barges and rafts were practised with care as instructed. Werner Schatke was in the Luftwaffe, paratroop trained, and served with an anti-aircraft flak regiment through the campaign in France. He recollected:

. . . I went right through France and finished up at a place called Fécamp on the coast near Dieppe. . . . It was straight away training and guard duty and training and then they had the crazy idea straight away to attack England. . . [We used] two barges and there were planks across there and hooks where you hang on to it flat out, and outboard motors and a big aircraft engine with a propeller and a big 88 millimetre anti-aircraft gun and some smaller guns and we used to go in the Channel for training like that. First gently to see how you hang on to it. They wanted to see if you fell off or anything like that. . . . There were Army as well as paratroops on these barges. Of course, there were just about 200 soldiers on each float like. It was very scary. Very scary it was. . . .

Mind, we had a nice time swimming in the sea too. It was training more or less every day, like, but we had some time for relaxation. I never found any French people that were hostile.[18]

Quite apart from the unusual requirements of debouching from landing craft, the Army had to restructure the attack force to get the key units ashore in the appropriate sequence. Mention has been made above of the first and second echelons of the first wave of landings, the need for which flowed from this reorganisation. The first echelon of each infantry division was planned to consist of two reinforced regiments; 6762 men. They were equipped with 49 tanks, 14 light field guns, 27 anti-tank guns, 54 light and 72 heavy mortars, eight rocket launchers and eight mountain guns. Their transport included nine light tracked vehicles, about 90 4×4 Pkw field cars, 300 horse-drawn carts, 34 trucks, 135 motorcycles and another 46 such machines with sidecars, and nearly 2000 bicycles. Then there were nearly 350 horses. The light arms included 80 heavy and 292 light machine-guns. This was a formidable, well-armed assault force.

The second echelon had twice the number of men, nearly 4500 horses and almost 2000 vehicles, as well as the heavy field guns and the howitzers; a solid reinforcement to assure the tenure of the bridgehead their forerunners had secured.[19] The weaponry of this follow-up force was entirely conventional whereas, in contrast, the first echelon were given the best and most modern equipment possible. The German 3.7cm anti-tank gun had been useless against British Matildas in France and the *Panzerabwehrkanone* or PAK issued to the first echelon was either a Czech or a French 4.7cm weapon. The light field howitzer was replaced with the 7.5cm *Gebirgskanone 15*, a weapon with a barrel length of only 112.5cm and thus handier for use in the circumstances. Self-propelled artillery was deployed and included 2cm flak and 4.7cm anti-tank guns, the latter mounted in place of the turret behind a simple shield on the old two-man training tank Panzer I chassis.[20] The 7.5cm gun was used as an assault gun when mounted on a Panzer III chassis. It was limited by the fixed forward-firing mounting which meant the whole machine had to be turned to traverse the gun, but the crew were well protected by heavy armour plate in front. Only eight batteries of six guns each were ready for Sealion.[21] Panzer IIs were converted into *Flammpanzer*, flame-throwing tanks, by removing the main gun and fitting two flame guns, each with a 180° traverse. While protected by conventional tanks these machines could attack bunkers with up to 80 two- or three-second flamings at a range of something under 35m. Those in the *Flammpanzer* had only a machine-gun for defence and so were dependent on their comrades for security against attack.[22] The troops issued with the weapon were Tank Detachment (Fl) 100 which comprised nine platoons organised in three companies. Each platoon had four *Flammpanzer*. Twenty fuel bowsers were needed in support given the ability of each tank to exhaust its on-board supplies in 15 minutes. The unit was broken up for the first stage of Sealion with ten tanks each being allocated to XIII and VII Corps of the 16th Army, the rest to come over with VII Corps in the second wave.[23]

Another entirely new weapon was the *Nebelwerfer* or 'smoke thrower', a cover name for a rocket-firing device. The Treaty of Versailles, after the previous war, had forbidden German development of new artillery but it failed to ban rocket artillery. A research station was therefore established at Kummersdorf in 1930 and there a novel design was created. Previous missiles had been unstable because the propellant was at the rear and the uncertain flight resulting made for woeful accuracy. Putting the elements the other way round, propellant in front and warhead behind, with the former's gases emerging through angled, narrow tubes further down the body gave a reliable trajectory. There were 26 venturis through which the exhaust passed, angled at 14° to give the missile spin, thus obviating the need for fins. The firing tubes were arranged in a ring of six and mounted on one of the old 3.7cm anti-tank gun carriages. A crew of four manned this revolutionary new weapon, as yet unproven in action.[24] The *Nebelwerferregiment 51* was assigned to the 16th Army and had eight batteries with nine weapons apiece. It was to cross in the second wave.

Final orders

By mid-September the preparations were sufficiently advanced to permit the issue of the orders for the operation. They read as follows:

Nr 32

14 September 1940

Orders to Army Group A

for the execution of Operation "Sealion"

SECRET COMMAND MATTERS

TOP LEVEL!

RECIPIENTS ONLY

(25 Copies)

Army Group Order Nr 1
For the execution of "Sealion"

1) Enemy

   The disposition of the British army (status as at beginning of September 1940) is to be assumed as follows:

   (a) *Some 17 divisions deployed in defence of the coast. Close cooperation between these divisions and the coastal defence sections of the Air Force and Navy is probable.*

   (b) *22 divisions as tactical and operational reserves in the area around London, whose task will be to throw back in a counter-attack any opposition that has penetrated that far.*

   The disposition of the British Army leads us to suppose that the British army command is expecting German troops to land on the east as well as the south coast, with the main concentration in the south.

   Details:

   (a) *Situation map of 10.9.40 relating to Situation Report Nr 415 Army Gen. Staff.*

   (b) *'The British Army', updated at 20.7.40 Army Gen. Staff, Dept Enemy Armies West Nr 2700/40 g.*

2) The task of the army *is to land with strong forces in southern England in collaboration with the Navy and Luftwaffe, to defeat the British Army, and to occupy London and, depending on the situation, other parts of Britain. The tasks assigned to the Army are the responsibility of Army Group A Command with the 16th and 9th Armies under their orders.*

3) The task of Army Group A *is firstly to capture the English south coast between Folkestone and Worthing, and* then *take possession of a wide continuous beachhead with a depth of 20–30km inland.*

   On the arrival of further reinforcements the Army Group will proceed to launch a concerted attack up to the line:

   Thames estuary–hills S of London–Portsmouth (1st operational objective)

   It will then send fast mobile forces west of London, in order initially to seal off the capital from the S and W and then advance to the line:

   Maldon (NE of London)–Severn estuary (2nd operational objective)

4) The task of the 16th Army is, *after setting out from a line Rotterdam–Calais (including both places), to force a landing on the English coastal sector Folkestone–St Leonards (incl.) and* initially *to gain a broad bridgehead along the line:*

   Canterbury–course of Great Stour river–Ashford–Tenterden–Etchingham.

> Under the cover of this bridgehead, the strongest forces possible, especially armour, are to be brought up. Folkestone–Dover is to be taken from the W and N, and then the important coastal sector Ramsgate–Deal is to be captured for later landings.
>
> To support the attack on Dover the 1st Paratroop Regiment will be assigned to the 16th Army.

5) The task of the 9th Army is, *setting out simultaneously with 16th Army, from the line Boulogne–Le Havre, to capture the English coast between Bexhill and Worthing, and then in conjunction with 18th Army to push forward initially to the line: Hadlow Down–Burgess Hill–Storrington and westward.*

> Under cover of this bridgehead further forces, including armour, are to be brought up as quickly as possible.
>
> Two paratroop regiments are tasked with capturing Brighton and the important high ground N of Beachy Head.

6) *In their bridgehead positions the* armies will initially *concentrate all available resources on defence.*

> We must assume that it will not be possible to break out from the bridgehead to attack and capture the 1st operational objective until the 8th day after the first landing, and that in this period the enemy will put his operational reserve into an attack.
>
> All measures necessary to hold the bridgehead at all costs *must be taken in advance.*

7) Separation-line *between 16th and 9th Armies:*

> Former corps boundary between VII and XXXVIII A.K. (any alterations to be made by the armies by mutual agreement)–Boulogne (9)–St Leonards (16)–Mayfield (16)–East Grinstead (9)–Reigate (16)–Windsor (16)–Banbury (9).

8) Disposition of forces: *see Appendix 1 [not reproduced in this work].*

9) Ports of departure:

> (a) 16th Army: *Rotterdam, Antwerp, Ostend, Dunkirk, Calais.*
>
> *Auxiliary ports Nieuwport and Gravelines, but loading cannot take place here.*
>
> (b) 9th Army: *Boulogne and Le Havre*
>
> The time required *for embarking and bringing across the 9th Army formations is disproportionately longer than for the 16th Army, which has five departure-ports at its disposal.*
>
> *Therefore from S-Day + 3 onward,* 16th Army will *make the port of* Calais *temporarily available to 9th Army.*

T. [Transport] will report to Army group Command as to how many days 9th Army will be able to count on having Calais available as a port of departure.

Apart from the ports listed under (a) and (b) every *opportunity is to be exploited, in* close co-operation *with the relevant naval authorities, to dispatch smaller formations from river estuaries and small harbours.*

10) The allocation of shipping capacity *is the responsibility of the Navy, who will as far as possible take account of the wishes of the armies and individual corps.*

11) The making ready *and disposition of forces, and the sequence of their embarkation will be determined by the armies.*

    (a)   The readying of the 1st wave *will in general be determined by shipping capacity provided for it.*

        However, depending on circumstances, *the organisation must be as flexible as possible, to allow for changes to be made* during *the day of the crossing.*

        The readying of the 2nd wave *is determined by the definite choice of Rotterdam and Antwerp as departure-ports for the 16th and Boulogne for the 9th Army.*

        The armies will bring the formations of the 2nd Wave punctually up to the designated ports in such a way as to avoid unnecessary troop concentrations on shore for a long time, and so that there can be flexible *movement to suit the situation – if necessary even of individual units.*

        The readying of the 3rd wave, *already under the armies' orders by train and on foot, will be controlled by the armies, or else they will call them up at the appropriate time from the Army Group Command. The scheduled times and unloading areas for the* tracked vehicles *of XXXI. and XV. A.K., as well as the 15. and 164. Divs., which are to be brought up by rail, are to be checked by the armies in conjunction with the Bv. T.O. Any requests for alterations are to be submitted without delay.*

        The readying of the 3rd wave must also take place in such a way that a flexible *embarkation can proceed in* different *ports as circumstances require.*

    b)   Disposition and sequence *are to be prepared in such a way that* first and foremost *combat units can be taken across, as well as those weapons which will be needed as an* urgent priority *by infantry*

*fighting hard throughout the day on the English coast, i.e. artillery,
flak units, panzer units, heavy weapons, ammunition.*

*In so doing it will often be necessary to abandon the battle-order
arrangement of the formations and units. Rather, it will be the job of the
first staffs (rgt., div.) arriving on the beaches to assemble tactically and
deploy the forces landing in their sector of the coast into highly varied
units.*

*Now is not too soon to establish divisional sectors for the landing and
the first engagements. All the elements landing in one sector – i.e.
including units that are not part of the same battle-order – will* initially
be under the orders of the relevant Div. Commander in that sector.

Not until *the defensive strength of the first landed* combat troops *has
been built up sufficiently, can senior staffs, essential supply services and
elements of columns be integrated.*

12) Home staffs

The task *of the home staffs, as the responsible bodies within their
commands operating from the continental mainland, is to provide smoothly
and continuously the crucially important back-up and supply of the fighting
formations, and to go on doing so even after they have crossed to England.*

*They must work closely with the naval departments in charge of sea
transport. They will receive their instructions from the commanders already
located in England, according to the situation there.*

*Because situations can arise at the mainland departure-ports (due to
enemy air-raids, blockading of ports, fire from artillery and enemy vessels),
which the commanders in England are unaware of, but which require swift
and effective intervention, the home staffs can only operate successfully if
they have faultless information links (radio, dispatch aircraft, motor-
launch) to their command posts in southern England.*

*Close contact must also be maintained with the office of the O.Qu. (Senior
Quartermaster) England.*

13) Co-operation with the operational Luftwaffe *is governed by Appendix 3
to Ob.d H. Gen. St.d H. – Op. Abt – Nr 480/40 g.Kdos.*

In urgent cases it may be necessary to consider combining the forces of
both Luftflotten *(2 and 3) and in certain circumstances Lfl. 5 as well;
requests to this effect to go via A.O.K. to the Army group Command, who
will pass them on to Ob. d L. and/or the Luftflotten.*

*Furthermore, the armies will direct all requests for their sectors – including
those to cripple enemy movements behind the lines – directly to the*

Luftflotten and/or Flieger-Korps assigned to cooperate with them, while keeping the Army Group Command broadly informed at all times. Army Group Command will, if necessary, control centrally any requests to attack targets deep inland.

T. By 21.9.40 the AOKs will report to Army Group Command the arrangements they have agreed with the Luftflotten and/or Flieger-Korps regarding:

(a) *Support for landing and advance by the close-range Flieger-Korps and paratroopers.*

(b) *Plans to use smoke-screens.*

(c) *Breaking up of enemy columns advancing towards the invasion area along roads and railways (a map with Army Groups' suggestions for key points at which to cut railways will be sent to the Luftflotten and AOK separately).*

(d) *Rearward limit for dropping bombs, and recognition-zones.*

By the same date a report is requested on the agreements reached with the Luftflotten about aerial reconnaissance (see Appendix 3, fig.2 [not reproduced in this work]). Once again you are particularly asked to pay special attention to the terms for the liaison service *between fighting elements of the army and the flying elements of the Luftwaffe (Ob.d. H. Gen.St.d.H./Ausb.Abt Nr 750/40 g of 29.3.1940), and to the terms of the* recognition service *between the fighting elements of the army and the flying elements of the Luftwaffe (Ob.d.H. Gen.St.d.H./Ausb.Abt. Nr 450/40 g of 8.3.1940).*

The flares and recognition signals and code-forms will in each instance be announced by Air Command and must be familiar to all responsible officers.

Planned battle HQs:

Luftflotten command 2: SW of Sangatte

" 3: *Deauville*

Flieger-Korps VIII: St Inglebert

" I: *Le Touquet*

14) Co-operation with the navy *is governed by Ob.d.H. Gen. St. d. H. – Op.Abt –(Ia) Nr 480/40 g.Kdos. of 30.8.40 and special instructions from the Navy.*

The release of smoke-screens at the time of landing *will be carried out exclusively by unit commanders of the* army *(Div. Cdrs) after prior agreement with the naval officers commanding the transport fleet.*

For this it will be necessary for the relevant army and naval officers to be in the same vessel.

For the naval command structure, see Appendix 4 [not reproduced in this work].

15) Regiment 51 *will be under the command of A.O.K. 16. Place and time for it to be brought up will be announced.*

16) Artillery Kdr *with the 10cm and 15cm cannon batteries assigned to it, is to be integrated by A.O.K.16 if possible at the start of the 2nd wave. After a successful landing on the coast, it is to be positioned* facing the sea *in such a way that it can cover the Calais–Deal and Boulogne–Hastings zones as soon as possible. In view of our own mine-fields and the coastal batteries remaining on the mainland, deployment of the artillery must be carried out in concert with the naval authorities. It is foreseen that individual sections will be handed over to 9th Army later.*

17) Time of day *of the S-day landing on the English coast will be the subject of a separate order.*

18) *To facilitate verbal and radio communications all English place-names will be pronounced* as written.

19) *On S-day minus 2 at 18.00, the* staff *of Army Group Command will be located in the barrack camp 7km NE of Amiens.*

  An advance HQ on the coast will be recce'd and announced in good time (probably N of Boulogne).

20) Inputs

  T. A.O.K. 9 and 16 are to report to Army Group Command by 21.9:

  a) Scheduled readiness *of waves 1–3.*

  b) First proposal *for the landing on the south coast of England and the capture of the line of the continuous beachhead, incl. the divisional battle-sectors.*

  c) Battle HQs *of the A.O.Ks and Gen. Commands.*

    a)–c) on map 1:250 000 or 1:1 000 000

  d) Possible alterations *to the approximate timetable*

  e) Intended deployment of Artl. Kdr. 106 with assigned sections (A.O.K. 16)

  f) Copy of the instructions for the home staff

  g) Survey of the shipping capacity planned for the individual ports and corresponding approximate troop distribution.

  For correctness;

  Chief of the General Staff of   *Deputising:*

  Army group A   *signed Busch*

  (signed) von Sodenstern   *Generaloberst*

  General der Infanterie

Appendices:
Appendix   1: Disposition of forces [battle order?]
            2: First combat actions
            3: Special orders for Luftwaffe formations with the army
            4: Command structure of the navy
            5: Orders for intelligence communications[25]
    [Appendix material not reproduced here.]

It is interesting to note that, in paragraph 1, the estimate of British forces is more accurate that that previously generated by the German intelligence services, but the disposition of those forces assumed is wrong, with far too much of the power placed north and west of the Thames at Reading. The paratroop units mentioned in paragraphs 4 and 5 came under Luftwaffe command and are discussed alongside air force arrangements. In paragraph 11 flexibility is emphasised, both in the bringing up of troops to be transported in the second wave and in the deployment of troops after landing. Indeed, it is made entirely clear that divisional commanders have total control in their landing sector and all troops within that sector come under that command, no matter what their formal place might be in the battle order. Paragraph 13 facilitates direct communication between ground forces and the air support units allocated to them. This dedication to adopting whatever tactics or organisational structure will lead to victory lay at the heart of the Army's plans. All it required now was for the Luftwaffe to achieve sufficient supremacy in the air and the Navy to secure the seaway, and the invasion of England could commence as soon as 21 September.

Notes and References

1 Schenk, Peter, *Invasion of England 1940*, London, Conway Maritime Press, 1990, pp. 10–13.

2 *Ibid.*, pp. 16–17.

3 *Ibid.*, p. 27.

4 *Ibid.*, pp. 48–55.

5 Ansel, Walter, *Hitler Confronts England*, Durham, NC, Duke University Press, 1960, p. 104.

6 Schenk, p. 28.

7 Quarrie, Bruce, *Encyclopedia of the German Army in the 20th Century*, Wellingborough, Patrick Stephens, 1989, pp. 194–200.

8 Quoted in Schenk, pp. 109–10.

9 *Ibid.*, pp. 114–24.

10 *Ibid.*, pp. 124–8.

11 *Ibid.*, pp. 141–4.

12 *Ibid.*, pp. 154–5.

13 *Ibid.*, pp. 160–2.

14 *Ibid.*, pp. 168–9.

15 Ansel, pp. 229–30.

16 Kieser, Egbert, *Operation Sea Lion*, London, Arms and Armour, 1997, p. 224.

17 Schenk, p. 187.

18 Schatke, Werner, 'The Memories of a German Soldier' in *Everyone's War No. 5*, Leeds, Second World War Experience Centre, 2002, pp. 16–17.

19 Schenk, p.188 [Horse-drawn carts are incorrectly listed as 'cars' in the English text, Schenk, e-mail, 27.1.04].

20 *Ibid.*, p. 184.

21 *Ibid.*, p. 185.

22 Perrett, Bryan, *German Light Panzers 1932–1942, New Vanguard 26*, Oxford, Osprey, 1998, p. 13.

23 Schenk, pp. 184–5.

24 Quarrie, pp. 176–8.

25 Klee, Karl, *Das Unternehmen Seelöwe, Vol. 2*, 1958, pp. 408–14, trans A. McGeoch.

chapter 5

Controlling the sea and the sky

The invasion of England depended on security at sea and domination in the air. The command of the sea was not the responsibility of the German Navy alone, for the crossing was to take place largely in the Straits of Dover, a narrow waterway easily covered by heavy artillery on shore. Indeed, there had been the suggestion that covering fire for a landing in England could be provided by heavy guns in France, but this was rejected as impractical.

Coastal artillery

The installation of heavy guns overlooking the Straits was begun by the Todt Organisation on 22 July 1939 with the erection of the *Grosser Kurfürst* battery from Pillau at the Pas de Calais. This installation was armed with four 28cm guns of the K (E) Bruno Class. These were designed originally for the 1917–18 *Von Der Tann* class battleships and in their various evolving forms hurled a shell of 325–525lbs (148–265kg) for something between 12–18 miles (20–37km).[1] In addition the Army deployed its railway guns. There was one 21cm K12 capable of sending a shell of 236lbs (107kg) a distance of some 70 miles (115km) but it was not to be used liberally. There had always been a problem with large weapons because of the wear that firing inflicted on the barrel. In order to counter this, the K12 was made with eight grooves down the length of the barrel and the shells had corresponding ribs.

The worst fault was the recoil; the gun carriage had to be jacked up lest the breech bury itself in the ground when the gun fired. It then had to be jacked down again to reload it. The other rail-mounted guns were six 28cm K5s which fired a shell of 560lb (255kg) to a maximum range of 38 miles (62km) and had the advantage that, with two sets of 12 bogie wheels, it did not need jacking up to fire and thus could be reloaded more easily.[2] There were more railway guns of Bruno class to give four batteries between Boulogne and Calais, *Friedrich August*, *Siegfried*, *Grosser Kurfürst* and *Prinz Heinrich* and one between Calais and Dunkirk, *Oldenburg*. They were placed under Navy command and first tried firing on British merchant shipping on 12 August. A firing of two and a half hours took place on 22 August, apparently with some success. The British hastened to install heavy guns at Dover to reply. A massive attack on British ships and on Dover itself was made on 9 September when 226 shells were fired. The presence of these guns was, therefore, no secret and they were clearly a danger to the Royal Navy's larger ships; the smaller vessels had time to take evading action after the first shot had been fired.[3]

Mines

Great emphasis was put on the protection of the flanks of the invasion fleet by mine barriers but the conditions of the Channel made it difficult to create such defences effectively. The currents and tides made the use of conventional moored mines impossible and so a new device, the *Gezeitenmine*, or EMG tidal mine, was developed. It hung from a tethered buoy, which had the disadvantages of showing the position of the mine to any observer close to it and of the necessity to place them quite far apart to avoid one snagging the next at low water.

The most westerly of the minefields, code letter D for Dora, was laid on a north–south axis off Start Point at the west of Torbay to defend against the Royal Navy approaching from Plymouth, and ships emerging from Portsmouth to harass the invasion fleet would have to face mines (code A, Anton) south of Selsey Bill. A major cross-Channel belt of mines (B, Bruno) ran between, approximately, Brighton and Dieppe, stopping clear of the French coast to permit part of the invasion fleet to come up from Le Havre. The line from Calais to Deal was substantially mined (C, Caesar) and other C minefields ran west to east from the east Kent coast. These minefields were not single, simple lines of weapons but a series of belts containing mines of various types and the laying of them took place in a succession of missions beginning on S−9, that is, nine days before the invasion. The principal use of the EMG was in mine barrier B and conventional, moored mines were used elsewhere. The minefields themselves were defended with cable-cutting buoys and floating explosive devices to interfere with attempts to sweep them. Five minelayers were based on Cherbourg and two at Le Havre to form the Western Group while four at Ostend and three at Antwerp made up the Eastern Group.

Other mines were deployed. The British minefields protecting the east coast were taken into the German scheme as an extension of barrier C. Additional mines were laid by the Luftwaffe to cut Portsmouth off from the open sea and inshore mines were laid by German motor torpedo boats. The number of EMG mines laid was 2700 and moored mines totalled 2845. Altogether the minefields formed, as remarked by Vice Admiral Ruge, 'a strong obstacle to the British Navy'.[4]

The German fleet

On and under the sea the German Navy added to the Royal Navy's problems in resisting invasion, in part because of the forces they could deploy and in yet greater part because of what the British thought they could do. The losses suffered in the Norwegian campaign were known to the British: three cruisers and ten destroyers. The status of the damaged ships was not. In fact *Scharnhorst* and *Gneisenau*, both regarded as significant threats by the Royal Navy, were unfit for service and although the German Navy wanted at least one of them ready for sea in September, RAF air raids prevented night work at the dockyards and held up progress. The damage done to the pocket battleship *Lützow* in the Norwegian campaign was even greater and she had no prospect of putting to sea before the following year. Two new ships were being made ready, the massive battleship *Bismarck* and the heavy cruiser *Prinz Eugen*, but crews had yet to be trained, the former was not even fully fitted out and the latter had not completed her trials. The pocket battleship *Admiral Scheer* was still undergoing reconstruction and the light cruiser *Leipzig* was still being repaired after a torpedo struck her nine months earlier. Thus the German Navy was seriously depleted and could only count on one heavy cruiser, *Admiral Hipper*, three light cruisers, *Nürnberg*, *Köln* and *Emden*, and seven destroyers.[5] The Royal Navy was basing its calculations on the readiness of *Bismarck*, *Scharnhost* and *Gneisenau* as well as the ships actually fit for sea and therefore Admiral Forbes moved a large part of his fleet to Rosyth on 13 September.[6]

In addition to providing the transport fleet as described above, the German Navy had to protect the routes it was to follow, escort the barges and ferries and create diversionary activity. The latter received a great deal of attention and accounted for the deployment of the most substantial ships. Operation *Herbstreise*, Autumn Journey, was a decoy the details of which have been described in Chapter 2, a feigned invasion strike from Norway directed towards northern Britain. The fleet of some ten steamers was to be escorted by the cruisers and by four torpedo boats that had been taken in the Norwegian campaign and nine World-War-I boats usually employed as training vessels. To these were added three fleet escort ships.[7] The Army raised a number of queries about this operation, seen as an unnecessary distraction and none of their business it appears. They were answered by Colonel Warlimont.

Nr 34

15 September 1940

Instruction from The Wehrmacht High Command

Concerning planned deception manoeuvres for Operation "Sealion"

SECRET COMMAND MATTERS

6 Copies

To: OKH, Gen. St d H., Op Abt. (E)

The deception measures planned from the Norway area are principally intended to deceive enemy naval forces *and divert them from the Channel if possible. It is therefore necessary,*

    (a) to carry out these deception measures early enough for counter-measures by the British fleet to be triggered, and

    (b) by leaving port, to bring about an actual counter-action

What follows from this is:

    As to your point 1)

    The transport ships must leave port. Equally, the troops must be embarked.

    However, they will then be disembarked in the same port, or an adjacent

one. This means that the deception movement itself will be carried out with empty *transports.*
As to your point 2)
Yes. The ships will turn back on S−day minus 2 after nightfall
As to your point 3):
That is correct from the army's point of view. *However, since Ob.d.M. (C-in-C Navy) intends to divert elements of the British fleet, he wants to keep to this timetable.*
As to your point 4):
It is sufficient to place the troops in readiness.

Chief of the Wehrmacht High Command
PP.
(Signed) Warlimont[8]

Thus the Army was obliged to cooperate with the Navy in this. Of itself Operation *Herbstreise* seems unimpressive. It was to finish two days before Sealion began and although the fleet would sail after elaborate charades of troop embarkation with the hope of provoking a British counter-attack the extent to which it would assist the true invasion given the true status of the German Navy is questionable. What the Royal Navy made of it would be crucial.

The rest of the German Navy's strength was devoted to Sealion. The orders of Naval Commander West on 14 September were, 'Three groups of five submarines each, all destroyers and T[orpedo]-Boats west of the western mine barrier, two groups of three submarines each and all motor torpedo boats east of the mine barrier'. On 6 August Rear Admiral Karl Dönitz, the Commander-in-Chief, U-boats, estimated that, assuming there were no further losses, there would be seven large boats (Type IX), 12 medium (Type VII) and 20 small boats (Type II), which included 13 training boats; 39 in all. However, a number of them would be unready to put to sea for lack of crew or because they needed repair and about ten of them might fall into that category. The boats were to be concentrated along the Channel with the small boats between Portsmouth and Le Havre, south of minefield A and west of B, and between East Anglia and the Netherlands, north of minefield C. The medium boats would be south of minefield D, between the Devon and Brittany coasts and the large boats would guard the approaches from the south Irish Sea and the Atlantic off Cornwall. In addition small boats were to be positioned off Tyneside and south-east of the Orkneys to take

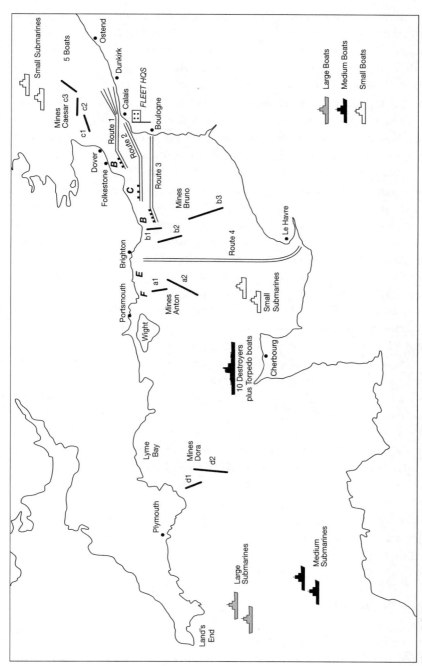

Figure 15 The German dispositions in the Channel, September 1940

advantage of a counter-attack stimulated by Operation *Herbstreise*. These flotillas would have access to supplies of fuel and torpedoes from bases at Rotterdam, backed up by Den Helder and Flushing (Vlissingen) in the case of the southern North Sea, at Cherbourg, with Le Havre in reserve, in the case of the central Channel and at Lorient, with alternatives at Brest and St Nazaire in the case of the Western Approaches. The positions were allocated in broad terms only as changes in events would demand changes in the deployment, and provision was made to leave gaps in the minefields to permit the movement of the larger boats from the west into the Channel as such. Meanwhile the campaign against merchant shipping continued, to the chagrin of the Royal Navy which was hamstrung by the need to stand guard against invasion. Admiral Raeder undertook, on 5 September, to be responsible for ordering the invasion deployment in person. Dönitz had small confidence in the Sealion plan and, when an officer under training expressed the fear that he would not have the chance of active service, told him the war would continue for many months. 'Don't forget,' he said, 'that we are fighting the most powerful navy in the world.'[9]

The destroyers were mostly of the Beitzen class, armed with five 5 inch (12.7cm) guns, eight anti-aircraft guns, half 37mm and half of 20mm, and eight 21 inch torpedo tubes. The exception was the *Karl Galster* which was somewhat larger but similarly armed and the only survivor of her class after the losses at Narvik. Of the torpedo boats, seven were ships commissioned in the late 1920s, of 800 tons displacement and armed with three 4.1 inch (10.5cm) guns, two anti-aircraft guns and six torpedo tubes.[10] They were robust enough to engage a destroyer, if need be. The motor torpedo boats, on the other hand, were smaller and armed only with a single 4.1 inch gun in addition to their torpedo tubes. There were three flotillas, some 21 boats, all of which were to be deployed in the eastern end of the Channel. Some had been damaged or destroyed when an explosion took place in the torpedo magazine at Ostend and a couple more were hit in air raids, but repairs and replacements seemed likely to make up the numbers by the time Sealion began.[11]

The Luftwaffe

The Luftwaffe's tasks for Sealion were to carry our reconnaissance, to give direct support to the army and airborne forces, to deny freedom of movement to British reserves and to give the invasion fleet cover from both the Royal Navy and the RAF. An aggressive action by transport aircraft was the lifting of the 7th Airborne Division to Kent, an operation for which about 750 aircraft and 150 gliders were said to be available. The Luftwaffe organisation was under three Air Fleets, *Luftflotten*, each of which was divided into Flight Corps, *Fliegerkorps*. Luftflotte 5 was based in Norway and played no direct part, being tasked with action against the Royal Navy in the North Sea. Luftflotte 2, under Field Marshal Albrecht Kesselring, was based in Belgium and acted in support of the 16th Army out of the Low Countries and north-east France while Luftflotte 3, under Field Marshal Hugo Sperrle, based in Paris, flew in support of the 9th Army from north-western France. From 29 August Sperrle exchanged his VIII Fliegerkorps, which included three *Stukageschwader (StG)*, Dive Bomber Wing, units with Kesselring's I *Fliegerkorps* with its three *Kampfgeschwader (KG)*, Bomber Wing, units. This gave, leaving aside training and other specialist units, three dive-bomber, six level bomber and four fighter wings to Luftflotte 2 and one dive-bomber, seven level bomber and three fighter wings to Luftflotte 3.[12] The Stukas were vulnerable to enemy fighters and had to be escorted by their own. Their range was some 370 miles (600km) when loaded with bombs and their usefulness was maximised by having them operate across the Straits of Dover where two wings were, initially, to attack Folkestone, Dover and Dungeness while others supported the landings between Hastings and Rye. This work was to be coordinated with the rail-mounted artillery. On 17 September the firing plan was confirmed thus: before the Stuka attack all batteries were to concentrate on Sandgate to neutralise the batteries there, after which they were to shift their fire to Folkestone before moving on to Dover.[13] The remaining Stuka wing was to be used against warships. The level bombers were to hit major military centres such as Aldershot, to disrupt the railway system at Watford, Reading and other points west of London and to bomb bottlenecks in the road network to prevent reserves moving south. The rest of the bomber effort was to be kept for the opposition to the Royal Navy. The weight of work to be done was too great for simultaneous action and the tasks were divided up into action to be taken over a period of days. Throughout the RAF had to be kept at arm's length and attacks on the airfields remained in the plans.[14]

The level bombers had proved dangerous against the ships of the Royal Navy in the Norwegian campaign, with the sinking by level bombers of the destroyer *Gurkha* on 9 April and the infliction of severe damage on *Suffolk*

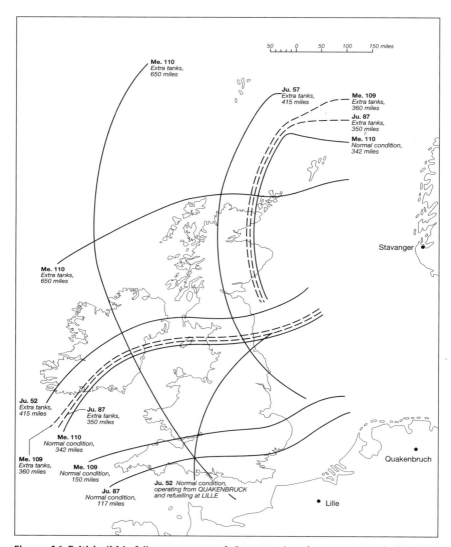

Figure 16 British (M.I. 14) assessment of German aircraft ranges as calculated in August 1941. The Ju 52 was a transport aircraft and the Ju 87 was commonly known as the Stuka, a dive-bomber. The Me 109 and Me 110 were the single-engine and twin-engine fighters. The Ju 88 and He 111 bombers were capable of reaching the whole of the British Isles and thus no limits are shown here. (After Appendix XIX, *Notes on the German Invasion of the United Kingdom,* 2nd edn, 1942)

by level bombers and a Ju 87 (Stuka) on 16 April. Both incidents were, however, the product of prolonged attacks and the extent to which the Luftwaffe could realistically claim to be able to hold the Royal Navy at bay was open to question. Here, once again, the reality and the perception of it by the British varied; having rejected the influence of air power for the previous two decades, the Royal Navy had now developed an exaggerated fear of it. The effect of the modified Junkers Ju 88, a medium/dive-bomber, had yet to be seen.

The Navy and the Luftwaffe were as ready as ever they would be to support Sealion. They only awaited the order to fix the day.

Notes and References

1 Quarrie, Bruce, *Encyclopaedia of the German Army in the 20th Century*, Wellingborough, Patrick Stephens, 1989, p. 181.

2 Quarrie, p. 183.

3 Schenk, Peter, *Invasion of England 1940*, London, Conway Maritime, 1990, pp. 323–7.

4 Schenk, pp. 328–33.

5 *Ibid.*, pp. 334–5.

6 Roskill, S. W., *The War at Sea 1939–1945, Volume 1*, London, HMSO, 1954, p. 257.

7 Schenk, pp. 335–6.

8 Klee, Karl, *Das Unternehmen Seelöwe, Vol. 2*, pp. 426–7.

9 German Naval History, *The U-boat War in the Atlantic 1939–1945*, London, HMSO, 1989, pp. 55–7.

10 *Jane's Fighting Ships of World War II*, London, Studio, 1989, p. 149.

11 Schenk, p. 336.

12 *Ibid.*, pp. 190–3 and 241.

13 Ansel, Walter, *Hitler Confronts England*, Durham, NC, Duke University Press, 1960, p. 277, footnote.

14 Schenk, pp. 242–5.

chapter 6

Assessing the terrain and the defences

The problems the Germans met in Norway were intimately connected with the mountainous character of the country which channelled their attacks into defensible valleys and obliged them to undertake costly operations using precious mountain troops. By contrast, the experience of the French campaign had shown what could be achieved when tracked, armoured vehicles were let loose in favourable country. Further to this, care had to be taken in selecting landing sites both for the purpose of getting ashore and for opening the way to favourable routes inland. The broad strategy had been decided with terrain in mind and the tactical outcome would be influenced by the accuracy and relevance of the facts as known to the Germans at that time. A great deal of documentation survives.

The basic decisions were taken on 27 August in the light of data gathered from numerous sources such as textbooks and reference works on the geology and geography of southern England, holiday photographs and postcards, and utility and Ordnance Survey maps acquired, presumably, before the outbreak of war. The Army's *Militärgeographische Angaben über England, Südküste*, was a volume of over 400 pages giving maps (reprinted from Ordnance Survey maps), photographs and drawn coast profiles of the English coast from Land's End to the Thames Estuary.[1] It was supplemented with extra pictures, many of Lyme Bay, on 28 August 1940 and again with yet more photographs on 29 August. A second volume covered the shore from the Thames to the Humber. Both volumes also had geological maps

showing soil types and their characteristics in relation to military requirements: suitability for tracked and wheeled vehicles, for siting artillery and
the effects of shellfire on the land, availability of water and of building
materials, among other topics. Maps in sheet form were also published. The
Military Geology map[2] was a more detailed version of the example included
in the bound volume. The *Befestigungskarte Grossbritannien*,[3] the fortifications map, was published in colour on a scale of 1:100,000 and in black and
white[4] at 1:25,000, giving the locations of pillboxes, gun emplacements,
barbed wire entanglements and so forth. The examples used in this book are
dated 3 September 1940 in the case of the former and 8 August 1940 in the
latter. Comparing the data on these maps with what has been identified on
the ground by the Defence of Britain Project suggests that possibly two-
thirds of the defences were accurately marked.

The evaluation – terrain

As the South Coast volume shows on its landform and communications
map (entitled in German *Beschaffenheit und Gliederung*), the coastline from
the South Foreland to Folkestone, marked 38 on the map, consists of chalk
cliffs whereas the Folkestone to Dungeness shore (part of 37) has a sloping
beach and is sheltered from the prevailing west wind. The disadvantage is
that the Varne and Ridge banks lie offshore and, while they can be crossed
at high water, they would have to be circumnavigated at other times. This
beach the Navy designated Landing Area B. The rest of the coast marked 37,
to Cliff's End just east of Hastings, is also suitable for landing and was given
the letter C. The text describing the terrain of shoreline 37 reads as follows:

K: Type of Coast (Küstenform): *Flat fenland coast, river delta.*
S: Shore (Strandes): *Varyingly broad, sandy, gently-shelving beaches, reinforced*
breakwaters.
H: Interior (Hinterland): *Delta landscape with marshes, no woods, open view.*
Complex network of drainage ditches. Road network only in northern area.
Isolated settlements. The Royal Military Canal separates the delta from the
hinterland. Canal connection from Hythe to Rye.

Immediately west of Landing Area C the map shows the dots that represent
cliffs and the higher land runs on towards Bexhill. In the areas marked 36
and 35, east of Beachy Head and Eastbourne, a landing space exists that

became Landing Area D. Originally Landing Area E was much further west in the area marked 32 and 33 on the map, between Selsey Bill and Brighton. In the later stages of the planning process the landings were reorientated to include the Cuckmere valley (mistakenly marked Ouse on the map) and the area east of Newhaven with the westernmost landings taking place at Brighton with an airborne element taking the high land, the South Downs, north of the town.[5] In the final plan the most westerly landing was pulled back to Rottingdean in area 34 (Brighton to Eastbourne), for which the handbook's description reads:

K: Type of Coast: Steep coastal cliffs, at Beachy Head high chalk cliffs. Steep coast broken by the mouths of the River Ouse at Newhaven and of Cuckmere River to the east of Seaford.
S: Shore: Narrow shingle beach in front of the cliff. Sandy beach in front of the mouth of the Ouse increasing eastwards from the foot of Castle Hill owing to longshore drift in an easterly direction.
H: Interior: Hilly hinterland criss-crossed with bushes and hedges. No sizeable settlements apart from Newhaven and Seaford. Road along the coast from Brighton to Seaford.

The advance from these beaches was intended to take the form of a grab and hold operation in the east and a curving thrust to the west and north. The first operational objective was the securing of a line from the Thames Estuary along the North Downs and south-west to Portsmouth. That done, the Panzer Divisions would push past Guildford and Aldershot to the line of the Thames and then head both west towards the Severn and east towards Malden to secure the second operational objective, at which point, with London surrounded, the British were expected to capitulate.

The South Coast book included a simplified version of the military geological map (p.174). It shows the great horseshoe of chalk upland, the North Downs, running from Dover towards Chatham and on north of Dorking to curve down west of Farnham and Petersfield before turning east once more north of Brighton to meet the sea at Beachy Head and Eastbourne. The steep, inward-looking faces of the hills are marked with hatching on the coast and communications map. Within the chalk hoop a line of sand and clay surrounds the clay lowlands which rise to the same sand and clay mix before, in the centre, giving way to sandy soils. The dark areas show river and coastal wetlands. The descriptions of the terrain provided in the more sophisticated map indicate the military perception of the land.

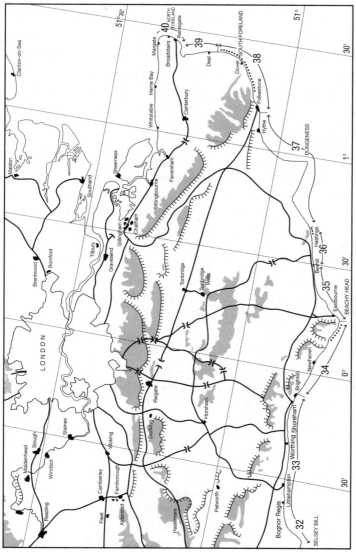

Figure 17 The landform map from the Coastal Handbook shows the steep slopes on the south face of the North Downs and the north face of the South Downs with comb-like lines. The solid, dark lines representing the railways are shown entering tunnels. The rivers were marked on the original, although the Ouse was mistakenly shown where the Cuckmere enters the Channel between Newhaven and Eastbourne. Dots along the coast include chalk cliffs. The numbers relate to detailed text descriptions given in the Handbook

If the landform map is examined along a line from Sittingbourne, west of Canterbury, to Brighton on the south coast, the terrain types are described as follows. The high land of the North Downs, where it is marked with shaded areas on this map, is said to be mildly undulating plateau, flat or gently rolling terrain, crossed at fairly wide intervals by shallow but quite steep-sided valleys. This renders it easily passable in the direction of river-flow and on high ground, but going across the grain of it is made difficult by the need to cross the valleys. It also shows, with a heavy line, the River Medway as a navigable waterway more than 1.8m (6ft) deep, constituting a military obstacle restricting vehicles to bridges or ferries.[6] The map also shows comb-like markings, lines with small marks along one side, running roughly east to west. These indicate 'steeply stepped sides' to the otherwise favourable terrain mentioned above, which 'present considerable obstacles (notable defence positions). On the tops the ground types present no difficulties for movement.' Immediately south of the North Downs the land classification reads: 'Flat terrain at any altitude. Height differences of adjacent points less than 20m [65ft]. Types of ground nowhere cause difficulties for movement.' This is the strip of land over which the Ashford–Tonbridge–Reigate railway line can be seen. South again, in the area curving through Tunbridge Wells and Horsham, north of a wooded region indicated by dark markings on the geological map, the description speaks of hill country with height-differences greater than 20 metres, but with gentle gradients. It continues: 'Still passable for horse-drawn artillery and motorised troops, but away from tracks often difficult for single-horse vehicles.'

The Weald, the high ground in the centre of the region under examination, is pictured in daunting terms. 'Low mountain country with height differences generally between 100m [325ft] and 300m from valley to summit. Away from tracks, ground presents considerable difficulties for vehicles, horse-drawn artillery and motorised troops. Visibility of terrain difficult.' This is the triangular area broadly from a base on the Hawkhurst–Battle line in the east tapering westwards through Crowborough and the Ashdown Forest to Crawley. The word translated here as 'mountain country', *Bergland*, does not convey such an extreme idea in German as it does in English, but none the less the terrain sounds unattractive for swift movement.

South once more and the pattern of land-types runs in reverse order with the exception of the South Downs which are classified as country as unattractive as the Weald for motorised troops. In the area north of Beachy Head small horizontal lines are shown for which the caption reads: 'Seasonally

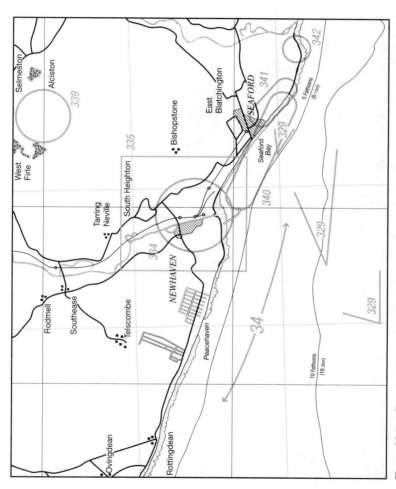

Figure 18 Landing Area E on Map 41 of the Coastal Handbook. The Ordnance Survey map from which the Germans took this predates the construction of Saltdean, east of Rottingdean, which was partly built by 1940

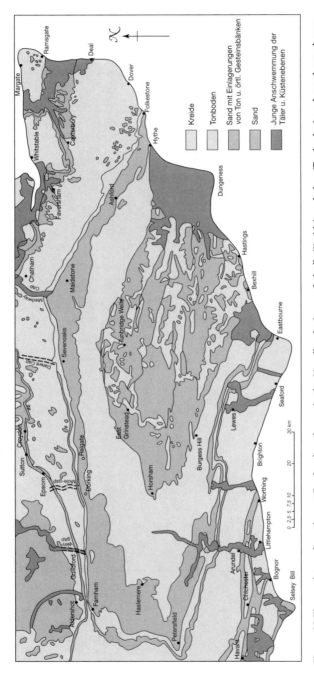

Figure 19 The geology of south-east England as shown in the Handbook. Areas of chalk (*Kreide*) and clay (*Tonboden*) and sand are shown and the wetlands of coast and river valley show clearly in dark tones

boggy and flooded land. Obstacle for horse-drawn vehicles and motorised troops especially in winter and spring. The conditions at a given time require reconnaissance.' Similar areas can be seen north of Hastings and of Dungeness. The region of Romney Marsh is characterised by heavy, continuous, horizontal lines. This is described as 'Marshland or moor, criss-crossed by ditches. Progress except on tracks is hindered by numerous ditches and heavy, soft ground. Trench-digging made difficult by high level of ground-water.' The map of south-east England shows the Straits of Dover and the coast of France and Belgium. There the same solid horizontal lines appear on the area inland of Dunkirk.

The *Militärgeographische Angaben über England: Südküste* also classifies the soil characteristics and the information on Romney Marsh relating to traffic movement on bare ground and temporary tracks is slightly less discouraging. It declares that it is restricted by the water crossing opportunities but that, where not inhibited by ditches, it was generally not unfavourable. The details of the obstacles to movement are given as watercourses, ditches and artificial obstruction of drainage systems leading to a bogging up of the ground.[7] It still does not sound like tank country. The same information book went into greater detail about the country near the intended area of advance near Guildford. The soil is said to be sand with clay layers and some outcrops of stone. As far as traffic is concerned, the ground is open and the going reasonably good except for those areas that are intersected with embankments or on hillsides. Particular attention is drawn to the example of Leith Hill, 'near Guildford' as it is described, although south of Dorking might be more accurate, as a hilly moorland capped with stone and with occasional coniferous woods. The map shows such land as running through Reigate and Dorking to Farnham and, with the Wey valley in between, northwards from Aldershot and Guildford. The book declares that, at the foot of the 'mountains', and Leith Hill is again mentioned, springs of water make the ground difficult for tanks, as do the stone banks and steep gullies that intersect the hillsides.[8] The break-out from the line of the 1st Operational Objective was evidently expected to present some difficulties in terms of terrain. The chalk uplands were also written about with a certain caution. Here the traffic would face problems in wet weather because of the soft, greasy condition of the ground although, if dry, it was classified as good going. For infantry on foot it was passable in all weathers, though somewhat slippery in the wet. As far as obstacles were concerned, the only problem foreseen was the artificial damming up of streams through the 'gaps', and here the English word was inserted, to add a water hazard to the natural cleft in the landscape.[9]

Water hazards were the subject of a special map which included roads and railways, the scale of the features being indicated by thicker or thinner lines and their nature by colour coding. Canals are shown by lines with bumps along them and the thickest waterway lines indicated a depth in excess of 1.8m (6ft). Continuous lines showed maintained waterways while dotted lines were for natural, unkept streams. From this map it appeared that a route from Hastings through Horsham to Guildford was almost hazard-free, very much like Guderian's route from Sedan to the Somme and on to Calais that was the foundation of the campaign in northern France in May 1940.

To the modern observer, used to travel by car, train or aircraft and rarely to be found plodding across the countryside on foot or horse, some of these descriptions may seem exaggerated or even false. To some extent inaccuracy in relation to the true nature of the terrain did exist, but the crucial consideration for the Germans making plans was that this was the best information they had at the time.

The defences

Information on the British defence provisions was being updated constantly. Some of the data had been available before the war and collected by spies such as Dr Hermann Götz, who had been arrested in November 1935 for gathering information on RAF stations. Other data were gathered by aerial reconnaissance and photography. The results were presented on the *Befestigungskarte*.

In the area from Dover in the east to Dymchurch in the west the delineation of the defences was thorough, if in fact incomplete. North-west of Dover great areas are shown with horizontal and vertical cross-hatching. The legend to the map defines these marks as: 'Terrain unsuitable for landing due to obstacles. Size of symbol indicates extent.'[10] These were the potential aircraft landing zones which the British had guarded with scrap motor vehicles, posts, ditches and other obstructions. The high ground around Dover is shown as dotted with triangle symbols, for 'small battle positions' (pillboxes) and the small 'x' marks for barbed wire. There are also numbered circles which are zones designated for bombardment. The area intended for both Stuka and artillery attack at Sandgate, for example, is

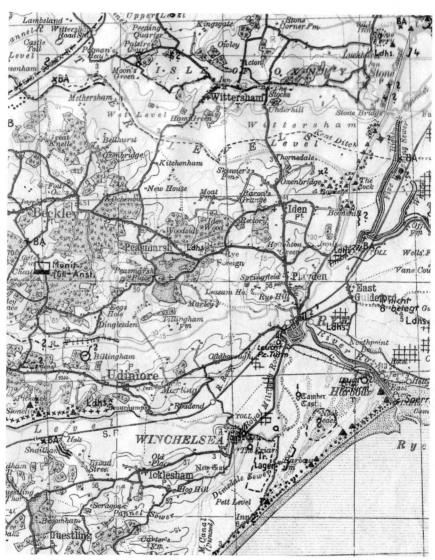

Figure 20 A detail from the original defences map of 3 September. Landing Area C, Rye Bay and north to the Isle of Oxney. North-east of Rye the defences associated with the Royal Military Canal face east. (Bodleian Library (17[42L])

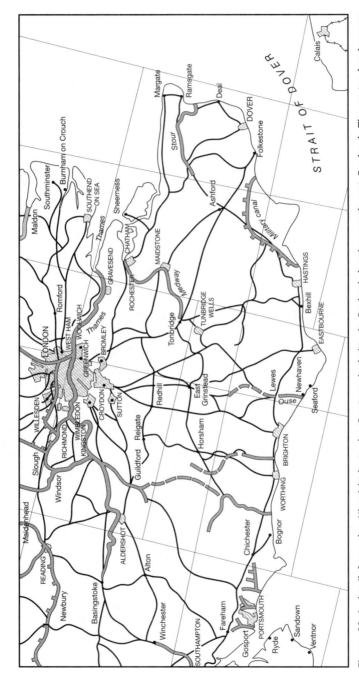

Figure 21 A detail from the *Übersichtskarte der Gewässerabschnitte in England* showing south-east England. The water barriers are shown as thick, tinted lines. (After Bodleian Library C16 [S15])

marked with the number five. North of Sandgate the airfield the British called Hawkinge is shown by an aircraft within a circle at Up Hill and the field at Lympne can be seen to the west of Hythe.

From Hythe, running to the west through West Hythe and beyond, the Royal Military Canal forms a defensive obstacle edged with the triangles and x-marks of pillbox and barbed wire. Between the canal and the coast, south of Lympne, a broad line flanked by two narrow ones marks an anti-tank ditch near a point labelled 'Ldhs.' which stands for *Landehindernis* or terrain obstacle; i.e. a trench. Other symbols showed further defence works and various types of anti-aircraft guns, radio masts and bunkers. Minefields were indicated by small crosses. A full key is given in the Appendix at the end of this book.

A study of the terrain information, taken together with the details of known defensive installations, influenced the tactical plans for the forces landing in England. Order Number 32 of 14 September (as given in Chapter 4, p. 141) outlined the tasks of the landing forces. The 16th Army, on the right or east of the German line, was to land in the Folkestone/St Leonards area, the latter being St Leonards next to Hastings. Sandgate, between Hythe and Folkestone, was marked for bombardment, so the landing area evidently lay to the west of that town. The 9th Army was allocated the coast between Bexhill, just west of Hastings, and Worthing.

From their landing zone the 16th Army had to secure a line along the river valley of the Great Stour from Ashford to Canterbury and some way beyond the Canterbury to Dover road to deny the use of the port to the British. Dover and Folkestone were to be captured from the landward side, making use of a parachute regiment. After that an advance to the eastern coast between Ramsgate and Deal was planned to remove the coastal batteries that prevented in-shore navigation by the invaders. On the western side, an advance of 20km (12 miles) north of Hastings was ordered to secure the hills west of Rye and north of the Brede and Rother valleys, through Battle and Tenterden to Ashford. The 9th Army was to take an area continuing this line through Hadlow Down, north of Heathfield, at the head of the Rother Valley, Burgess Hill, north of Brighton, and Storrington, north of Worthing. Two parachute regiments were allocated to the taking of the South Downs north of Brighton and Beachy Head. In effect, the initial beachhead was to include the South Downs as far west as the River Arun and the line would run along the southern edge of the Weald to the Great Stour River and Canterbury and the port of Dover.[11]

On the high ground north of Hythe and the Canal the maps showed a comprehensive network of barred landing areas with only the slopes of the hills left uncluttered. The landings would, therefore, have to be by parachute and thus by 7th *Fliegerdivision* without support from 22nd Air Landing division. A major constraint was the equipment that could be deployed by parachute alone. The Parachute Division was organised on very similar lines to the Mountain Divisions, that is, in battalions of five companies of which three were armed with light machine guns, three 8cm and three 5cm mortars. The support companies had four 7.5cm LG40 recoilless guns. These weapons had been developed during the 1930s for airborne forces, but were called LG, light guns, to conceal their true purpose. The design overcame the recoil usual in ordinary field artillery pieces by balancing the force that sent the projectile on its way with the force required to vent the explosive gases through a fine tube. This could be costly both in injury to troops caught by the backblast and in the revelation of the location of the firing weapon. The weight of the gun was 145kg (320lb) and that of the shell 5.8kg (just under 13lb).[12] The task of the paratroops was to seize the heights above the Canal to the north of Hythe and establish a perimeter as far north as Lyminge and west as Sellinge to allow reinforcements to come up from the Marsh and turn towards Folkestone and Dover.

The other end of the 16th Army's line was at Cliff End, immediately east of Hastings; the western end of the flatlands that are bisected by the Royal Military Canal. The whole area is subject to the weather and the roads are vital to moving heavy vehicles off the beaches and into the hills. One complex of roads leads from Littlestone-on-Sea through New Romney where one branch leads west to Appledore to cross the Canal on the road for Tenterden while the more northerly road pushes towards the Canal at Warehorne on the way to Ashford. Both canal crossings are shown with pillboxes and defences under construction on the map of 3 September. The coast west of this, round Dungeness, appears uninviting for invading troops until west of the River Rother which enters the Channel south-east of Rye. The shore south of Winchelsea is shown as lined with anti-tank obstacles but it does look possible to pass vehicles, once they have escaped from the beach, up the hillside behind Hastings overlooking the Brede Level, the flat plain of the River Brede running due west of Winchelsea, towards Battle. Hastings marked the southern end of the dividing line between the 16th and 9th Armies while Reigate, to the north-west under the North Downs, was the northern end of the divide. The thrust of the 16th was therefore on the right of that line, taking in the eastern Weald and the valleys below the North Downs and south of Maidstone, but success hinged uncomfortably on the ability to get off the marshes and into the hills beyond the Military Canal.

The territory allocated to the 9th Army had a similar combination of hazard and opportunity. Between Hastings and Bexhill a seductive band of 'hill country ... generally gentle gradients' runs broadly west leaving the woods and valleys of the Weald to the north and the more risky terrain of the Pevensey Levels to the south. It continues almost without interruption to Burgess Hill and Horsham. The geological map indicates a single hazard, the valley of the River Ouse north of Lewes with a stream more than 1.8m to overcome. The defences map of 3 September adds the fortification of the Cuckmere River north-west of Hailsham between Michelham Priory, near Upper Dicker, and Horsebridge, but that appears to be possible to outflank to the north. Also shown is a new road under construction, the modern A22. The Pevensey levels do not carry the same, dire classification as the marshes to the east in 16th Army's sector, but they are still 'seasonally boggy and flooded ... obstacle for horse-drawn vehicles and motorised troops ...'. Close examination of the map reveals, however, an opportunity to get off the beach quickly and onto higher ground immediately west of Pevensey itself to run up the ridge to Polegate. The area was fortified. The usual line of tank-traps and pillboxes threaded along the shore and inland the old castle at Pevensey, first a Roman and then a Norman fort, was again given a defence-work classification. Just north of Eastbourne the railway station of Hampden Park stood in open country a mile and a quarter (2km) from the outskirts of the town. A force landing near Langney Point could also aim to climb to Polegate, clear of the maze of valleys north-west of Eastbourne, and then head west for Lewes. The Cuckmere River was a minor obstacle, but might be secured with a landing where it met the sea at Cuckmerehaven.

The next major attraction was Newhaven. The River Ouse had given Lewes status as a seaport until, some 400 years earlier, a storm completed the failure of the river as a navigable waterway for sea-going vessels and the new haven came into being. This port was used, in peacetime, as a cross-Channel departure point for Dieppe and was the only harbour of any size between Shoreham and Dover. The entrance is guarded by a massive redoubt on the high ground west of the harbour from which the low land east of the river could be threatened by artillery. The redoubt was marked for bombardment. The road from Seaford is shown on the defences map as covered by anti-tank ditches and pillboxes as well as anti-aircraft guns, but the beach itself appears to be unfortified with a railway line alongside it. As an objective, Newhaven does not seem to have been given much attention by the planners of Sealion; they were interested almost exclusively in Dover and the east Kent coast. Between the Ouse at Newhaven and Brighton the coast is formed of cliffs with one narrow valley breaking the line at Rottingdean, none of it fortified. Above Brighton, on the road to the Devil's Dyke, numerous anti-aircraft installations are shown as being under construction and another crop of anti-aircraft guns with two searchlights is marked on the road north to London at Patcham. What the paratroops made of this fortification of their intended landing-ground is not recorded.

The first wave of the invasion force was tasked with securing the first objective, the line from the Medway to the Portsmouth area, breaking out from the bridgehead area described above. As it was expected that it would take eight days to achieve the bridgehead, a counter-attack was probable and the first wave was therefore ordered to prepare defensive positions as soon as they completed their initial advance.[13] The arrival of the second echelon of the first wave would provide the strength to proceed to the 1st Operational Objective, itself the start line for the armoured divisions due to come over in the second wave. The advance from the bridgehead to the 1st Operational Objective appeared to be quite straightforward in the north, from Ashford through Maidstone and Sevenoaks, under the North Downs, broadly along the route of the M20–M25 motorway system built later that century. This was subject mainly to possible flank attack from the hills to the right and to getting over the river Medway, presumably between Tonbridge and Maidstone. In the centre, across the Weald, the terrain description was not encouraging; 'low mountain country'. South of the Weald, reasonably favourable country was indicated on the maps until the South Downs were met and the obstacle of the valley of the River Arun ran from north to south across the hill-top route towards Chichester and the Southampton–Portsmouth line. The western curve of chalk uplands where the North and South Downs meet, beyond Farnham and Petersfield, is the eastern edge of the great, open terrain that includes Salisbury Plain and it was the northern edge of this area that formed the principal part of the 2nd Operational Objective, the line running along the chalk hills of the Berkshire Downs and the Chilterns where the going could be expected to be good even in poor weather. From the area of Hertford the land stretches east towards Chelmsford and Malden as a broad plain by way of Dunmow; easy riding.

In terms of anticipated resistance, the major difficulty was likely to be met in the Guildford to Aldershot area, where the Rivers Wey and Blackwater, the numerous lakes and the gravel diggings near Staines and Heathrow formed serious obstacles when combined with the fact that the headquarters and home of the British Army was found there. It was to provide the Panzer divisions with the jumping-off point to smash their way through to the chalk downs north-west of this region that the first wave needed to secure the 1st Operational Objective. Details of the defences are not to be found on the September map. There are, however, some indications of defence works and it was certainly known that a series of forts, the London Defence Positions, was built along the North Downs in the late nineteenth century.[14] That these might be the core of a renewed line of resistance was an obvious inference, but the maps do not make any special mention of them.

The German Army was thus excellently briefed on the military geography of England and on the defences on and near the coast. The further inland they advanced, the more sparse their knowledge would become.

Notes and References

1 *Generalstab des Heeres, Abteilung für Kriegskarten und Vermessungswesen*, Berlin, 1940.

2 *England (IV Militärgeographische Beschreibung)*, Berlin 1940, Bodleian Library, C15e12/1.

3 Berlin, 1940, Bodleian Library, C17(42L).

4 *Stellungskarte Grossbritannien*, Berlin, 1940, Bodleian Library, C16(16).

5 Klee, Karl, *Das Unternehmen Seelöwe, Volume 1*, Göttingen, 1958, Chapter 4, Section 2.

6 Key to *England (IV Militärgeographische Beschreibung)* translated by A. McGeoch.

7 Berlin, *Generalstab des Heeres Abteilung für Kriegskarten und Vermessungswesen*, 1940, pp. 26–7, translated by Chris Sylge.

8 *Ibid.*, p. 25.

9 *Ibid.*, p. 24.

10 Key translated by A. McGeoch.

11 Klee, Chapter 4, Section 2.

12 Quarrie, Bruce, *Encyclopaedia of the German Army in the 20th Century*, Wellingborough, Patrick Stephens, 1989, pp. 117 and 175.

13 Klee, Chapter 4, Section 2.

14 Saunders, Andrew, *Fortress Britain*, Liphook, Beaufort Publishing, 1989, p. 201.

PART 2

9 September 1940 to 29 September 1940: Conjecture

The invasion of England: introduction

On 25 August German bombers, possibly lost or dumping their loads to facilitate escape, hit London. In immediate retaliation a raid on Berlin was ordered and on the night of 28/29 August the German capital was bombed. The damage was trivial, but the blow to German pride was significant. The Luftwaffe had, for some time, been advocating attacks on London, but Hitler had continued to forbid them. The airmen's theory was that massed bomber strikes against London would force the RAF to fly in defence of the city and thus expose themselves to a fighter battle which they would lose. On 9 September the Luftwaffe Operations Staff proposed:

The continuous attack on London will be carried out during the day by Air Fleet 2 under strong fighter escort, whilst Air Fleet 3 will operate at night; the offensive will continue until London's docks, supply centres and power stations have been destroyed.[1]

Hitler, however, had his eye on the larger prize, the conquest of England, and the campaign against the fighter stations was the key to the success of that plan.

Göring therefore ordered an intensification of attacks on the fighter airfields, even at the risk of interfering with their use once Sealion had brought them under German control. Bombers which their commanders would have preferred to send in great mass raids on London were used in smaller groups to hit Biggin Hill, West Malling, Manston, Kenley, Redhill and Gatwick as well as the grass-strip airfields of Detling, Lympne, Hawkinge and Friston. Industrial targets were also attacked to interrupt the supply of arms and aircraft to the defenders. The only slackening of the assault resulted from adverse flying conditions. Between 16 and 19 September only one day, 17 September, was sufficiently favourable to permit raids in significant number. Meanwhile the British were doing their best to disrupt German invasion preparations. By 18 September 1,004 invasion vessels had been observed in the Channel ports and day raids by Blenheims and night bombing by Wellington, Whitley and Hampden bombers delivered some 1400 tons of bombs to their neighbour's shores.[2]

For Air Chief Marshal Dowding the battle had reached a turning point. His pilots and aircraft were not being destroyed at an intolerable rate, severe though the damage was, but the ability to operate was being denied to him. The craters in the runways could be filled and the damaged machines repaired or replaced, but the operations rooms were mostly above ground in inadequately fortified buildings and communication was by land telephone line. These vital components of the system could not, he decided, be maintained or replaced quickly enough to keep the airfields operating for many more days. The radar stations had not suffered sustained attacks and it was deemed likely that the Germans had no understanding of their significance. However, if they were left for examination by an invading force their secrets would soon be revealed and the rest of them would be subjected to severe assault. Whatever happened the land forces would remain in place to face invading forces and they needed as much air cover as possible. Dowding was thus confronted with one of the most demanding manoeuvres of warfare, the fighting withdrawal.

His principle weapons, the Hurricane and the Spitfire, had a fighting range of some 400 miles which was great enough to permit the abandonment of the forward airfields without ceasing opposition to intruders into British airspace. These airfields still had to appear operational in order to attract attacks the Germans might otherwise direct elsewhere, so runways would continue to be repaired, damaged aircraft made to look good and new dummies put in place to give the appearance of a squadron being caught on the ground. Radio signals traffic would be faked and anti-aircraft guns would remain in place and in action or be relocated to enable them to serve a second purpose: the destruction of land targets. Air Vice-Marshal Park was to remain in his underground headquarters at Uxbridge, but his operational squadrons south of the Thames and east of and including No. 600 (City of London) Squadron at Redhill[3] had to be repositioned to the north and west. For the time being, at least, Tangmere and the stations around Portsmouth, would remain operational to protect, among other targets, the important Supermarine aircraft factory at Woolston, east across the Itchen from Southampton. If it became necessary to pull back even more, the arrangement Park had made with 10 Group, and which underpinned his orders of

5 September 1940 for the protection of these installations, would be extended by basing his squadrons on their airfields. The movement of squadrons was, by now, a routine although complex activity. On 5 September, for example, No. 504 Squadron was ordered south from Catterick to Hendon. Part of the personnel flew down in transport aircraft that day while the rest came by train. The aircraft and pilots flew down that afternoon and the squadron was operational on 7 September.[4]

The information network had to be maintained at the same time as it was redeployed and, in part, made ready for destruction. There were Chain Home stations at Dover, Fairlight (east of Hastings) and Pevensey which, given the assembly of invasion craft on the other side of the Channel, were evidently in the potential invasion area. They were prepared for the removal of vital components and the destruction of the rest. The station at Dunkirk, between Faversham and Canterbury, was similarly prepared, though it might be able to remain active for much longer if Dover and Canterbury remained in British hands. Ventnor, on the Isle of Wight, had been put out of commission on 13 August, but a new station had opened ten days later at Bembridge.[5] This, too, had to be made ready for destruction. The loss would result in a restriction of radar information, for the Chain Home range was 120 miles (190km) and the Mobile Base apparatus had only three-quarters of that range. They were, none the less, useful supplements to the low-level Chain Home Low stations with their 50-mile (80km) vision. The Chain Home Low installations at Foreness, Dover, Fairlight, Beachy Head, Truleigh Hill (north of Shoreham) and Poling (east of Arundel)[6] would all have to go if the Germans got anywhere near. The Mobile Base units were to be withdrawn north and west as needful; there were 12 of these available altogether of which five were placed in support of the south-eastern sector. In spite of this loss of existing coverage it was predicted that adequate warning of the approach of enemy aircraft could be maintained, but the tracking of shipping which Chain Home Low was able to offer would be lost. The network of Observer Corps posts and communications was also slated for progressive withdrawal as an invasion developed. The centres at Maidstone, Horsham and Winchester were made ready for early destruction if need be and arrangements made for their stations to be in contact with Colchester, Watford, Bristol and Yeovil in that circumstance.

On 1 June Lieutenant Colonel Kennedy, Commanding Royal Engineer of the 23rd Division, addressed the staff officers of 2nd Anti-Aircraft Division on the experience gained in the fighting in France in the preceding weeks.

Among other things, he related what he considered the outstanding action of the anti-aircraft guns, the use of a 3.7 inch (9.4cm) gun against two German tanks. The muzzle was lowered and the enemy's machines were 'blown to smithereens'. 'Used as such,' Kennedy reported, 'it was undoubt-edly a magnificent weapon.'[7] Others told similar tales. It was also generally agreed that these heavy guns were not useful against low-level or dive-bomber attacks but had their chief importance in fire against high, level-flying enemies. Major-General Sir Frederick Pile, who commanded Anti-Aircraft forces, was not slow to appreciate the significance of this, but his resources were limited. At 24 July the number and distribution of 3.7 inch mobile anti-aircraft guns in the south-east was as follows:[8]

Thames-Medway (South)	8
Langley/Slough	4
Hounslow	4
Brooklands	16
Dover	8
Portsmouth	4
Southampton	23

These locations were not random. At Langley, Kingston and Brooklands there were Hawker aircraft factories and Supermarine was at Slough. However, at Brockworth, east of Gloucester, there were 24 of the 3.7 inch guns, 20 in south Wales, and so on. It was clear that, endangered though the manufacturing centres were from the air, keeping the Germans away on land was yet more important. In addition the production of guns and stand-fasts for fixed sites protecting airfields was stepped up to release mobile guns and, further, fixed gun sites were modified to allow weapons to be trained on land targets.[9]

By 20 September the RAF had pulled its squadrons back but the vacated bases displayed all the signs of continuing occupation and attracted all the venom of which the Luftwaffe was capable. The fields had been booby-trapped to deny the Germans use of them should they ever come and were defensible as strongpoints in a land war. Nearly 200 3.7 inch guns were now available and deployed with the army as anti-tank weapons. The Royal Navy stood nervously on the fringes. The RAF was still locked in a mighty battle for air supremacy, its true strength disguised. On 20 September General Sir Alan Brooke wrote '. . . unfortunately weather is improving!' He went on to remark:

... PM [Prime Minister Winston Churchill] sent me paper from [Ambassador] Sam Hoare in Spain giving details of talk with reliable American who had come from Germany. Speaking on the 7th of this month he said he was certain that Hitler would attack within a fortnight. Today ... must be the last day of that fortnight! Weather prophets predict a perfect sea.[10]

Notes and References

1 In fact a report of action already in hand. Jacobsen, Hans-Adolf, and Rohwer, Jürgen, *Decisive Battles of World War II: the German View*, London, André Deutsch, 1965, p. 88.

2 Wood, Derek, with Dempster, Derek, *The Narrow Margin*, London, Hutchinson, 1961, p. 235.

3 *Ibid.*, pp. 300–1.

4 *Ibid.*, p. 207.

5 Collier, Basil, *The Defence of the United Kingdom*, London, HMSO, 1957, pages facing p. 149 and p. 184.

6 Locations from Collier, facing p. 149.

7 True to this point. Dobinson, Colin, *AA Command*, London, Methuen, 2001, pp. 191–2.

8 *Ibid.*, pp. 512–16.

9 *Ibid.*, p. 204.

10 In fact written on 21 September. Alanbrooke, Field Marshal Lord, *War Diaries 1939–1945*, London, Weidenfeld & Nicolson, 2001, p. 110.

chapter 7

Landing Area B – Hythe to Dungeness

The time had come for the final decision on the German side. The arguments for and against proceeding with the invasion were finely balanced. An essential pre-condition had been the destruction of the RAF and that had not been completed. It was clear that great damage had been done and the speed with which Luftwaffe incursions were challenged suggested that the more southerly of the RAF fighter squadrons were now approaching extinction and were not being replaced. New methods were being tried such as General Paul Deichmann's scheme of using Me-109s of 2nd Wing of No. 2 Instructional Group each fitted to carry a 250kg bomb to hit the British airfields installations.[1] The invasion fleet was assembled. If 21 September 1940 was to be confirmed as the date for Sealion, the order had to be given on 11 September.

The plans were reviewed at a conference attended by the High Command of all three services under the eye of Adolf Hitler himself. He looked closely at the dispositions made and was not entirely satisfied. The great triangle of Romney Marsh, so crucial to the concept, was shaded in just the same way as the lowlands inland of Dunkirk, the country he had forbidden his Panzers to enter on 24 May; a decision the wisdom of which was confirmed by General Guderian's report of 28 May.[2] The same error was threatened again! Hitler's rages were legendary and he now gave a demonstration of anger that put previous performances in the shade. Was this, he demanded, deliberate sabotage of his armoured divisions or simple incompetence? Fortunately the subject came up shortly before the great man's

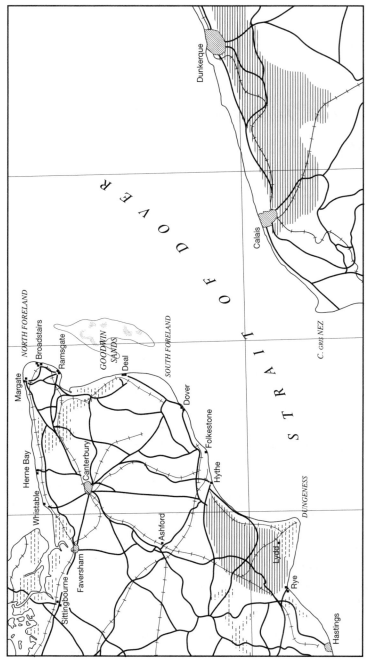

Figure 22 Part of England (*IV Militärgeographische Beschreibung*), the detailed geological map, which includes the French coast and shows the Dunkirk area classified in the same way as Romney Marsh. (Bodleian Library C15e 12/1)

customary break for exercise and there was time to allow him to calm down and the Army to come up with explanations and modified plans.

The plans were for the landings to be supported by relatively small numbers of specially modified tanks, the Unterwasserpanzer units, while the principal armoured strength was to form part of the second wave of the invasion. In the region of Romney Marsh the 16th Army was to have landed XXXXI Armoured Corps comprising 8th and 10th Panzer Divisions and 29th (Motorised) Infantry Division reinforced with two regiments, Grossdeutschland and SS Liebstandarte Adolf Hitler. The justification of the use of the modified tanks was not difficult and so the argument was when and how the Panzer divisions themselves should be deployed. The Army was forced to agree that they would either be landed when Folkestone or Dover had been secured, or put ashore close to Hastings or even in 9th Army's sector at Bexhill. On no account were they to be committed to Romney Marsh. Hitler's concern to preserve his tanks from failure in unsuitable country, based on Guderian's warning that they should not be used where 'the armoured attack will break on the terrain'[3], was consistent with his decision in the Dunkirk battle. Subject to this limitation, the order for Sealion to proceed was given.

The loading of the craft destined for Zone B from Rotterdam began six days prior to S-Day, the designated invasion date of 21 September, and took two full days. The fleet sailed on S-Day minus two, 19 September, to form Convoy 2 under Captain Schirlitz. It consisted of 49 transport vessels and 98 barges.[4] Convoy 1, under Captain Wagner, consisted of eight transports and 16 barges and pusher boats. They had four hours to load in contrast to Convoy 2's 48 hours. The tow formations from Ostend and Dunkirk were given eight hours for troop embarkation, but the support ships were being loaded from S-Day minus eight for two days. Ships and barges were loaded and moved to the outer harbours in readiness for sailing. Horses were loaded two days before the invasion and the men of the 17th Infantry Division the day before. The protection screen of minesweepers and patrol boats made their rendezvous with the invasion fleet the day before the landings. In overall command, and also commanding Tow Formation 1 from Dunkirk, was Vice-Admiral von Fischel and Tow Formation 2 from Ostend was commanded by Captain Hennecke.

As General Brooke had remarked, the weather was calm. Thursday, 19 September was cloudy with rain-squalls in the afternoon and a west-south-westerly wind was whipping up a sea that was just verging on too rough for the barges. The forecast was encouraging over the next two days with winds falling as a low pressure area moved away north-east. On the Friday the winds were forecast to drop. Low tide at Dover was at 0831 hours on the morning of Saturday, 21 September so a landing that began at 0600, 15 minutes after sunrise,[5] would be able to float off its barges and transports mid-morning for a second journey.[6]

For all that the Channel could be crossed in the sea conditions prevailing, the journey was uncomfortable in the extreme. The brisk wind of the previous day had dropped to a westerly breeze, but the seas still ran along the length of the Channel making the barges pitch and roll heavily as they were tugged or pushed towards England. After a whole day on board, the troops found that the efficacy of their sea-sickness tablets passed off and the stench of vomit was added to the damp, dark and crowded misery of the crossing. As the great body of ships in a column some 10 miles (16km) long pitched and rolled across the narrow waterway the heavy artillery sent its huge shells howling overhead, targeted on Sandgate and Folkestone.

As the miserable seaborne force approached the dark coast of Kent, the airborne element was on its way to land at the same time. The successful commander of 7th Airborne in the invasion of the Netherlands, Lieutenant-General Kurt Student, had been severely wounded on 14 May and was still recovering from the damage to his head. The division therefore had to go into action without its charismatic leader. Major-General Herbert Loch of the 17th Infantry Division had to use parachute troops allocated to him unsupported by airlanding men in transport aircraft and gliders because of the comprehensive blocking of potential landing grounds undertaken by the British made so clearly visible by the cross-hatching on the maps. Two detachments were to land at S-Hour, just as the landing force hit the beaches. Meindl Detachment was destined to drop between Hythe and Sandling Park, near the modern Junction 11 on the M20 motorway. The area, on a small plateau on the ridge above the marshes and the seaports, is almost surrounded by woodland. From here Meindl, disposing of some 950 men, was to seize positions across the Military Canal to the south either side of Hythe. Stentzler Detachment, a force of the same size, was to drop between Paddlesworth and Etchinghill. The former is on the heights of the North Downs while the latter lies at the foot of the steep slope that faces south-west, so the landing zone included a remarkably perilous hillside. This detachment was then to proceed to the south-east, through the area which is now the site of the Channel Tunnel Terminus, to take Sandgate.

They were to be reinforced by Bräuer Detachment scheduled to drop about an hour later when two further drops would provide defence from attack from the north and from the north-west, on the hilltop and in the valley respectively.[7] Once the beaches to the south were secure, these parachute units were to spearhead the advance east to take Dover, north to take Canterbury and north-west to open the way to surround London.

Landing

The invasion fleet approached from the east along the coast and then began the difficult manoeuvre of making a turn northwards into a line facing the shore before running in on their final approach. In the van were two advance detachments, one from Ostend aiming for the beaches either side of the Grand Redoubt midway between Dymchurch village and Hythe. This force, drawn from the 21st Infantry Regiment and commanded by Major Schuler, was nearly 1000 men strong and equipped with two mountain guns, three light field guns, three anti-tank guns (PAK – *Panzerabwehr-kanone*), ten heavy mortars, eight heavy machine-guns, two smoke launchers, two flame-throwing tanks and one standard, unmodified tank as a command vehicle. Various engineer units completed the force. They deserved, according to Walter Ansel, the designation *Himmelfahrtskommando* – heaven-bound commando. The other force, under Major Panwitz of the 55th Infantry, was to land to the south, near Littlestone-on-Sea, east of New Romney.[8] The first men to head in to the beach were in assault boats, with men in large rubber dinghies close behind. They had covering fire from the jury-mounted field artillery pieces on the coasters behind them, but they had expected the landing to be difficult and it was.

The approach of the invasion fleet, so long anticipated by the British, did not go unnoticed. RAF Coastal Command's regular patrols made observations that were confirmed when the Chain Home Low installations at Dover and Fairlight reported the fleet more than two hours before it closed with the beach. The Dover station was kept in commission for the time being, but, given the direction the fleet was moving, Fairlight was ordered to destroy its mast and remove what it could of its electronic apparatus before setting fire to the rest with incendiary bombs. The RAF were not merely informed of this destruction, but briefed to make use of the blaze as a navigational aid. The Chain Home stations were also reporting activity; a swarm of aircraft of which the hard core was heading for, it appeared,

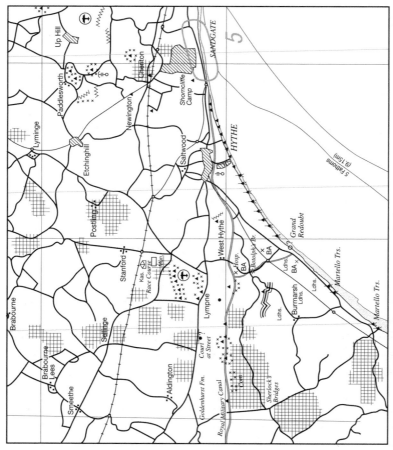

Figure 23 The part of the defences map of 3 September showing Landing Area B. Bombardment targets are ringed and numbered (5 in this case), and were to be avoided by German troops. Two further areas were similarly designated at Dungeness. (After Bodleian Library C17[42L])

Folkestone. The British were expecting them and as the fleet approached the beaches defensive artillery opened fire from the Redoubt, which was marked on the 3 September Fortification map with a question mark, a question now answered by its two 6 inch guns,[9] from machine-guns on the Martello towers and from gun positions at Dungeness and Sandgate, both of which were enduring shelling from German positions in France.

From Dover the British heavy guns turned their attention from cross-Channel targets to enemies closer to home. For the advance party coming ashore on the sands south-west of the Grand Redoubt things were bad enough, but for the group on the right the situation was worsened because they were on shingle. The stones of which the northern section of the shore is formed shattered into innumerable fragments which cut through flesh and sinew like flying razor blades. Here also the beach was too steep to risk the submersible tanks, so the armour was to be unloaded by ramps under the light machine-gun fire spraying from positions optimistically marked 'observation post' with a little chess-piece, pawn-like symbol. The sandy beach had what became both a hazard and a shelter, the Dymchurch Wall. The wall between the village and the Redoubt was built to exclude the sea and it also formed an obstacle to the invaders. Equally, those managing to get close under it were sheltered from at least some of the English fire and, a few at a time, they were able to rush over and find cover in the fields and their surrounding ditches or 'sewers' between the wall and the light railway. The beaches themselves were thronged with obstacles to the landing troops. There were barbed wire entanglements, minefields and lumps of concrete known as coffins and pimples.

The amphibious tanks were directed to go ashore either side of Dymchurch village. Here the sandy beach was favourable but scattered with artificial problems. The engineers worked valiantly to clear mines and paid highly for their courage until ship-borne artillery fire suppressed the gunners on the Martello towers. They began to land, chugging under the waves towing their little floats which held the pipes that kept them alive, about 45 minutes after the first men hit the beach. Tank Detachment B, east of Dymchurch, was seen from the Redoubt and came under fire from the heavy guns. To get off the beach they had to negotiate the vehicle ramps in the wall as well as the specially built obstacles on the beach and the delay allowed the Redoubt to destroy one machine, although the other two succeeded in getting inland. The smoke screen laid by the Germans and the mist of battle obscured Tank Detachment D, on the far side of the village,

**Figure 24 A Panzer III (U) going ashore, trailing its breather tube and radio link.
(Coll. Peter Schenk)**

from view and that set off in the direction of Ivychurch by road. The build-
up was steady, though costly. Two hours after the landings began more than
2000 men were ashore, but without any heavy weapons apart from the first
few tanks. The establishment strength of a Panzer Detachment was three
companies of four platoons (*Zug*), two with four tanks, two with five and
two tanks in the company command. It was rare for the full strength to be
operational at any one time, but something rather fewer than 60 machines
of Detachment D and 40 of Detachment B had been intended for these
beaches. At Hitler's insistence the numbers had been halved but even those
would take a considerable time to bring ashore. Meanwhile a fierce battle
had developed on the hills inland.

The Airborne attack

The approach of the 7th *Fliegerdivision*, the Airborne Division, was observed by the Chain Home stations when it was nearly an hour away from its drop zones. The Junkers Ju 52 three-engine transport aircraft cruised at 132 mph (212km/h)[10] and carried 18 paratroopers, so more than 50 machines were needed for each of the detachments. The signal received by British radar was similar to the patterns of bomber raids with which the operators were so familiar by now, but something did not quite ring true about them. The screen of fighters was entirely normal, but the mass of heavier craft was not. Those to whom the intelligence came were also looking at reports from Chain Low radar which indicated the probability of the invasion fleet and it did not take much imagination to guess that the paratroop invasion, the long-expected terror from the sky, was approaching. The RAF scrambled its fighters. Visibility was poor that Saturday; it was not until late afternoon, when the wind died away entirely on the Kent coast, that it cleared. The German pilots were at a disadvantage, for they were new to this airspace and the requirements of an airborne drop were demanding lest the troops be scattered across the land. Scattered they were. First, the Spitfires of the RAF fell on the escorting German fighters leaving the airfleet at the mercy of the Hurricanes. What the British had not anticipated was that the intended drop zone was so close to the coast; they thought they had the whole of Kent over which to cull the intruders. Nevertheless 15 Ju 52s were shot down and although some of the troops they carried were able to jump to save their lives they landed alone. Other transports turned for home too soon, giving the word to jump as they did so and another 10 per cent of the force was dropped off target, near Dover and Deal. This was exactly the circumstance for which the much criticised Home Guard had been trained. Single Germans were rounded up, outnumbered by the poorly armed but determined amateurs. Some groups of paratroops resisted with vigour and were not attacked, but just pinned down and left to think about it. Given their isolation, most thought it wise to surrender.

The most organised formation to land was Meindl's near Sandling Park. They were lucky in having the larger landing area and, although some landed in the woods, few were injured. What was even better was the safe arrival of their heavier weapons with a company each of the machine-gun battalion and the artillery battalion. That gave them four heavy machine-guns and four 7.5cm recoilless guns, but with limited ammunition. They already had wounded to care for; the anti-aircraft guns and machine-guns surrounding the airfield at Lympne had fired both on the transports and the descending men. Now Meindl found himself with a fight on two fronts. The airfield defence was not the only threat on his western flank, but the guard for the munitions store on Folkestone Racecourse to the north of the RAF station had been supplemented with coastal defence reinforcements, forming a substantial block of enemy between the railway and the slopes above the canal. To the south-east, his planned line of advance, the forces along the line of the canal were alerted. Much now depended on the arrival of the 2nd and 3rd Regiments to protect his rear as he pushed towards Hythe.

Stentzler's men were less fortunate. Their landing area was, in any case, more dangerous, covering, as it did, the steep hillside above the Lyminge to Hythe road. Coupled with the disorder spread by the RAF attack and the scattering of the transport aircraft, his detachment came down east of Paddlesworth and north of Up Hill and the Hawkinge airfield. From the anti-aircraft guns it took casualties in the air and from the line of pillboxes south of Paddlesworth it took more. The air drop dribbled on towards the north-east leaving a trail of isolated bands of brave but disorientated *Fallschirmjäger* to be mopped up piecemeal. The few who landed west of Paddlesworth suffered more than 50 per cent casualties on the steep hill and the survivors, aware of Meindl's position, made their way to join him. Fewer than half of the first wave of paratroops remained. It was chillingly similar to the landings north of Rotterdam the previous May.

The British, while aware of both landings on the beaches and the air drops, were uncertain about the German intentions. The local commander at Lympne, his airfield free of RAF aircraft for the past week or so, had organised his men and guns into a strongpoint and was unwilling to emerge from it, but Home Guard and 1st (London) Division troops based at Dover and covering the Military Canal were prepared to act. Contact with the paratroops was made some 40 minutes after they had landed and while they were still gathering themselves together and retrieving their heavier weapons and ammunition. As the first exchange of fire took place the next wave of Junkers transports could be heard through the noise of battle though they were not yet visible in the murky conditions. Again the RAF attacked and the drop was broken up. The rest of 1st Parachute Regiment, Bräuer Detachment, was intended to land close to Stentzler but his force had been badly scattered and the newcomers found themselves straddling the Paddlesworth to Arpinge line of defences as well as being challenged by

British troops arriving from Shorncliffe and Dover. The best they could do was to dig in and hold until their comrades could break out from the beach.

On the opposite flank the 3rd Parachute Regiment was to drop on the water-meadows north of the railway and west of Stanford, a target area surrounded by landing-blocked fields and woods. The establishment of a parachute regiment was 14 companies, of which numbers 13 and 14 were field gun and anti-tank companies and the rest were in three battalions of some 700 men organised in four companies.[11] The greater part of this number had succeeded in landing on the fields in which aircraft would have got bogged down. They prepared to defend themselves against the expected counter-attack from the west but none came. Instead they came under fire from the south, the munitions store and barracks at the racecourse. They returned fire but, wary of being distracted from their primary task, contented themselves with a holding action here and sent two companies probing around the flank to the south. They skirted the airfield defences and took a small British detachment by surprise from the rear as the defenders watched the flashes of gunfire on the beaches below.

The last of the drops, that of 2nd Parachute Regiment, was north of Postling. The place was not well chosen. In addition to the disorder in their transport formation caused by fighter attacks, the landing zone straddled a ridge of the North Downs with a particularly steep slope on the south-western side which caused numerous moderate injuries. The field gun and anti-tank companies came down well to the north-east, elements of two companies landed on the ridge itself and dug in, and the equivalent of one company was able to establish a defensive front to hold the valley against troops approaching from the north-west. The 7th Airborne Division was not deployed as planned, but was still capable of making a significant contribution to the landing enterprise. On the northern and eastern sides of their enclave all they could do was hold against counter-attacks, but Meindl was in a position to push towards Hythe leaving Lympne on his west and 3rd Parachute Regiment could both threaten Lympne from the west and support efforts to cross the Royal Miltary Canal below Court-at-Street and at Goldenhurst Farm. In the Netherlands, immediately after 10 May, the Parachute Regiments could cling on in confidence that they would receive reinforcements in the form of the Airlanding Division, brought in by Junkers transport aircraft landing, in some cases, on the roads. Here the precautions taken by the British and so carefully mapped by the Germans had forestalled any such plan. They were on their own until they could link with men from the beaches.

The thrust over the canal

In order to blaze a trail for regular infantry the 1st Brandenburg Battalion was to be used. The original idea was that they would be landed from fast motor boats to seize Dover Harbour, but the defences were so formidable that the German Navy declined to place its men at risk in so foolhardy an exercise.[12] Instead two groups were organised to go ashore, a commando unit under Lieutenant Dr Hartmann and another to land with tanks of 17th Division's advance detachment. The former consisted of two officers, 15 non-commissioned officers and 114 men on 50 motor bicycles, and went ashore with Tank Detachment D south-west of Dymchurch. The latter were committed with the three reconnaissance tanks, of which one was destroyed, to make for the canal. Here a problem arose. The strength of the Grand Redoubt had been underestimated and the 6 inch guns were doing unacceptable damage to vessels, men and equipment attempting to come ashore west of them. The tanks were ordered to hook around to fire on the Redoubt from inland and the Brandenburgers were required to lead an infantry assault to silence the position. The essential momentum to push inland was lost in the two-hour fight to overcome the strongpoint.

Hartmann's progress was not diverted. By now, mid-morning, the position in the Martello tower at Dymchurch had been silenced by field gun fire from the German ships and the Brandenburgers were able to assemble and take up formation almost undisturbed before moving, together with tanks of Detachment D, inland. They moved northwards, along the roads, some through Burmarsh towards Botolph's Bridge and others further west, towards Sherlock's Bridges and the canal bridges west of Goldenhurst Farm. Past Burmarsh the first group ran into fire from the pillbox on the road south-west of Botolph's Bridge and the tanks were held up by an anti-tank ditch on the left and the brimming drainage channel that ran to the sea near the Redoubt. It was approaching midday and the tide, which would reach a high water mark of 17.6 feet (5.36m) at Dover at 1332 hours, was coming in. The sluice near the Redoubt was open and fixed in that position by an explosive charge ignited by the garrison as the invasion fleet approached, but only now was the result apparent. The tide would soon flood the land south of West Hythe. The Brandenburgers changed direction to outflank the anti-tank ditch on the west, but found the ground yielding and their vehicles in danger of bogging down. The direction of advance shifted westwards and it seemed that the 21st Infantry could be in danger of

Figure 25 The drain running from the Royal Military Canal past Botolph's Bridge to the sea near the Redoubt with the steep hills above West Hythe in the distance

being cut off east of the waterway that afternoon. What was more, a second sluice, near the Martello tower a little way west near Blackhouse, had been sabotaged at the same time, jeopardising the way inland from the beach between the two. Over the coming days the liability to fresh floods decreased, for the high water mark on 19 September had been 18.4 feet (5.6m) and on 26 September it would be neap tide at 14 feet (4.27m), but the damage would have been done; the ground would be unsuitable for tracked or wheeled vehicles just as Hitler had feared.

From the hilltop north of the canal, men of the 3rd Parachute Regiment saw the tanks and men incline west, heading for the bridges which still stood across the canal below Bonnington. The bridge at Goldenhurst Farm was overlooked by a pillbox to the east, but the next bridge, on the road to Bonnington, appeared to be undefended and the leading tanks made for it. The first drove onto it as the concealed British engineers depressed the detonator and the bridge took the first machine with it as the second, failing to stop, plunged into the water. At nearly 6 feet (1.8m) deep it was enough to put the tank out of action for the time being. Detonations at the nearby bridges followed at once, but the destruction was insufficient to deny passage everywhere. Near the farm the bridge fell into the water neatly and offered a fordable route. A couple of Brandenburgers leapt from their motor bikes and started to wade across, only to be cut down by machine-gun fire from the pillbox on the right.[13] The 7.5cm guns of a Panzer IV, one of six among the machines of Detachment D, silenced the position and, one by one, tanks began to cross the canal. Two of the underwater machines made an effort to cross the canal using their special equipment, but while it was easy to get into the water and drive across, getting out on the other side proved impossible. A canal bank is vertical and the Royal Military Canal was well maintained, with banks in good repair. It was clear that, unless they could find a suitable slipway to form an exit, the amphibious machines gave no advantage.

On the shore the unloading continued in spite of the growing number of wrecked craft drifting on the incoming tide. By early afternoon four motorised heavy field howitzer batteries had been hauled over the sea wall and deployed on the roadside to bring down fire on positions above the canal. After 15 minutes' work they received a message pleading with them to cease; the 3rd Parachute Regiment had suffered a number of casualties already and no-one was sure where Meindl's men were. Until the Panzers were in a position to pin-point British defences the howitzers would have to remain silent.

By mid-afternoon Tank Detachment D had clambered up the hill towards Aldington. Instead of pressing on towards Ashford as intended they were needed now to support the drive east for Folkestone and Dover. Tank Detachment B was baulked; unable to move north or east because of the floods. It was therefore ordered to drive down the road to Dymchurch, turn inland through St Mary in the Marsh and Ivychurch and then to cross the canal further west to take over the task of reaching Ashford. Detachment D formed up across the road to Lympne and, in company with the paras, roared forward. At Court-at-Street there was momentary resistance from a pillbox built into the side of a garage[14] but the real resistance was encountered as the formation broke from the shelter of the hamlet into the fields to the east. Here the defences of the airfield came into play and the modifications to render them effective against ground attack showed their worth. The anti-aircraft guns at Lympne included the usual Bofors or the Vickers 2-pounder and Lewis light machine-guns, but more important were the mobile 3.7 inch guns that had proved themselves in France and had been allocated to strongpoints here, at Hawkinge and at Shorncliffe. The first wave of fire halted two German tanks and cut down Brandenburgers and paratroops moving up with them. An attempt was made to turn the southern flank through the woods but this was prevented by a line of concrete 'pimples' that can still be seen there today. The Germans were determined, but they lacked air support because the Stukas were allocated to coastal battery targets at Sandgate and Dungeness. By the time eight of the 20 or so machines of Detachment D that had made it to the hilltop had been hit they decided to withdraw behind Court-at-Street and wait until the following day for reinforcements.

Three of their tanks had not climbed the hill, but had explored eastwards along the southern bank of the canal. They came under small arms fire from the pillboxes on the opposite bank, but nothing to disturb their progress. On reaching West Hythe they crossed the ruined bridge which still gave passage in water knee-deep and turned up the steep hill. Immediately they came under fire from their right, a position high on the steep hillside. They hesitated. There was no room to deviate and attack from a flank, for the narrow gully up which the road ran was flanked on one side by a small field but otherwise the slopes were severe. Then, as they prepared to pull back, the skyline swarmed with the familiar silhouettes of German parachutists' helmets as Meindl's men over-ran the small British position from the rear. To his 700 or so men Meindl added two Panzer IIIs armed with 3.7cm guns.

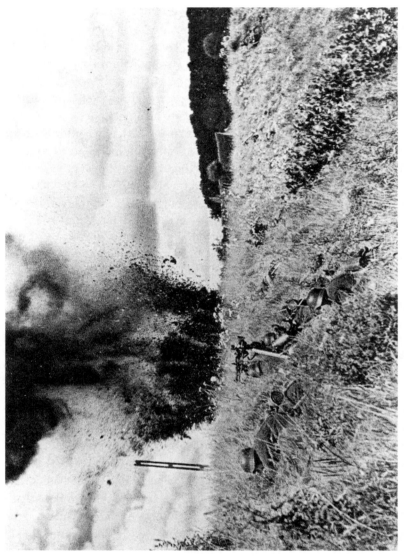

Figure 26 German troops under fire. (Tank Museum)

The parachute troops east of the Lympne enclave had been intended for an advance either side of Hythe to link with 17th Division troops landed west of the little town. The party on the right kept to the high ground and had been making their way past Pedlinge when they heard the fight above West Hythe in which they intervened. Now they had to make contact with their comrades who had come ashore on the sand and shingle of the rifle ranges south-west of Hythe so they advanced cautiously along the high ground planning to enter the town on the road past the barracks. The British were there, not in force, for many of the soldiers based there were manning posts along the canal, but enough of them, together with cooks, orderlies and even some civilians, to handle the small arms available to them. It took another hour to get past, the tanks making the difference. On the left the rest of Meindl's force came along the railway north of Saltwood Castle and they came under fire from the high ground to their left. Troops from Shorncliffe Camp, above Sandgate, were deployed up there and, staying under cover on the heathland, pinned the paratroops down. Now they were in a known position, Meindl's men were targets for shellfire from the east as well. Hythe, a ghost town, was in German hands, but they could not move on. The thrust to take Dover was stalled.

Sunset was at about 1800 hours and, as evening drew on, the invaders in Landing Zone B had achieved much, but not enough. Around Dymchurch they had come ashore in force, but the flooding of the marsh between there and Hythe constricted their front and prevented the use of tanks to break out. On the east they had been halted at Hythe and in the west the smashed sluice at St Mary's Bay was allowing the land near Brodnyx to soak up water. The best performance had been by Tank Detachment B which had managed to cross the canal at Ruckinge and gain the hills on the road to Ashford, but of the 20 tanks with which they started the day, only ten were still serviceable; two lost to British shell-fire and the rest simply broken down. They took up defensive positions for the night. It appeared that at the eastern end of the invasion front the advance had been halted and success would depend on how well their comrades fared to their west.

Notes and References

1 Jacobsen, Hans-Adolf, and Rower, Jürgen, *Decisive Battles of World War II: the German view*, London, André Deutsch, 1965, p. 89.

2 Marix Evans, Martin, 'The Error that lost the War?', *Osprey Military Journal*, Vol. 2, Issue 3.

3 Guderian, Heinz, *Achtung-Panzer!*, London, Cassell, 1999, p. 206.

4 Schenk, Peter, *Invasion of England 1940*, London, Conway Maritime, 1990, p. 252 *et seq*. All fleet and army unit details are based on this source.

5 Sunrise and sunset details based on data for 0°E/W and 51°N, 21 September 1940, Astronomical Applications Department, US Naval Observatory, http://aa.usno.navy.mil/data/docs/RS_OneYear.html.

6 Cox, Richard (ed.), *Operation Sea Lion*, London, Thornton Cox, 1974, pp. 187–90 from which weather and tide information at Dover is taken throughout Part 2.

7 Ansel, Walter, *Hitler Confronts England*, Durham, NC, Duke University Press, 1960, pp. 274–6, based on conversation with Loch.

8 Schenk, pp. 256–7 and 260. Ansel states that the 21st and 55th were to land either side of the Redoubt and may be correct.

9 Burridge, David, *20th Century Defences in Britain: Kent*, London, Brassey's, 1997, p. 7.

10 Mondey, David, *Axis Aircraft of World War II*, London, Temple Press, 1984, p. 103.

11 Schenk, p. 264.

12 Almost true; Schenk, p. 238.

13 ADS Online Catalogue, http://ads.ahds.ac.uk/catalogue/search/map.cfm?SN=11.

14 Burridge, p. 36.

chapter 8

Landing Area C – Rye Bay

Transport Fleet C sailed for the other side of the Dungeness peninsula, on the western flank of the marshes, where the River Rother enters Rye Bay, east of Cliff End and Hastings. The greater part of the fleet loaded in Antwerp where 50 transport ships and 370 barges were gathered, Calais was the starting point for 250 barges and 200 motor boats and 40 barges and 40 motor boats put out from Gravelines. The Antwerp convoy faced the greatest problems in putting to sea as the port is located on the River Schelde, some distance from the open sea. The navigable part of the river is narrow with sandbanks and turns as well as being tidal. Just getting out of the docks and onto the river proper took half an hour for transport vessels and four times that even in ideal conditions for a batch of eight barges. Loading there started nine days ahead of S-Day and the first craft to assemble on the river were obliged to do so four days before S-Day. At Calais loading began on S-Day minus five and the same schedule applied to Gravelines.

The detailed plans for the voyage prepared by Captain Kleikamp survive[1] and from them a clear picture of the landing approach is to be had. The pontoon ferries were placed at the head and rear of the fleet in order to have them available for guarding the flanks of the landing area when the line turned through 90° to make its final approach. The pontoons carried the 8.8cm anti-aircraft guns of Flakkorps II together with their entire combat units and could provide protection not only against aircraft but, like the

British 3.7 inch batteries, against armour as well. The Calais fleet sailed at 1000 hours on S-Day minus one and the vessels from Gravelines five hours earlier to be assembled off Calais by 1700 hours. Eleven hours before the scheduled landing time the 4th Raumboot Flotilla, inshore minesweepers, led the way, clearing any obstacles and followed by two minesweepers which marked the swept channel with buoys. The speed was raised to three knots and then, as the transport ships joined, to five knots. The column approached the coast on a line virtually from east to west, so once the turn north had been made the left of the line had to heave to while the right made north to take a position an equal distance from the shore.

The shore itself was, for the most part, gently sloping; only at the western end, close to Cliff End, was it steep enough to allow craft to come close in. For the greater part this area was described as flat, alluvial coast with sandy shores all the way to Sandgate. Vessels that beached at high tide would be stranded until the next tide floated them off and, at a time when the spring tides were giving way to neap, a robust beaching at high tide might leave the vessel stuck for many days. The military geography handbook contained an aerial photo-graph of the tidal sea-canal to the harbour and mouth of the River Rother which gave a fairly good idea of the sand and marsh east of it and what appear to be, though the quality of the image is not good, pillboxes.[2] Low tide was half an hour before the time at Dover, that is, at 0803 hours,[3] so care had to be taken to keep the barges from getting stuck at 0600 and having to wait at least four hours before being able to get off. At Cliff End that meant disem-barking troops more than 220 yards (200m) from the beach and at the other end of the landing area, Camber Sands, they would be half a mile (800m) away from dry land, forcing the men to wade thigh deep to the sands. The tanks, by contrast, could anticipate an easy run, battened down in underwater mode, with few hazards until they met the beach obstacles.

The defence map of 3 September[4] shows a continuous line of *Panzerhindernis*, tank obstacles, along the beach between Cliff End and the sea-canal, interspersed with pillboxes and, covering the entrance to Rye, the possibility of (that is, signed with a question mark) an anti-tank fort. The final length of shore west of the sea-canal is marked with the upright crosses of a minefield. It also shows a curiously complicated set of anti-tank ditches around the road and Royal Military Canal north-east of Rye but very little inland of the beach to the south-west. Indeed, the Military Canal there, south of Winchelsea, is shown as 'disused'. The selection of Pett Level behind the inn on the beach for the tank landing thus seems logical.

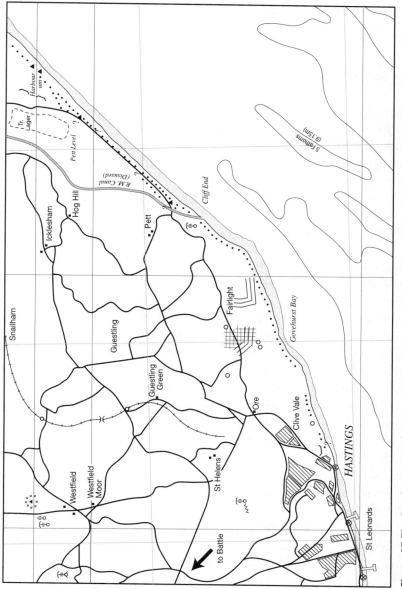

Figure 27 The Rye Bay to Hastings part of the defences map, Landing Area C. The Chain Home installation at Fairlight, just north-east of Hastings, is not marked. (After Bodleian Library C17 [42L])

The task of the 7th Infantry and 1st Mountain Divisions was to take and hold the high ground beyond Battle, at Robertsbridge, to connect with their comrades' line through Ashford to the north-east and to make contact with the 9th Army on their left or west.

The landings

The final approach was made as dawn was breaking, in fine drizzle and poor visibility, with a gentle breeze from the west and a calm sea. While it made navigation difficult, it also concealed the fleet from watchers on the shore who had been expecting them as the result of radar reports. For the men and guns of the British 45th Division it made the enemy hard to see and hard to hit. The Germans anchored their 57 transport ships outside the sandbank that shows on the defences map with the 15th Minesweeper Flotilla and part of the 1st forming a protective screen against possible attack by British submarines. The other sweepers and the patrol boats were allocated to ferry duties, unloading troops from the ships.

The 1st Mountain Division, with the 98th and 99th Regiments, were to land on the left between Cliff End and Pett Level to head immediately for the high ground north of Hastings. They waded ashore in the murk, eventually coming under fire from the anti-aircraft machine-gun post at Cliff End and from other light arms fire from the pillboxes on the beach, but the shooting was poor and light. Their casualties were trivial. Within an hour they had secured a line through Pett and Icklesham, protecting the landing ground of their armour on which Tank Detachment A was already starting to appear from the waves. They were slightly delayed by the line of concrete pimples, but the engineers' demolition teams soon blew holes in that obstacle. Part of the 98th Regiment turned west to scale the heights above Hastings with a platoon, four Panzer II tanks with 2cm guns, of Tank Detachment A in support. Here the going was much more demanding.

For whatever reason, the British appeared to have left a soft spot south of Winchelsea which the Germans were swift to exploit, but facing east on the slope were two substantial anti-tank ditches and a clutch of unidentified defensive positions, indicated by a small circle on the 3 September map. The two-floored brick observation post at Cliff End[5] and the machine-gun position that had given a little sting to the troops coming ashore were overcome with little effort, but the first attempt to advance along and beside the road to Fairlight failed. The positions of an unidentified nature turned out to be equipped with Vickers heavy machine-guns and an anti-tank gun. The small calibre weapons of the tanks were useless against the concrete fortifications and two of the tanks fell victim to the British gun. The Germans, for the time being, withdrew. To the Mountain Divisions the chalk cliffs offered no serious obstacle. By late morning a company of the 98th Regiment had made its way along the beach and was starting up them. At the same time the tank commander, irritated at the loss of two of his machines, was looking for a way round the northern flank of the defence complex. The tanks had pushed west from Pett to Guestling Green where, the commander of Detachment A could see from his map, the railway line from Winchelsea curved up towards a tunnel, offering a route through a cutting and a place, before the tunnel was entered, at which the Panzers could turn south-east to engage the anti-tank defence system from the flank. It would take more than an hour to make the move, which was time enough to arrange for support by Stuka dive-bombers. Ten *Flammpanzer* of Tank Detachment (Fl) 100 had been assigned to VII Corps and now was the time to use them.

The flame-throwing tank was a recent development. It was a Panzer II with a pair of flame throwers instead of the conventional main gun. The Detachment was usually organised in three companies of three platoons each and each platoon was led by a conventional Panzer III with a 3.7cm gun and had four flame-throwing machines. For the purpose of landing with the Advance Detachments one barge with these tanks was allocated to each Division, and as that vessel could carry only three tanks the regular formation was slightly reduced.[6] The tanks had to be unloaded from the barges and did not come ashore until early afternoon when the tide had risen and they could get close in. Then, accompanied by two Panzer IVs with their 7.5cm guns, one of the *Flammpanzer* platoons ground up the hill, along the railway line and on to engage the blockhouses. Each of the tanks carried enough fuel for 15 minutes' flame-throwing action. It was enough. First the positions were hit by the Luftwaffe's Stukas and then the tanks went in amongst the ruins of the British positions. By 1600 hours all resistance east of Hastings had been burned out. Two or three individuals escaped to spread word of these ghastly weapons. Coming ashore in support of the two *Flammpanzer* platoons were ten tanker trucks to refuel the thirsty machines, and the victorious unit withdrew to fill up.

The landings to the east placed the burden of a long wade ashore on the men of the 7th Division's 19th and 62nd Infantry Regiments. The 19th were

Figure 28 The shore of the south-west of Rye with the tree-covered ridge running inland from Hastings on the horizon

landing to the right of the tanks with the intention of passing to the right of Winchelsea to advance between the River Brede, to their south, and the Tillingham which drains into the Rother at Rye and then to thrust north towards Northiam and Beckley. The 62nd had to land east of the river mouth on Camber Sands and, having placed a rearguard to cover the approaches from Dungeness to the east, an objective to be dealt with later, the main body was to head for Rye and then north in the direction of Tenterden to link with the 35th Infantry Division which had landed south-west of Dymchurch and made for Appledore. To achieve this the 62nd had to cross the Rother without sustaining serious damage from the complex of bunkers and pillboxes around the confluence of the river with the Royal Military Canal, take the higher ground of the Isle of Oxney, cross the waterway north of it, Reading Sewer, and attain the hills beyond. In doing this they had to maintain touch with the forces of 19th Infantry on their left in a mutual flank-guarding role.

The first problem was getting ashore at all. The fleet gave what covering fire it could from its offshore anchorage but the fixed defensive positions at the mouth of the sea canal were formidable. On the western bank, behind the minefield, stood a coastal strongbox, a concrete emplacement with six

Figure 29 A substantial coastal strongpoint, possibly a variant of a Type 26 pillbox, on the west bank of the sea-canal to Rye

Figure 30 German troops attempt to move forward with their rubber boats in readiness for crossing a water obstacle ahead. (Tank Museum)

wide embrasures for Vickers heavy machine guns[7] from which a withering stream of fire cut the men down. On the other side of the water a rectangular pillbox housed more heavy machine-guns[8] and along the waterway towards Rye was a coastal gun battery[9] which was contesting matters with the pontoon ferry on the eastern end of the German fleet's line. South-east of Winchelsea two gun batteries marked on the 3 September map overlooked the area but only one of them was armed; none the less it did its share. Added to that was fire from the big guns at Dungeness, still in action for the time being in spite of the attentions of the Stukas bombing target area 7, as it was shown on the defences map. If it had not been for the intervention of the 99th Mountain Regiment on their left, the 19th would have sustained crippling casualties, for they, working with tanks of Detachment A, were able to deal with the first pillbox east of Pett Level and swarm into the parked trucks to the rear of the gun emplacements near Winchelsea. Then the map let them down; the minefield ran further down the shoreline than marked. Three tanks were immobilised with tracks blown off and the engineers spent a dangerous 45 minutes establishing that the hazard was a narrow strip laid to prevent exactly the flanking attack they were mounting. Once through they engaged the next pair of pillboxes and the combination of tank and infantry working along the sea shore and the weight of numbers of men pushing through the water eventually overwhelmed the defenders. From the Martello tower on the south-western side of Rye the local coast command could only watch the tide of Germans lap against and over his emplacements. Rye was abandoned. Once the fire on their flank had ceased, the 62nd's assault was renewed on Camber Sands. By early afternoon the shoreline was in German hands, but at a cost; they might have been better advised to wait for the *Flammpanzer* platoon now ready for action. Of some 4000 men of the 7th Division nearly a third had become casualties. The provision of hospital ships in the invasion fleet might even turn out to be insufficient.

The men of the 99th Mountain Regiment cut back across the flat land towards Winchelsea to rejoin their unit. It was a careless move made in the false relaxation of believing their job had been done. Where the Rye to Winchelsea road bends west alongside the Military Canal another Vickers machine-gun emplacement[10] remained operational until tanks of Detachment A had rescued what remained of the Mountain Regiment's men and a *Flammpanzer* had had the last word.

With the high tide now on the turn there was still enough water for the

Figure 31 An aerial photograph from the Coastal Handbook showing the *Seekanal*, the canalised River Rother, to Rye Harbour and the surrounding terrain

transport ships to make use of the channel to Rye Harbour in spite of the efforts that had been made by the British to disable the facility. The Germans had no need of the docks as the engineers used ramps and bridging equipment to hurry guns and men ashore. By 1600 hours field guns and howitzers, many self-propelled, were ready to move.

Since the defences map (Figure 20, p. 157) had been prepared, on the basis of information gathered up to 3 September, the British had built a good deal more. The road west of Rye through Udimore was blocked and barbed wire barriers had been swung into place to complete the line already made north of the Brede Levels. The Levels themselves worried the tank men; they appeared to be water meadows in which their machines could easily bog down. The tactics adopted were to let the infantry engage the defences at a distance and find a way to push the Panzers round a flank to roll up the British line. As the map showed, the picture was of a series of linear installations, in fact what had been Ironside's coastal crust in the original defence concept. The preferred approach, smashing a hole in the defence line and pouring through it, was not an option in the absence of dive-bombers to create the first breach.[11]

The 62nd Infantry Regiment on the right moved out of Rye in the late afternoon to engage the defences north-east of Iden while the 19th left a force to cover the road to Udimore. It had been decided to leave the Brede Level line alone, isolated on its ridge between the Brede and the Tillingham, and to make quick progress to a line between Beckley and Broad Oak, posing the British the dilemma of staying and being besieged or of attempting to withdraw north-westwards under fire from two sides. The move was entirely successful. By 2000 hours the 7th Division held the land south of the Rother Levels and elements of the 62nd Regiment had taken the Isle of Oxney without serious opposition.

On the left the 1st Mountain Division had started to move in the direction of Battle, the site of the previous English defeat by an invasion force in 1066, half an hour after their tank-assisted victory over Hastings's eastern defence line where their climbers had mopped up the last of the scattered resistance on the outskirts of the town. The machines of their prized *Flammpanzer* platoon, the lead tank, four flame-throwers and the four tankers remaining after the refuelling had taken place, were close behind the leading men. In the cloudy but now clear evening, the commander of the leading machine viewed the world from his turret with some satisfaction, for his formation had already proved its worth. From the undulating spine of the ridge the view between woods to the right was down towards the Brede Levels where nothing was happening and to the left, when the roadside banks permitted, the sight glimpsed from time to time was of the activity attending the landing of the 9th Army at Bexhill and beyond.

The approach of the *Flammpanzer* machines and the Mountain soldiers was not unobserved. An Operational Base of Brigadier Gubbins's Auxiliary Units had been established at Blackhorse Hill, off the road south-east of Battle and Telham.[12] The function of the Auxiliaries was, of course, to operate behind enemy lines rather than oppose them in their advance, but the commander here knew that the Home Guard were absent, having been drawn into the action earlier in the day, and that the means existed to inflict significant damage on the approaching column. A four-barrel flame *fougasse* installation was in place on the edge of Beauport Park. One man was positioned to ignite the array and the unit's best marksman was ordered to use the sharpshooter's rifle[13] to distract the commander of the leading tank. The telescopic sights enabled him to do rather more. The cheerful student of the countryside, apparently master of all he surveyed from his tank, died instantly when the .22 bullet struck him in the forehead. The tank halted as the man collapsed into his machine and as the *Flammpanzer* tanks made a hurried stop the *fougasse* was blown. The road was filled with burning tar and fuel and the newly refuelled flame-throwers were soon ablaze. The tankers exploded and the fire was so fierce that the tarmac melted, fusing the armoured column into a massive roadblock. The shock for the Germans was severe, but the practical outcome was, in strategic terms, minor, for the landings immediately left and right of the ridge made it easy to by-pass the blockage and the advance would certainly be able to reach Battle early the next day.

By nightfall the men from Landing Zone C were safely ashore and in reasonably defendable positions on the hill above Hastings, on the slopes south of the Brede Levels and solidly across the Rother. The British would have no choice but to withdraw from the Brede Levels line and the water obstacle the map showed along that river valley as the linear defences were thoroughly compromised. Contact had yet to be made with the forces from Landing Area B near Appledore, but it would surely be achieved on Sunday morning. Already the engineers were at work in Hastings, repairing the piers to create unloading facilities for the second invasion wave and a port that could be used for two hours either side of high tide, and longer during spring tides, had been secured at Rye. So far, so good.

Notes and References

1 This is true. Schenk, Peter, *Invasion of England 1940*, London, Conway Maritime, 1990, p. 274 *et seq.*

2 *Militärgeographische Angaben über England: Südküste*, Berlin, Generalstab des Heeres, 1940, p. 382.

3 Data provided by Proudman Oceanographic Laboratory Applications Group, www.pol.ac.uk.

4 *Befestigungskarte Grossbritannien 1:100,000, Blatt 40*, Berlin, Generalstab des Heeres, 1940.

5 *Defence of Britain Database*, http://ads.ahds.ac.uk/catalogue/specColl/dob/ai_full_r.cfm?REFNO=8586.

6 Schenk, pp. 184–5 and 281.

7 *Defence of Britain Database*, REFNO=6988.

8 *Ibid.*, REFNO=6993.

9 *Ibid.*, REFNO=12462.

10 *Ibid.*, REFNO=9769.

11 Bacon, Reginald, Fuller, J.F.C. and Playfair, Patrick, *Warfare Today*, London, Odhams Press, 1944, p. 35.

12 *Defence of Britain Database*, REFNO=11759.

13 Lampe, David, *The Last Ditch*, London, Cassell, 1968, p. 78.

chapter 9

Landing Area D – Pevensey Bay

The shape of Pevensey Bay has changed markedly since first the Romans and then the Normans had landed here. The flat area north of Pevensey itself that shows up as a dark shape north-east of Eastbourne on the geological map (Figure 19, p. 154) in the South Coast Handbook was then a lagoon dominated in the west by the peninsula on which the castle was built.[1] The Levels are classified as seasonally boggy and flooded land, an obstacle for horse-drawn vehicles and motorised troops especially in winter and spring. The conditions at a given time require reconnaissance, the handbook concluded.[2] For land that is a silted-up lagoon, this is reasonable. South of the spit on which Pevensey Castle stands is another, smaller marsh area of similar character. However, the ground west of Bexhill looks solid enough and the more doubtful terrain between Pevensey and Eastbourne is small enough to cross quickly at the end of a long, hot summer. The 9th Army's 34th Infantry Division was allocated the beach west of Bexhill as far as the mouth of the watercourse called Waller's Haven (now the settlement of Norman's Bay) and the 26th the area west of Pevensey and east of Langney Point.

Transport Fleet D sailed from Boulogne.[3] The port had been crammed with vessels almost beyond its capacity. There were 165 tows, groups of barges and tugs, to move 330 barges and 330 pusher boats. It was a major challenge to load the craft in the limited space and the device of mooring them bow shorewards was used to pack them close. It took ten hours to move the fleet out of harbour and the process began at noon two days before S-Day. At 1600 hours on S-Day minus one they sailed in a column 2400 yards (2200m) wide and 12.4 miles (20km) long. The 2nd and 18th Minesweeper Flotillas were responsible for leading the way and clearing dangers, but the flanks of the convoy were unprotected except for the Herbert and pontoon ferries with the anti-aircraft guns, including the heavy 8.8cm weapons. The Royal Navy, it was anticipated, would attack from the west. No such attack took place; the Royal Navy was at a safe distance.

The landings

The beaches were gently sloping in this sector, similar to those at Rye and imposing the peril of a long walk ashore. Low tide here would be at about 0745 hours, so a landing starting more than 90 minutes earlier would leave a beached barge static for over three hours before it could be floated off. It was therefore important to hold them off, the first echelon using rubber boats and assault craft to get ashore quickly and cover the unfortunates who would, in their greater numbers, be wading vulnerably to the beach.

General von Manstein, commanding XXXVIII Corps, organised his landing force into Assault Companies in order to get them off the beaches, over the marshy ground and onto the surrounding hills as fast as possible. Two detachments were from the 34th Infantry Division, 80th and 107th Regiments, and one from the 26th Division's 39th and 78th Infantry Regiments. The Assault Companies (*Sturmkompanie*) were not all equipped alike and the 34th's advance detachment had 12 such units while the 26th had six. The 34th's command companies included radio and telephone communication units, a mountain battery and the three rifle platoons had four heavy mortars and two heavy machine-guns. Two of the companies had anti-tank rifles (*Panzerbüchse*), weapons of modest performance, 30mm (1.18 inch) penetration at 90° at 100m (110 yards) range,[4] and one a PAK (anti-tank) gun[5] of rather more useful power, and probably sufficient to penetrate a British Matilda tank. The formation was completed with an engineer assault platoon and medical staff. The Assault Company B had three rifle platoons each with four heavy mortars, two heavy machine-guns and a 3.7cm PAK which was only marginally more powerful than the anti-tank rifles. The advance detachments also had two self-propelled PAKs with 4.7cm guns, two 2cm anti-aircraft guns and two assault guns. One company

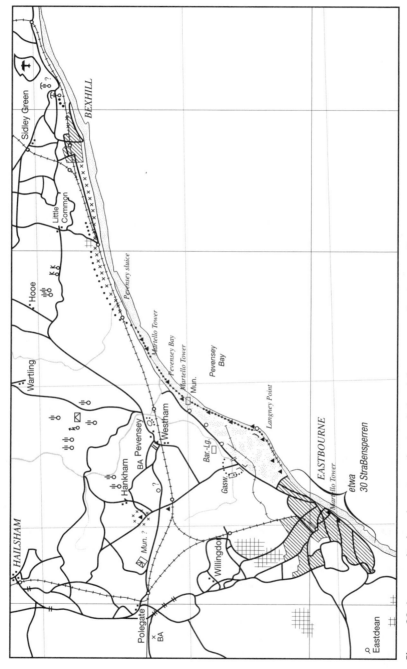

Figure 32 A composite based on two sheets of the defences map showing Landing Area D. The annotations suggest some 30 roadblocks around Eastbourne. (After Bodleian Library C17 [42L])

Figure 33 The shingle beach in Landing Area D looking from Norman's Bay towards Bexhill, with the sea wall on the left

of Tank Detachment (U) C was allocated to each of the two advance detachments and heavy pontoon and Herbert ferries were to be positioned to give flank coverage by five 8.8cm and ten 2cm anti-aircraft guns. This was the landing force destined for the Bexhill end of the Landing Area.

More modest was the force that the 26th Division was to land between Pevensey and Langney Point. The six companies were of three rifle platoons each, an engineer platoon and demolition and flame-throwing units. They had two heavy mortars, a light field gun and two PAK anti-tank guns. A company of the Tank Detachment was also allocated to them. General von Manstein had requested either mountain troop or paratroop participation to take the heights of Beachy Head, west of Eastbourne, but this was not forthcoming. What he did get was two *Brandenburg* commando units, one of 72 and one of 38 men, to go ashore with the 26th Division and silence the battery on the cliff tops. They were to be mounted on motor-cycles and would be lightly armed;[6] speed and surprise would be their principal assets.

After their surprisingly uneventful voyage from Boulogne, Transport Fleet D closed with the English coast soon after 0600 hours that Saturday morning in continuous drizzle and poor visibility. Their approach, as elsewhere on the coast, had been observed, but their precise positions could not be seen, until daylight came on at 0544 hours, in part because of the weather and in part as a result of the smoke screen laid down. The defences were not well-defined on the 3 September map, and a number of sites were labelled 'xBA', meaning a construction site which might have been completed by now and equipped with some kind of weaponry only experience would reveal. The shoreline showed the dots representing anti-tank obstacles and the saltire crosses of barbed wire beyond the railway line. Inland, at Barnhorne, two searchlights and two light anti-aircraft guns were shown at the eastern end of an anti-tank ditch. Clarity was not helped by the need to refer to two sheets of the map, 39 and 40. Further inland, at Lunsford's Cross, north-west of Bexhill, a clutch of defensive positions were shown as under construction and yet further north, among the muddle of valleys and hillocks rising towards Battle, more anti-aircraft installations. Along the shore to the left stood a Martello tower, from which machine-gun fire was already being brought to bear on the approaching boats, and further towers and pillboxes, but at the point designated for the landing of the 34th Division there was very little. It was hard to understand, but easy to explain; the planned defences were not yet built.

The first of the Assault Companies hit the beach at 0620 hours and, with a little light machine-gun fire coming from their left, crossed the shingle beach, swarmed over the anti-tank wall and made ready to deal with the barbed wire. The engineers radioed for ramps from the barges to be brought up with the tanks so that, with the tanks providing shelter from the small-arms fire, they could create a roadway up from the beach to the top of the wall. It proved to be a slow business, for the shingle itself gave poor footing to tank tracks and the ramps had first to be used to make a road over the unstable stones. Infantry probing forward discovered a weak point at the railway halt where the anti-tank obstacles and barbed wire could, once the section of soldiers of the 45th Division had been disposed of, be moved aside. The area turned out to be severely under-defended and the Assault Companies were quickly established around a beachhead from which they immediately launched an assault on the guns at Barnhorne. Mortar fire inflicted casualties on the small force manning the guns and defending the anti-tank ditch and by 0830 hours the 34th was holding the road running west from Bexhill. The landing of the rest of the first wave was going smoothly, with very little harassing fire to trouble the procedure.

The shore allocated to the 26th Division was more substantially fortified. The map shows Martello towers with pillboxes spaced out between them and, at Langney Point, a coastal battery. A ring of defences is marked around

Figure 34 The Pevensey Levels seen from Norman's Bay. Martello Tower 55 stands to seaward of the houses at the end of the defensive wall with the South Downs beyond. 'Coffin' anti-tank blocks survive near the tower

Pevensey Castle and on the roads fanning out from there pillboxes and anti-aircraft installations are marked. It was the battery on the shore that did the first serious damage to the approaching convoy before it got its smoke screen working, sinking one of the two Herbert ferries on this flank when the ammunition it carried with its guns went up, and damaging the guns on the other. The *Brandenburg* commandos were pushed into action and covering fire was given by the auxiliary gunboats of which there were two on this flank.[7] Their premature deployment laid them open to fire from the machine-guns mounted on the Martello towers on either side and a sharp little battle developed on the beach and in the water. The groynes, wooden barriers that prevented the shingle being swept along the length of the beach, offered some cover from view even if imperfect cover from fire. As the barges, carefully prevented from beaching, unloaded their troops to wade ashore, the pillboxes and guns on the road inland, across the stream, Pevensey Haven, that drained the sector, opened up as well. The water was filled with dead and wounded men, their comrades trying to tug them to the beach and others trying to return fire as they struggled on. Still the barges came in and the sheer pressure of numbers put more of the invaders ashore. The commandos took the battery and fire from the ships knocked out the Martello towers. An engineer unit with a flame-thrower attacked the pillbox left of the battery and put it out of action. Their problems were not at an end, for another battery, not marked on their map, was firing on the Germans from a position near the Martello tower on the front at Eastbourne.[8] It was necessary to concentrate the fire of several escort ships to silence the British guns.

The cost of landing here was high and the fight to reduce the defences on the shore and immediately inland took a long time. Two of the 34th's Assault Companies that had trotted inland so freely were hurried westwards along the narrow road inside the sea wall to start working their way, pillbox by pillbox, from Pevensey Sluice towards Pevensey Bay but it was late morning before the whole beach was under German control. The setback on the left had prevented progress on the right but by early afternoon they were ready to renew their advance.

The whole battle had been observed in detail from the look-out post in Pevensey Castle and accurate estimates of the nature of the landing force had been passed to divisional headquarters. It was clear that a counter-attack that day could not be mounted, particularly in view of events east and west of Pevensey Bay, and that the only option open to the British was

Figure 35 Steam trawlers ready to serve as tugs moored in Rotterdam. Field guns shrouded under canvas are mounted on wooden platforms in their bows. (Coll. Peter Schenk)

to inflict as much damage as possible during a fighting retreat. The castle itself, built of stone capable of generating a mass of lethal splinters under shell-fire, was being evacuated and the garrison was already on its way west by road, taking with it the light machine-guns and small arms, having rendered the heavier weapons inoperable. The modern emplacements in the ancient structure were not to take a direct part in the action.

The *Brandenburg* commando units had suffered seriously in their unplanned intervention to take the shore battery, but there were 48 of them still fit for action and their motor-cycles were undamaged. They reorganised in two units one of which was to take the shortest route for Beachy Head, circling Eastbourne through Willingdon, while the other would head for the road junction at Polegate before turning south towards Eastdean. The Willington squad rode straight up the hill and swung left-handed round the railway station, across and left again to get to the Eastbourne to Eastdean road. The town was, of course, deserted except for servicemen and civilians supplying essential services; nurses, for example, working at the sanatorium which was still an operational hospital. No-one opposed their progress; some soldiers marching north even saluted the officer riding at the head of the well-ordered column. They arrived at the rear of the sole fortification, a half-built emplacement south-east of Eastdean, without being challenged. They had been taken for reinforcements against the invaders. There was no great battery to threaten the invasion fleet. Leaving a guard to prevent their prisoners attempting to rejoin their units, the commandos turned east once more and with great care started to make their way down towards the sea-front. The town appeared just as shown in the handbook, with the exception of empty, sand-bagged look-out posts and unmanned road-blocks. They moved with immense caution, expecting at any minute to discover a centre of resistance. There was none. The Wish Tower, the Martello tower on the promenade, was abandoned and the guns of the adjoining battery had been rendered inoperable. The huge Redoubt was empty. At about 1700 hours they were challenged in their own language; they had completed the circuit of the town and were back close to Langney Point once more.

The Polegate detachment rode off equally briskly and similarly in parade-ground formation. The route took them over the railway line south of Stone Cross and the Pevensey garrison saw them coming. From the cover of the railway platforms they opened fire as the convoy slowed and halted to have one of their number open the gate over the rail crossing. None of these *Brandenburg* soldiers survived.

As soon as the beachhead on Pevensey Bay had been stabilised General von Manstein ordered the 34th Division to get moving again. Their task was unchanged. They were to get up off the Levels to make a common front with the 26th on their left by taking Windmill Hill, north of Wartling, and advancing north and west while, in the east, they were to envelop Bexhill from the landward side and push up towards Battle to link with the 1st Mountain Division coming from Rye Bay. The work in the west went quite smoothly and steadily. The few anti-aircraft installations north of Pevensey offered no lengthy resistance to the Assault Companies of the 34th which were ordered to head inland after their relief mission on the right flank of the 26th's beachhead. They were reunited with their comrades at Wartling, together with tanks of Detachment (U) C whose machines had been con-verted back to land use. Skirmishers fell back before them, irritating mainly by wounding and worrying their men, for few were killed, delaying their progress by enforcing caution, but making no stand. To their left the 26th was passing round the south of Eastbourne and up to the downs above the Cuckmere River and by nightfall the objective of the river valley was before them. On the hills close to the sea where the chalk cliffs called the Seven Sisters stand they encountered exhausted men of the 6th Mountain Division.

Stubborn men defended the approaches to Battle and the country inland from Bexhill. The woods and narrow valleys gave cover the British used well and uncomfortably accurate sniper fire was brought to bear on anyone in uniform suggesting a higher rank; someone out there was using telescopic sights. The self-propelled guns were engaged by anti-aircraft guns that were certainly heavier than the defence map suggested. Radio communication with their artillery to the rear was eventually successful in eliminating the British weapons, but the irregular nature of the terrain made accurate sighting and correction of shell-fall a difficult business. The emplacements at Lunsford Cross had been finished and held until pounded to fragments by shell-fire, and that took time. It was getting dark before they entered the outskirts of Bexhill and halted, wary of going further until the light of the next day. Once past Catsfield, progress towards Battle picked up, but they had not yet made contact with the 1st Mountain Division and the clear evening light was fading. Suddenly a huge gush of flame erupted away to their right on the crest of the ridge running down to Hastings. The fire burned bright and steady in the growing darkness and the blackening sky was streaked with even darker smoke. They decided to stop, sleep and wait for dawn before moving on.

Notes and References

1 Gravett, Christopher, *Hastings 1066*, Oxford, Osprey, 1992, p. 50.

2 *England (IV Militärgeographische Beschreibung)*, Berlin, 1940.

3 Schenk, Peter, *Invasion of England 1940*, London, Conway Maritime, 1990, p. 286 *et seq.*

4 Quarrie, Bruce, *Encyclopaedia of the German Army in the 20th Century*, Wellingborough, Patrick Stephens, 1989, p. 146.

5 Calibre uncertain. Schenk states 4.7cm, but Quarrie, p. 164, cites this weapon only on a *Panzerjäger I*.

6 Schenk, p. 238.

7 *Ibid.*, p. 288.

9 ADS Online Catalogue, Refno=15180.

chapter 10

Landing Area E – Rottingdean to Cuckmerehaven

The western landing zone was not to the German Navy's taste. It was, in their opinion, exposed both to the westerly weather and seas and to the Royal Navy which was so close at Portsmouth. The Army insisted and a compromise was struck; the Army could have its landing as long as the Navy chose the route and shipping.[1] The long voyage from Le Havre was to be made by sailing at high speed, seven knots, in ships towing empty barges. The barges could not make this pace when loaded, but were needed to ferry the troops ashore on the English coast.[2] The route was protected left and right by minefields, but was evidently vulnerable in the west and also dangerous should the invasion fleet deviate into a minefield or if mines should drift. The evolution of the final invasion fleet illustrates the problems the Germans had in balancing naval practicality with the needs of a land army capable of achieving its assigned tasks.

Not only were there fears about getting across the Channel, the problems of finding moorings for assembling and loading the fleet, originally conceived as 50 transports, 200 barges, 25 tugs, 200 motor fishing boats and 100 coasters, were insuperable. Le Havre overflowed and Trouville, Rouen, Caen and Fécamp were pressed into service for loading which gave the additional advantage of avoiding dependence on the locks at the major port. It had the disadvantage of making movement dependent on the state of the tide. British air raids had threatened both ships and locks. Another problem was the state of the barges that arrived for the invasion. Many were incompletely equipped and as many needed to be degaussed, that is, desensitised to magnetic mines. On top of all that the quality of crew was poor; Germany was a largely land-locked country and finding seamen was difficult. In order to deal with these problems the number of barges was cut and the number of small, powered vessels increased so the new scheme was as follows: The Advance Detachment consisted of 200 motor fishing boats and 100 coasters sailing 20 abreast. Convoy 4 (Echelon 1a) followed with 25 transport ships towing 50 empty barges and 25 trawlers with three empty barges each. Convoy 5 (Echelon 1b) had another 25 transports with 50 barges.

It was then necessary to allocate space to the various units of the 8th and 28th Infantry and 6th Mountain Divisions. Spreading them over a large number of small craft was intended to increase the survival rate and guarantee a viable force when landed, but small ships could not handle heavy armament and the Advance Detachment would be in serious trouble without heavy guns. Their ships were augmented with the addition of ten transports, four of which towed Herbert ferries and their associated support barges and the others a pair of half-loaded barges, and two trawlers with three empty barges each. Further, four heavy, ocean-going tugs were added to bring 1 Company, Tank Detachment (U) D and its support across. Echelon 1a was reduced to 15 transport with half-loaded barges and four more Herbert ferries and the mass of empty barges, three towed by each of 21 trawlers, and two half-loaded barges with each of 25 transports formed Echelon 1b. The weight of guns and tanks had been increased, but the speed and flexibility of the fleet had suffered. The final phase of the operation was the arrival of Echelon 2 which was to embark from Boulogne.

The Herbert ferries, each of which mounted an 8.8cm anti-aircraft gun, contributed to fleet defence during the voyage, but the bulk of the protection was given by three patrol flotillas and five heavy auxiliary gunboats. The gunboats were judged to be effective against light naval opposition and also to be capable of coastal bombardment, again making up for the shortage of heavy artillery.

The planned landing areas were three separate zones, for the coastline is one of cliffs with three limited entry points. In the east, Cuckmerehaven is a narrow river valley, very flat near the sea and narrowing inland, the River Cuckmere running from the north through a cutting in the South Downs. In the centre the River Ouse flows south past Lewes, once upon a time a seaport itself, to enter the sea at Newhaven on the western side of the flat, alluvial valley on the eastern side of which is Seaford. On the cliffs west of

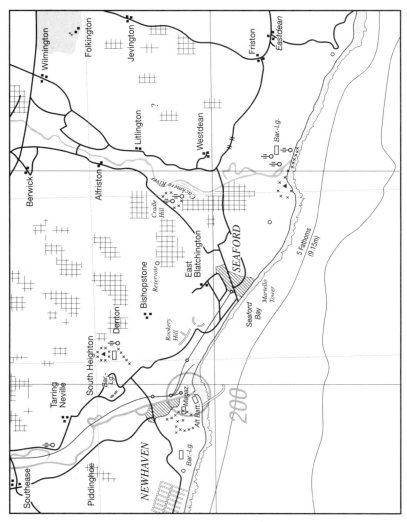

Figure 36 The section of the defences map covering Landing Area E, the coast from Rottingdean, just east of Brighton, to Cuckmere-haven, west of the Seven Sisters and Beachy Head and the immediate area inland to Lewes. (After Bodleian Library C17 [42L])

the harbour mouth is Newhaven Redoubt, a fort which the British started building in 1864 and finished, for the time being, ten years later.[3] It was now equipped with slightly more modern guns, the Germans thought four medium weapons. The defences map of 3 September[4] shows that the fort is targeted for bombardment, presumably by Stukas and then by gunboats, as it is marked to be kept clear, avoided by the German troops. To the west the original idea of landing at Shoreham and putting paratroops on the Downs north of Brighton was abandoned. The Luftwaffe was not willing to undertake the airborne operation and the seaborne element went as a result. The 28th Division was therefore directed to Rottingdean, a cleft in the cliffs that ran from Newhaven to Brighton that gave access to a little valley going north to Falmer. The area had been developed to some extent after the date of the map the Germans were using and Saltdean, immediately east of Rottingdean, was coming into existence as a resort and retirement town and the undercliff walk, to which there was access by way of a tunnel, was shown under construction in the handbook to the coast.[5]

On the morning of Saturday, 21 September 1940 the tide at Newhaven was at low water at 0734 hours, giving problems similar to those experienced in Pevensey Bay, and high water would follow at 1324 hours.[6]

The landings

The Cuckmerehaven landing was carried out by 6th Mountain Division, supported by the tank company. The defences map suggested that the fortifications were modest. There are three light anti-aircraft guns shown east of the river on the hillside at the western end of the Seven Sisters cliffs, and a fortified barrack building alongside them. On the shore are barbed wire entanglements and on the western hill a defence position classified as being of unknown type. Above the river valley north of the Seaford to Eastbourne road, at Cradle Hill, another anti-aircraft gun stands surrounded by tank obstacles, and the higher, flatter ground is hatched to show aircraft landing obstacles. Altogether not too daunting. Unfortunately it was misleading.

As elsewhere that morning, visibility was poor and a light rain was falling. The British were aware of the Mountain Division's convoy approaching, but found it hard to make out the details. The Herbert ferries took station on the east and west and the gunboat stood off awaiting developments. The first men ashore encountered no gunfire but, to the right of the river viewed from the sea, found themselves looking at a long earth bank. The priority was to get the underwater tanks ashore and no attempt was made to advance until the machines had descended their ramps and begun creeping beneath the waves towards the beach. The Mountain infantry cut wire and probed cautiously forward. Some fire was directed at them from the emplacement on the west. The engineers did what they could to open a channel between the tank obstacles on the beach and the first tanks rolled in, shed their air pipes and breasted the slope before them. As they tipped over the top a yet steeper slope hasted them down into an abrupt ditch: it was a massive trap. Immediately the 3.7 inch guns and the machine-guns in the pillboxes tucked against the hillside opened fire. Two tanks burst into flames at once and another slewed sideways down the slope, a track blown off. A tank at the top of the bank attempted to back away and smashed into the machine following it up. The poor visibility had worked in favour of the defence. The troops began at once to seek flanking opportunities and attacked the slopes to their right, the cliffs of the Seven Sisters. Progress was slow but sure, although fire from a pillbox sited on the hillside took its toll. The motorised 10cm artillery was ashore, but the problem was getting it off the beach and into a position to fire on the British without exposing itself fatally. An attempt to creep around the left, along-side the river, almost led to the loss of one machine as it started to bog down, but it was towed out successfully.

The Mountain Division then put men ashore west of the river where, making use of their mortars, they began to cause difficulties for the British pillboxes which had, like all fixed positions, the disadvantage of turning into a trap when opposed to highly mobile forces. The 3.7 inch fire ceased as the mobile guns were pulled back and the tanks tried again. One gun remained and another tank caught fire, leaving little space for others to pass. Echelon 1a was now sending men and equipment ashore and, as the day brightened, British resistance faded. On the right a platoon rushed the first pillbox and burst in. Except for two dead men, it was empty and silent. Then it exploded. After that lesson the Germans would enter apparently inactive fortifications with care.

The 6th Mountain Division regrouped and advanced once more. The river meanders widely across the valley floor and drainage ditches, blocked and overflowing, added to the hazards of progress. As they neared the road from Eastbourne the tanks came under fire again and a pillbox on the

Figure 37 View west across Cuckmerehaven towards Seaford Head. The anti-tank ditch runs from left to right towards the river and one of the pillboxes, possibly an anti-aircraft Type 23, stands in the foreground

Figure 38 On the valley flank a cylindrical Type 25 pillbox looks over the River Cuckmere

eastern side of the valley opened up as well. There was no prospect of assistance for the invaders from comrades on their flanks as they were cut off from the 26th Infantry Division by the mass of Beachy Head and from the 8th by the ridge east of Seaford; the only course open to them was to inch their way forward in a series of platoon engagements, leapfrogging one unit past another and working to find a place in which their remaining tanks would be of use. Here, picking their way through the mud between ditch and river, they had no room to use their strength.

The Mountain Division's objective was the open country north of the Downs, past Alfriston, to protect the flank of the 26th Infantry coming west from Polegate and later to guarantee this flank to allow the passage of the Panzers due in the second wave. Stubbornly they bit and held their ground through the valley. A patrol sent towards Seaford alongside the road found no defenders at all; they had withdrawn having inflicted what damage they could and apparently without loss. From the hills above Seaford they saw that the axis of advance of the 8th Division was clearly north-west and they could not look to them for help. The road towards Eastbourne was blocked with tank obstacles but apparently not covered by guns. The infantry mounted a carefully prepared assault on them and found then undefended, but that all took time. The men now on the high ground to the right above Seven Sisters found the anti-aircraft installations blown up and the guns lacking breech blocks, rendered useless. There was, as yet, no sign of the 26th Division; they were not encountered until late afternoon when they discovered that they could pass around Eastbourne along the seashore unopposed. The advance north towards Alfriston was delayed for a while by fire from the anti-aircraft guns at Cradle Hill and, by the time they reached the Polegate to Lewes road near Berwick, Tank Detachment (U) D's company had been reduced to less than half its operational strength through loss, accident and mechanical breakdown.

On the western flank the 28th Division's landing at Rottingdean was, by comparison, a mild and uneventful affair. The defences were trivial, consisting of Home Guard road blocks and lacking sophisticated pillboxes. They entered the ghost town of the partly-built resort of Saltdean in a series of house-to-house rushes, sections leapfrogging ahead while covered by their comrades, expecting to be fired upon at any minute. All remained silent. The tunnel to the undercliff at Saltdean gave the invaders pause because of the bomb-blast baffle walls which made them think of the possibility of sabotage, booby-traps or unknown hazards, so they worked their way through with hand grenades hurled round corners and found nothing to resist them at all. They moved on with care, up to the Brighton to Lewes road and waited. A defensive position facing Brighton was established and then patrols moved north and east, towards Ditchling Beacon and Lewes.

Meanwhile the 8th Division were making their assault on the Newhaven to Seaford shoreline. Here the railway runs within the shoreline on a high embankment and beyond that the broad, flat valley floor that is the flood plain of the Ouse spreads to the steep hillsides on either flank, crossed with small streams and drainage ditches. The two principal roads to and from the north-west and Lewes run just above the foot of the hillsides and the west-to-east road from Newhaven to Seaford is raised on a causeway across the plain with a branch north towards Lewes. In the centre of the 8th's landing area the apparently unremarkable Bishopstone Halt railway station, high on the embankment, overlooks the beach. The September defences map does not indicate that the Martello tower at Seaford is fortified, although it was, and suggests that the principal defence works were inland of the railway halt at Rookery Hill and also, quite a complex, at South Heighton. More defensive positions, mainly anti-aircraft are marked on the road to Lewes.

Figure 39 The view towards Newhaven Redoubt and harbour mouth from Bishopstone railway station, overlooking the shore

The Advanced Detachment of the 8th had four motorised guns with them and the 28th *Jäger* (Light Infantry) Regiment. As they closed with the shore the Stukas of Luftflotte 3 began their attack on the fort at Newhaven. The RAF was aware of their approach but unsure of their objective, so the attack, from the German point of view, got off to a good start. The slow Stukas gathered speed in their banshee-shrieking dive and released their bombs into the area of the Redoubt. The inside of the fort was a series of arches faced with windows and doors, bolstered with sand-bags and glass shielded with wooden shutters, but by no means armoured against explosives. The guns were mounted above the massive, earth-covered external walls and came to no harm at all, but the garrison suffered serious casualties before they found shelter. Before the dive-bomber wing could finish its business the British fighters were among them and their escorts and drove them off. Two British guns remained in action throughout and the invasion fleet hastened to bring Herbert ferries and gunboats into action against them. The landing beach was hit repeatedly, but perhaps unwisely as the shells did as much to clear the carefully erected obstacles as they did harm to the enemy. The old naval guns were slow and worn, and while they did significant damage they were not effective enough to turn the Germans back. The invaders persisted, making what use they could of the cover of the railway embankment and readying their own artillery to reply. The trouble was that the seaward side of the embankment was exposed to the fort while crossing the railway attracted fire from the tower on the railway station at Bishopstone and other emplacements inland. Within an hour they had two howitzers in action and the defenders of Newhaven Redoubt were exposed to the firepower of an experienced and skilled unit of gunners. By mid-morning all the coastal defence power of the fort had been silenced. On the right flank the Martello tower at Seaford was repeatedly hit by shelling from both a gunboat and an 8.8cm anti-aircraft gun mounted on a Herbert ferry, but it was a high-trajectory missile from a German howitzer than ended its active service.

Quite early in the day a platoon of the 28th Regiment had risen to run across the railway. They were startled to be fired upon from the railway station tower by machine-guns. The weapons were light and the fire they laid down, though serious, was not substantial, and more than half the invaders made it into the cover of the reeds and ditches beyond the line. It took their artillery half an hour to reduce the little railway halt to rubble and by 0900 hours the serious fire from both flanks had ceased.

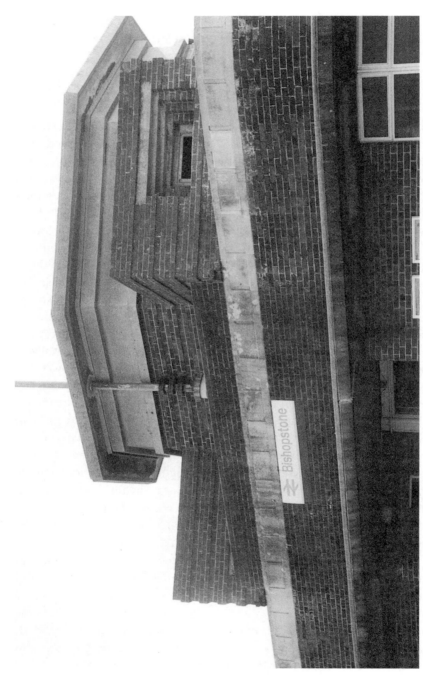

Figure 40 Bren-gun, i.e. light machine-gun, emplacements built into the tower over the booking hall of the railway station

The infantrymen could then advance in earnest, moving close under the seaward side of the embankment towards Seaford before turning inland west of the railway station and pushing uphill behind the defences facing Bishopstone. Meanwhile their artillery was putting down shellfire on the works north of the road below Rookery Hill and in a well coordinated infantry and artillery action the complex was taken before noon. On the west a gunboat and a minesweeper made a tentative approach to the harbour overlooked by the now silent Redoubt. From the inner harbour's landward defences on the west small-arms fire began, but did little to distract them. The waterway was free of mines but an attempt had been made to block the port by scuttling a cross-channel ferry which would clearly be a nuisance at low water but failed to close the dredged channel entirely at high tide. Motor and fishing boats of the Echelon 1a were sent in carrying men of the 84th *Jäger* Regiment who were put ashore on the west of the harbour to work their way up to the cliffs alongside the Redoubt and, eventually, to take the fort itself where surviving members of the garrison, their heavy artillery gone, were still resisting with rifles and light machine-guns. They were told to leave the emplacements further west, above Friar's Bay, until one of the self-propelled assault guns could be unloaded to support them. In the meantime a company started to advance towards Piddinghoe on the right bank of the Ouse.

By early afternoon the invasion had gathered momentum and the boats of Echelon 1b were unloading. Lacking tanks, the advance was not dramatic, but steadily the shell-fire reduced the pillboxes and emplacements at South Heighton and the tide of light infantry rolled north-west on both sides of the river. There were unforeseen centres of resistance, for not all the fortifications were known to the Germans, but the British lacked the mobile strength to counter-attack and bring relief to besieged positions. At about 1800 hours the 84th met men of the 28th Division's 49th Regiment at Kingston near Lewes in time to see the bridges at Beddingham and Glynde disappear in a cloud of explosive. Shortly afterwards another detonation was followed by a cloud rising from a location beyond the castle at Lewes. The main bridges over the Ouse had all gone before the Germans could reach them.

In spite of that, for their engineers would certainly be able to build temporary bridges within a couple of days, the 28th and 8th Divisions had every reason to be satisfied with the day's work. Their casualties had been no greater than expected and they now held the crossing of the Ouse with

Figure 41 An aerial photograph from the South Coast Handbook of the port of Newhaven with the Redoubt on the left, the harbour facilities centre and the low, marshy ground of the Ouse delta on the right

troops firmly established on both sides of the river. As evening came on the 8th's eastern advance north of Seaford made contact with the 6th Mountain Division at Cradle Hill and the task of securing the high ground south of the Eastbourne to Lewes road the next day was not demanding. They had done the job of gaining a bridgehead that would protect an advance westwards below the South Downs and, in their own estimation, the yet more important task of capturing a viable seaport.

The port of Newhaven was not considered such a desirable prize by the German Navy. The proximity to Portsmouth and the exposure of transport ships to attack by the Royal Navy, not that the Royal Navy had attacked any-thing yet, made it, in their estimation, far too vulnerable a supply port in the short term. Only when German lines were established west of the Solent would the use of Newhaven suit Admiral Raeder.

Notes and References

1   Schenk, Peter, *Invasion of England 1940*, London, Conway Maritime, 1990, p. 301 *et seq.*

2   Ansel, Walter, *Hitler Confronts England*, Durham, NC, Duke University Press, 1960, p. 263.

3   Saunders, Andrew, *Channel Defences*, London, Batsford/English Heritage, 1997, p. 91 *et seq.*

4   *Befestigungskarte Grossbritannien 1:100,000, Blatt 39*, Berlin, Generalstab des Heeres, 1940.

5   *Militärgeographische Angaben über England: Südküste*, Berlin, Generalstab des Heeres, 1940, pp. 331–3.

6   Proudman Oceanographic Laboratory Applications Group, www.pol.ac.uk.

chapter 11

The British reaction

General Sir Alan Brooke had planned to meet the Director of Military Training after spending the morning of 21 September in his office. He then had an appointment with the New Zealanders' commander, Major-General Bernard Freyberg, VC, who was on the point of departing for the Middle East.[1] He was woken at 0500 hours with the reports of radar sightings of large groups of vessels on the move in the English Channel and the assessment that Sealion was starting. Although he felt that preparations were far from complete it was a relief to be in action again. The first of his appointments was cancelled and he put a call through to Freyberg at once. The New Zealand Division was near Maidstone and Brooke ordered them to stay there unless directly attacked; they were a card to be played later.

The great temptation was to start issuing orders and getting people to do things. This Brooke avoided. The RAF had already withdrawn from airfields in the invasion sector, orders were in place for the destruction of installations and landing strips at the discretion of local commanders and the security of the radar stations' secrets was arranged for with instructions for removal of equipment and demolition of installations if they were threatened with capture. Indeed, the Chain Home stations at Fairlight, near Hastings, and Pevensey were already in ruins. For the time being Dover remained operational and was feeding back information on the dive-bomber air-fleets heading for Folkestone, Sandgate and Dungeness which enabled Air Vice-Marshal Park's controllers to scramble fighters to oppose them. The forward positions of the Observer Corps had already been evacuated and the communication system was, as planned, redeploying accordingly. The Auxiliary Units' radio system, such as it was, had already become active with information on the landing of airborne troops above Hythe. In towns and villages in Kent and Sussex those garages and service stations not already decommissioned were pumping out their fuel tanks and some adding sugar and water to the small residue of petrol left behind. In south-east Kent the 1st (London) Division was already in action to oppose landings but, more importantly, to prevent an attack on Dover and the 45th Division was fighting all along the south coast up to Eastbourne with orders to hold if possible, delay if holding could not continue and to undertake a fighting retreat at the last. The 29th Brigade west of Eastbourne was giving the 6th Mountain Division a hard time at Cuckmerehaven and their comrades problems near Newhaven. The extension of the invasion area towards, but not beyond, Brighton allowed Brooke to ask for 1st Independent Brigade to move east to prevent further western movement of the invaders. For the time being the German attack lacked a clear direction and Brooke elected to wait.

It was vital to be sure that this was not just the real thing, but the real thing in its entirety. For months the British had been convinced that the blow would fall on East Anglia and the four divisions and the Independent Brigade of XI Corps were deployed there with an armoured division, an infantry division and a brigade in reserve. They might yet be needed there, but they were put on notice of a possible move. Enigma decrypts[2] suggested that the ports from Rotterdam to Le Havre were involved, which led Brooke to believe the South Coast was the only region being targeted, but he had already weathered the tension of Operation *Herbstreise*, Autumn Journey, the diversionary action on 16 September.[3] Brooke was wary of falling for another.

By nightfall on Saturday 21 September the situation had become that much clearer. The Germans had succeeded in establishing a beachhead from Hythe to Rottingdean and were solidly positioned from Dymchurch to Eastbourne. They had failed in what was a clear effort to open a route inland to Dover and were without a foothold on the North Downs. On the South Downs they were east of Brighton and could, perhaps, be halted on that side of the London road. They had already gained a presence on both sides of the pillbox line on the River Ouse through Lewes. The development of their invasion was apparently inclining to an advance through Horsham, south of the pillbox line from Burwash through Uckfield, then, perhaps, north-west to Goldalming and Guildford to envelop London; in fact the true concept of Sealion with a modification of the north-eastern end of the First Operational Objective. Alternatively, the Germans might have it in mind to gain control of the Solent with the ports of Southampton and Portsmouth; only time would tell.

The work of MI 14, that part of Military Intelligence concerned with gathering information on Germany and German intentions, had included the study of preparations for the invasion. Part of that work was an assessment of the capacity of ports and beaches to handle the supplies an invading force would require. The report states:

The success of the invasion must stand or fall on the ability of the Germans to maintain their forces after the initial landing supplies have been expended, and it is clear that their difficulties in this respect will be very considerable. While the enemy would not expect that all their assaulting forces could succeed in getting ashore, they would probably have to arrange for landing supplies and replacements at the rate of some 8–10,000 tons per day.[4]

This figure was reached by taking the requirement for a British division at 200 tons a day for basic needs, excluding engineering and ordnance supplies, and at 350 tons for all needs and guessing that the Germans might be prepared to operate at 300 tons in the first phase of an invasion campaign. Thus, for 30 divisions, a figure of 9000 tons emerges. The landings so far had put about ten divisions on English soil, but obviously there must be more to come, so 30 was the number assumed. The facilities required were then examined.

The proportions of these supplies which could be landed on open beaches would depend on the number of special craft which had been provided, e.g. the craft designed to beach themselves, remain upright, and land supplies via special prows direct onto the shore. . . . The continued supply of invasion forces, as opposed to any improvised arrangements for the first few days, can only be carried out through properly equipped ports, in view of the high wastage rate of special craft and of other difficulties, including weather. It will be essential, therefore, for the Germans to secure, within or near the area of the main attack, ports capable of dealing with the volume of supplies envisaged.

The study continued with consideration of the throughput that might be attained using beaches and ports between North Foreland, the north-eastern extreme of Kent, and Dungeness. It assumed that the ports of Ramsgate, Dover and Folkestone would be in German hands and that the only beach suitable for the purpose would be those between Sandgate and Dungeness, Landing Area B in German terms. The report concluded that, in the early days of the campaign, the ports would handle 350 tons per day and the beaches 5200 tons. This would rise, after a week, to 1600 tons through the ports and 6800 tons over the beaches. It was pointed out that the figure for the beaches was '... not based on experience, of which there is none available, but an exercise in combined operations has provided some evidence.'[5]

The importance of the conclusions was underlined by the assumptions made in the study and by the actual situation Britain faced. The Intelligence officers worked on the basis of the RAF being in a position to interfere substantially with German operations, so the figure had already been cut to take that into account. What they came up with was four supply barges per mile of beach unloading 100 tons of supplies per 12-hour day, and thus the 13 miles of beach east of Dungeness would take the 52 barges needed to produce the figure of 5200 tons they suggested for the initial stages of the invasion. The fact was that the Germans had more beach at their disposal than they actually needed. The lengths from Hastings to Rye and from Newhaven to Seaford were already occupied and the Rye to Dungeness beach, although exposed to the west, might also be pressed into service. Further, there were piers at Eastbourne and Hastings which had not been destroyed in their entirety but merely lacked a span or two and could be repaired to use as jetties. In this light the failure to capture Folkestone and Dover was not a severe blow to German plans, and they might yet be able to use Newhaven.

The disruption of German supply lines was clearly a priority. Air Chief Marshal Sir Edgar Ludlow-Hewitt was four years younger than his opposite number at Fighter Command, Dowding, but a similarly dedicated professional. He had become Commander-in-Chief, Bomber Command in September 1937 and made himself deeply unpopular with his political and civilian masters by pointing out the woeful inadequacy of his force to carry out the actions on which the whole strategy of a future air war would be based. The poor equipment, the lack of an effective bombsight and the inadequate navigational aids were all problems with which he grappled, but most serious of all was the inability to do the bombing itself. The bombs were poor, failing to explode or, if they did, to do any serious damage. Further, the bomber crews had difficulty in finding and identifying targets and then, assuming that had been achieved, hitting them; largely the result of limited opportunity to train realistically.[6] The first year of war was, therefore, a swift course in all the skills years of peace had eroded or denied, and it was expensive in men and machines. By September Bomber and Coastal Commands were capable of turning the French coast from Dunkirk to Calais into what some called 'Blackpool Front' – an area alight as if it was a holiday resort.[7] Ludlow-Hewitt was now charged with turning the coasts of Sussex and Kent into similar displays and with maintaining the pressure on the French, Belgian and Dutch ports from which the supplies originated. When people had said, before the war, that it would be the bomber that would win it, they had a different scenario in mind, but they may well have been speaking the truth. Perhaps the Lutwaffe's concentration exclusively on the destruction of the RAF's fighter capability had been a mistake.

The other weapon available for the disruption of supply lines was the Royal Navy, so much feared by the German Navy and against which they had taken precautions in laying minefields and deploying submarines. Admiral Forbes was unwilling to commit ships larger and slower than destroyers and it would be with destroyers and motor torpedo boats that he would act. The fight had to be taken to the underwater threat and the minefields had to be swept to allow the surface ships to carry out search and destroy missions against the supply fleet. In this enterprise the Royal Navy had ASDIC, standing for the Allied Submarine Detection Investigation Committee which undertook the development of a sound-pulse detection system to combat submarines in 1917. The device was well-established by 1938 and, within its limitations of indicating only distance and direction of the enemy boat, effective. Against mines the British had introduced a magnetic sweep that summer, but for counter-measures against acoustic mines there was, as yet, no fully operational acoustic sweep. It would be necessary to use an experimental sweep in this crisis.[8] Ship-borne radar for vessel-to-vessel detection was still in the future. What soon became apparent, however, was the existence of a German submarine screen in the western Channel. Of the 57 boats they possessed, including training boats and vessels undergoing trials and working-up exercises, 17, their large and medium boat strength, were off Cornwall, nine off Sussex and six off East Anglia and the Netherlands.[9] The Royal Navy did not know the detail, but the concentration of the enemy close to the shore, once appreciated, offered a superb opportunity to wage war on the enemy Admiral Forbes had been so keen to engage: the opposing navy. That was undertaken by both day and night in the western Channel. In the central sector minesweeping cleared the way for a number of night attacks on German supply convoys, but again the principal target was the submarine flotilla. By the end of Sealion, Admiral Dönitz's force would be reduced to almost half its number. The Royal Navy also had the Fleet Air Arm to contribute. The Blackburn Skua had already shown its powers as a dive-bomber in the Norwegian campaign and, provided the RAF could give fighter cover for the comparatively slow aircraft, 806 Squadron at Eastleigh, near Southampton, was available.

The defeat of the BEF in France was the result, in part, of factors beyond its control but also because of flawed attempt to defend in depth against the sort of thrust that gave the Panzers victory in Poland. The British had neither the manpower nor the number of weapons to achieve their aim; long fronts were covered by too few units with too few guns.[10] Attempts to create strongpoints were irrelevant when they were too far apart to give mutual support or when no mobile force existed to carry out a counter-attack. Above all, the Germans in France had room to manoeuvre. At Flavion, in Belgium, west of Dinant, Rommel had simply by-passed the French armour, leaving it to his motorised infantry and artillery to fight them, and driven on towards Cambrai.[11] One way or another, the German invasion had to be channelled into a constrained strike towards a narrow front and, as had been imagined but not achieved in France, sliced up by attacks on the flanks.

Another major problem the British had created for themselves in France was their clumsy communications system. It relied on land lines almost com-pletely, and those were in the hands of their allies, the French. Linking the command posts to the telephone system was difficult for an army constantly on the move and the lines themselves were vulnerable to bomb and shell. The radios were limited in number, about 75 sets for each division, and in type, for many could not transmit speech but used Morse code. Further, the fear of interception led to the laborious use of cipher instead of simple code words for units and locations.[12] Given the time since Dunkirk and the losses of equipment sustained there, the faults could not be overcome entirely, but the experience of keeping RAF stations in touch through the attacks of the summer and the energetic replacement of radio sets, coupled with a less formal approach to framing and sending messages, improved matters.

A serious effort had been made to learn from the experience in France by setting up a committee under Lieutenant-General Sir William Bartholomew as early as 12 June and the results were ready on 2 July. Quick though this was, it did not give time to make sweeping changes and, indeed, some senior persons still spoke of the importance of parade-ground drill, instant and unquestioning obedience to orders and deference to higher command when better training to foster swift decision making and initiative nearer to the action was needed.[13] Brooke's view was summed up in a meeting on 6 August when he set out his concept of the effective defence of England. Linear defence was to be abandoned and fixed defences would be around ports and along beaches. They would check the German advance and give the British the opportunity to organise a decisive counter-attack. He called it 'all-round defence in depth with the maximum number of troops trained and disposed for a rapid counter-offensive'.[14] The troops were in place and the check to the German advance was in hand, though incomplete. The overall concept was clear and, in the next day or two, he had to decide in detail and issue orders to complete the check and make the counter-attack.

The 1st (London) Division had taken a good deal of the strain so far. They needed reinforcement and the route north of the Weald towards the Medway should, if possible, be denied to the Germans. Freyberg's New Zealanders were ordered to attack the flank of the 17th Infantry Division as it attempted to join the 7th Airborne in an advance on Dover. He was given more of the 3.7 inch guns which, although lacking an optical sight and weighing a cumbersome nine tons, were actually capable of killing Panzers, and without tank support he would certainly need them. That it was sending most of Freyberg's men on a self-sacrificial mission was understood and ignored by all concerned, including the Kiwis. The 45th Division was to hold the Weald by any means possible, so that the Germans would be drawn into a series of attempted western flanking movements. The reserves, the 1st Canadian Division, 1st Armoured Division and the 1st Army Tank Brigade were to hold position north of the Weald while the situation developed, ready to move east or west, while the 42nd Division covered the route to Reading past Aldershot. In the west, Montgomery's 3rd Division, the Australian Division, the 4th Division and the 2nd Armoured Division's single brigade together with the 21st Army Tank Brigade were in readiness to strike from the high chalk plains when the moment was ripe. It seemed likely that the Germans would have more than twice as many troops in the field, so the army alone was not going to settle the matter. Success would depend on all arms doing their uttermost and in particular those attacking the enemy's supply lines. It would be, so to say, a mobile siege, in which the Germans were to be starved out.

Notes and References

1 Alanbrooke, Field Marshal Lord, *War Diaries 1939–1945*, London, Weidenfeld & Nicolson, 2001, p. 110. True to the end of the second sentence, imagined thereafter.

2 Based on October 17 events. Gilbert, Martin, *Finest Hour*, London, Heinemann, 1983, p. 852.

3 Based on Schenk, Peter, *Invasion of England 1940*, London, Conway Maritime, 1990, p. 317 *et seq.*

4 General Staff, War Office, MI 14, *Notes on the German Preparations for Invasion of the United Kingdom (2nd edition)*, 1942, reprinted Uckfield, Naval & Military Press, 2004, p. 90 .

5 MI 14, p. 182.

6 Terraine, John, *The Right of the Line*, London, Hodder and Stoughton, 1985, p. 81 *et seq.*

7 *Ibid.*, p. 209.

8 Dear, I. C. B., *The Oxford Companion to World War II*, Oxford, OUP, 1995, pp. 588–9.

9 *German Naval History Series: The U-Boat War in the Atlantic, Vol. I, 1939–1941*, London, HMSO, 1989, pp. 46 and 56.

10 French, David, *Raising Churchill's Army*, Oxford, OUP, 2000, p. 174 *et seq.*

11 Marix Evans, Martin, *The Fall of France*, Oxford, Osprey, 2000, pp. 67–70.

12 French, pp. 180–1.

13 *Ibid.*, p. 189 *et seq.*

14 *Ibid.*, p. 196.

chapter 12

The final round

S atisfied with their progress so far, the Germans pressed on with their
campaign. In the words of the order of 30 August, they had to 'broaden
out these isolated beachheads to form a single cohesive landing-zone, the
occupation of which covers the disembarkation of the subsequent troops
...'. And then, 'As soon as sufficient forces are available, the assault begins
against the first operational objective: the line from the Thames Estuary,
over the high ground south of London, to Portsmouth.' Three days were
required for the execution of the order for the second wave to land, bringing
the strength of four Panzer Divisions and three Motorised Infantry to the
fight.[1] Although they had advanced inland at the western end of the
landing area, they had by no means achieved what the Luftwaffe had noted
as the first step, 'Hills midway between Canterbury/Folkestone-
Ashford–hills 20km N of Hastings, and the coastal strip at least as far as the
line: hills 20km N of Bexhill–hills 10km N of Worthing.'[2] The centre section,
north of Bexhill and Hastings, was near to being secured already, but the
progress north of Folkestone had been minimal and the far western advance
north of Worthing had been curtailed by the abandonment of the Brighton
operation. Consideration now had to be given to the possibility of attaining
these objectives in the short term as against the overall concept of the
invasion in the longer term.

The Second Operational Objective was the line from Maldon, in Essex,
to a point on the route west from London, Reading, perhaps, that would

have London surrounded and the British forced to negotiate peace terms if not surrender outright. As the ports of Folkestone and Dover had not been seized on the first day their later capture would doubtless put the Germans in possession of a heap of ruins and blocked harbours, so the purpose of adhering to the plan in that respect was now doubtful. If the German Navy could defend the cross-Channel route, the port of Newhaven was already available, virtually undamaged. On the other hand the British were still able to fire from Dover on the beaches west of Hythe to interfere with landing supplies, and suppressing the shelling was a worthwhile objective. Further, the roads across Romney Marsh were still open as causeways in spite of the flooding, and if the shelling could be stopped the Dungeness to Hythe beaches could be used for landing supplies and even troops and equipment of the Second Wave. The route to Reading appeared to be open south of the Weald, so the expenditure of men and machines in taking the hills south of London was arguably an extravagance. It was, however, premature to conclude that the road to Canterbury was unattainable and, even if Dover was left to long-range artillery and the Luftwaffe, the North Downs route was worth having. It was decided to continue the effort on the eastern flank at the same time as developing the rest of the front to satisfy the criteria summarised by Jeschonnek in the Luftwaffe's orders.

Landing Area B: the second day

The first night in England was not a peaceful one for the men of the 17th Division along the Royal Military Canal below Lympne and in Hythe. The weather was dry with broken cloud and a soft wind from the south was coming up, but it was noisy. Overhead the drone of British bombers seemed continuous and the sound of their work at Calais and Boulogne kept many from falling asleep. Then, later in the night, the bombing came closer as the beaches behind them became targets. The aircraft were flying high and the bombs fell all over the place, doing little damage to the barges still being unloaded or to the roads along which the men and supplies moved inland, but the very random fall of the bombs undermined confidence and forbade rest. In addition it was impossible to hear if the British were creeping up to attack and more than one German life was lost to friendly fire as nervous sentries reacted.

West of Lympne the force that had attacked and fallen back the previous day, supported by Tank Detachment D, could now look to reinforcement from Tank Detachment B which had been re-routed by way of Dymchurch. The mobile combat unit it had been hoped to form under the command of Colonel Hoffmeister the previous day was now assembled as best as could be managed from the units to hand, the rest having been reduced in numbers or holding positions on the shoreline as a result of unexpected developments like floods. The force now put together comprised the better part of a Tank Detachment, some 35 tanks, from Detachments (U)B and (U)D, two companies of self-propelled anti-tank guns, a battery of II Battalion, Artillery Regiment 67 with self-propelled heavy field howitzers, two heavy and one light batteries of I/Flak Detachment 61, an engineer company, two companies of the 21st Infantry and most of a company of Brandenburgers.[3] It was no mean force.

Having attempted to break through the British line at Lympne the previous afternoon and failed, something more sophisticated than a frontal assault was tried. A task force of about two dozen tanks with the Brandenburgers and a company of the 21st Infantry was sent north to pass round the munitions dump on the racecourse and push east, on the other side of the railway track, towards Hawkinge. One company of anti-tank guns would go with them and Hoffmeister himself took command. The rest of the force would, at least to start with, keep the British busy with another, but rather different, attack on the airfield and munitions depot defences.

The presence of the howitzers made a great difference. The Germans approached the airfield in a series of small-unit jumps, working with the ten tanks remaining. As the tanks attracted the fire of the anti-aircraft guns around the airfield the howitzers brought down counter-fire and the steady, disciplined application of artillery, tank and infantry attacks took out the pillboxes and guns positions one by one. The assaults eventually concentrated on the weak join between the airfield and the munitions dump through which the tanks broke and encircled both positions. It was not swift work but by late morning the garrisons had surrendered and the Germans found themselves with the added burden of prisoners of war. The front-line, fighting troops surprised their captives by offering them curious cigarettes and ardent spirits from hip-flasks; the courage and determination of the mixture of RAF Regiment, Home Guard and 1st (London) Division aroused respect in their adversaries. The prisoners plodded off towards the beaches under escort, destined for a trip in a barge across the Channel. The closer they got to the sea the more the men around them changed in character from assault troops to lines of communication men who had been shot at while manhandling supplies and, unable to respond, were now the more hostile towards their enemies. One of the British prisoners later wrote:

... You could smell there had been a battle, apart from the debris of war. It's a curious mixture of smells, containing petrol, diesel, dust, cordite, burning and horse manure. The Germans used a lot of horse transports, especially in the rear. ... If you happened to drop behind and got to the rear of the column, the German guards hit you in the back with their rifle butts or pushed and banged their bicycle wheels into the backs of your legs, yelling at you to go faster. If you complained, they threatened to take you into the fields and shoot you. This did happen, these troops were a different type to the elite corps on the front lines – these were mean and spiteful.[4]

The flying column heading for Hawkinge encountered little resistance as they crossed the railway and turned east. Their radio system was working well and the paratroops of Meindl's force were able to join them north of Saltwood. In the style that had been demonstrated so convincingly in France, they decided to leave the Shorncliffe Camp garrison where it was, engaging the token German force remaining in Hythe, and continue their rush towards Dover. The route had to be decided. The fortifications map of 3 September[5] showed a line of pillboxes and anti-aircraft positions running up north of Sandgate through Newington and up onto the Downs towards Paddlesworth, but north of that village the density of defences appeared to decline and the way east open up. They had to tackle the steep climb to the open downland and chose a route through Beachborough and Etchinghill, there to incline right between Lyminge and Paddlesworth. They were observed all the way, but nothing more worrying than light machine-gun fire was experienced. They swung round Paddlesworth and attempted to conceal themselves from anti-aircraft gun fire from the Hawkinge airfield by smashing their way through Reinden Wood. Nothing warned them that the wood concealed the dispersed site of RAF Hawkinge. The wood held air-raid shelters, open-topped anti-blast shelters and a gas decontamination building;[6] robust brick and concrete structures from which even the primitive Boyes anti-tank rifle could perform useful service against the more tender parts of a tank. What was more, the British had manned the position and as the task force entered the infantry were riddled with heavy machine-gun fire and the armour, seeking shelter from the anti-aircraft fire which had taken out three of their number west of the wood, found their way blocked by their lead tank catching fire after a couple of well-placed rounds. What had been a brave, Rommel-like foray broke down in the confusion of burning tanks, trees, smoke and explosions. Under the cover of their own 8.8cm anti-aircraft guns they pulled back and tried further north again. The infantry ran clinging to tanks or huddled in the remaining trucks but they had been moving for only a few minutes when another hail of fire hit them. Down the road and from the western flank a swarm of tracked carriers, bren-gun carriers as they were known, rushed amongst them, twisting and turning, guns blazing. The advance party of Freyberg's New Zealanders had been unable to resist making an attack, and, moving fast, were gone almost before the Germans could return fire, leaving almost 50 of the invaders as casualties. What was most serious was the death of Colonel Hoffmeister. As one of the little carriers bounced past his command vehicle the khaki-clad officer standing in it casually fired his revolver in the Colonel's direction. The bullet took Hoffmeister in the head.[7] The losses were mounting and, with their leader gone, the offensive spirit drained out of the task force. They pulled back to Lympne.

The plan to break through to Dover was recognised as too difficult to fulfil. It was therefore decided to establish a defensive line from Hythe through Saltwood, where the castle was vandalised in converting it to an artillery fort, and west along the high ground to Lympne. The task of dealing with British guns at Dover was passed to the Luftwaffe's dive-bombers and the heavy guns in France.

Without a significant number of tanks the progress of the 35th Infantry Division towards Tenterden was modest. The expected thrust towards Ashford on their right was not happening as the 55th Infantry Regiment, also tankless, made tentative probes northwards, but little more. The whole attention of the 17th Division was on the Dover sally and the rest stalled. By the end of the day the 35th had made contact with 7th infantry near Appledore and their platoon of five tanks, four of them *Flammpanzer* machines that had yet to see action. The centre of gravity of the whole operation was leaning west.

Landing Area C: the second day

Above Hastings on the road to Battle the 1st Mountain Division had hesitated only for moments when the *Flammpanzer* platoon had been destroyed

Figure 42 A column of bren-gun carriers on the move. (Tank Museum)

and they hurried forward to take up defensive positions for the attack they expected would follow. Nothing happened except a few whoops of joy from the dusk ahead. They sprayed the gloom with fire until ordered to stop wasting ammunition. There they spent the night. The 7th Infantry Division on the other flank also settled down, content to be off those exposed beaches and now into country with reasonable cover and, apparently, few of the enemy. These men, too, spent a disturbed night as the aircraft roared overhead. The harbour of Rye was a target for the British. No bombs fell in the river or on the quays, but a number of sheep in the marshes to the east were blown to bits. The bombers also attacked Hastings, and here they had better luck. The pier which might have been useful as a jetty was destroyed and the damage to the promenade immediately inland was also great. A potential supply line had been hit.

The 7th Infantry were within easy reach of their objective on the Tenterden to Ticehurst line, in effect the ridge north of the Rother valley, from which the British seemed to have withdrawn. The 62nd Regiment moved on from their overnight positions on the Isle of Oxney and over Reading Sewer which ran down to Appledore. The movement up to Tenterden, more by luck than judgement, outflanked the incomplete anti-tank defences protecting the approaches to Sandhurst and Rolvenden to their left and they exploited the opportunity, driving quickly westwards to secure the high ground where they were reunited with the 19th Regiment which had had a similarly easy journey. The noise and dark of the night had been used by the British to creep away to the north-west, vacating their works on the Brede Levels and along the Rother. It took a little time for the Germans of the 7th Division to appreciate that their right flank was hanging in the air. While there appeared to be no danger because the British were absent, their own people were absent as well. A company of the 62nd together with their *Flammpanzer* platoon, was sent east through Tenterden and down to Appledore to renew contact, and they did so during the afternoon.

The 1st Mountain Division was on the move again at dawn, but lacked tanks. Almost at once they ran into men of the 34th Division together with tanks of Detachment C and self-propelled guns from Landing Area D who had overnighted near Catsfield. The Mountain Division was keen to have tanks in what they anticipated would be a hard slog north. The problem was referred upwards and contributed to the pressure for the Second Wave, with its substantial Panzer element, to be sent as soon as possible. In the event there was little to worry about. Again, the British had withdrawn and even the anti-tank ditch at Etchingham was undefended.

Landing Area D: the second day

The 34th Division had to be slowed down on the second day. On their right the 1st Mountain Division distracted them with an argument about who should use the surviving tanks, but in moving north they met only token resistance. They could not exploit their advantage further because of more problems that the 26th ran into. North-west of Hailsham a major defence work obstructed progress. Along the Cuckmere valley from Michelham Priory to Horsebridge a massive earthwork, an anti-tank ditch, had been dug and the attempt by a company of Tank Detachment (U)C to cross it had been a disaster. The position was covered by two of the 3.7 inch guns that had been hurried into service as anti-tank weapons and they had inflicted serious losses. The woods and valleys to the north-east appeared to be full of concealed marksmen and the rumours of snipers and sharpshooters began to circulate to the detriment of morale. The advance here was losing momentum and immediate steps were taken to set matters to rights. The 34th were ordered to get their tanks back from the Mountain Division at Battle and to outflank the British position by driving for East Hoathly. It was harder to do than it appeared on a map, for the country was dotted with woods and little streams, offering excellent cover for defence. Not that it was held in strength, but impulsive action was clearly too dangerous and the Germans picked their way forward with care. Most of the day was spent in this activity, with little to show for it. In the end the tank obstacle was taken by men of the 6th Mountain Division advancing along the river from the south, by which time the guns had been put out of action by their crews and fewer than 30 men were made prisoner.

Landing Area E: the second day

The major action of the second day in the most western of the invasion zones took place around Lewes. The tanks of 1 Company, Tank Detachment (U)D were released from the ill-chosen narrows of Cuckmerehaven once the wreckage of the first to come ashore had been cleared from the anti-tank ditch close to the beach. As the 6th Mountain Division had made good

Figure 43 German infantry working their way forward in the company of a Panzer II. (Tank Museum)

progress up the river valley the armour was switched to the west to join the 8th Infantry in developing their hold on the Ouse valley. They took the road to Seaford and crossed the Ouse at Newhaven before turning north for Lewes. There, to the north-west of the town, close to the site of the battle that had curtailed the power of English kings in 1264, were suspect structures; defensive works of some kind not clear to the Germans.

The tanks clanked and creaked up the road and headed around the west of the town where His Majesty's Prison dominated the scene. It had been emptied of its usual inmates and taken over by a unit of the Auxiliary Military Pioneer Service, an arm of the service drawn mostly from veterans of the previous war, but here including some who, as a result of recent, involuntary residence, were already familiar with the building and had been given the option of remaining with the Pioneers. Their tasks had been the construction of many of the defences that had hindered German progress and now they were resentful of the presence of these invaders. As the tanks clambered past the cross-roads with the 8th Infantry troops trotting alongside, a thin hail of small-arms fire came from the prison. The tanks turned to protect the foot-soldiers and as they did so two men with pickaxes broke from cover and attacked. With their picks they wrenched the tracks from the two leading machines before they were themselves cut down by German machine-gun fire.[8] The disabled armour blocked the road and had to be towed clear. In the meantime the German infantry fought a house-to-house action outside and a cell-to-cell action inside Lewes Gaol. It took more than an hour to quell the Pioneers.

The remaining tanks then made cautious progress towards the racecourse and the unspecified defence works. They were unmanned and unfinished.

Waiting for the Panzers

At the end of the second day the beachhead had been expanded and consolidated, but it did not comply with the original scheme. The centre, the hills north of Bexhill and Hastings, had been taken thus putting the Germans in control of the broad valley south of the Weald, but the eastern objective of Dover and the high ground of the southern end of the North Downs remained in British hands. What was more a bunch of mad New Zealanders was on the loose, apparently unwilling to play by the rules. In the west the Germans were comfortably placed on the South Downs east of Brighton, overlooking the low land south of the Weald and in an eminently defensible position. As evening approached it rained heavily.[9] The forecast was for moderate winds and seas, but with good visibility, so the Channel crossing and the unloading process would be reasonably easy to achieve, but the convoys would need protection from air attack. The Second Wave was ordered to sail on Wednesday evening, 25 September, and to start unloading at first light. Landing Area B was no longer to be the principal disembarkation point. It was vulnerable to attack from the north, jeopardised by inland flooding and now drenched with rain. Newhaven had been rejected as too close to Royal Navy interference. The Second Wave would therefore be divided between the Rye Bay zone, including, if rain ceased, Camber Sands, and the Pevensey Bay zone including the Glyne Gap, between Bexhill and St Leonard's.

The next three days were busy. Although the arrival of fresh troops and equipment to pursue the conquest of England had to be awaited, supplies were coming in all the time and the perimeters of the beachhead were being patrolled and consolidated to protect the flanks of the launching ground for the new assault. The work did not proceed undisturbed. The Royal Navy's sweepers were clearing the minefields and by dawn on 24 September craft attempting the direct route from Le Havre to Landing Area E had been attacked and turned back; it would now be necessary to reach the Newhaven–Seaford beach by way of Boulogne or, perhaps, cease sailing there at all. The western cross-Channel flank was looking more vulnerable. From the air the RAF's attacks continued. In daylight the FAA Blackburn Skuas they escorted from Eastleigh sank two transports bringing drums of fuel crucial for the advance. The night of 23–24 September and the early morning of 25 September saw clear skies with some cloud giving enough visibility for night bombers to strike with a reasonable chance of hitting their targets all along the south coast. Frantic work began to clear the wreckage of sunken barges and coasters sufficiently to allow the Second Wave to come in. Doubts were expressed in the German Army High Command about the wisdom of committing the Panzers to the invasion, but things had gone too far to permit withdrawal. If the Navy could not supply the invasion forces, Göring claimed, the Luftwaffe would supply them by air. The German Navy pointed out that they had used small boats to supply Norway and could do the same here if need be.

On the ground the Germans suffered a series of small, but irritating and depressing, attacks. They could do little to discourage them by exacting reprisals on civilians or by taking them hostage because there were no civilians around. The villages and farms stood empty for the most part, only a few ancients too wedded to their homes to move remaining. The disadvantage of shooting them was that there was no-one else to watch and be terrified. On the night of 24–25 September the growing fuel store of petrol drums stacking up in the transport depot at Winchelsea caught fire. Two guards had been on duty on the fence and both were later found dead of knife wounds. Four loaded trucks were blown up by explosive charges and another three went up, killing troops who had rushed in to search the site and to fight the fires, as a result of delayed action devices. Another man was killed by a bullet apparently fired from the ground through his foot and into his belly, though how this could be achieved was a puzzle.[10]

One of the men of the Auxiliary Unit responsible for the raid later told of how close he came to being caught by one of the sentries.

I'd crawled slowly all the way. . . . I was absolutely caked with mud. I was cold and miserable, too, and as brown as the field. . . . And – suddenly I heard [the sentry] coming. . . . I thought, "Well, here's where I lie still." And so I lay still. But my hands were up on the grass, poised to crawl over it. Brown and muddy, but there. And he came so close to me – he must have been within an inch of my fingers – that I felt the muddy ground give slightly under his foot. He walked off and I lay there for a bit, and then I . . . [did] the thing . . . I'd got to [do] . . . and went away. He never saw me. . . .[11]

General Brooke was not idle either. By Sunday night his staff had concluded that the Kent and Sussex landings were the principal undertaking and the Enigma intercepts supported this, giving news of the movement of the German 16th Army's XXXXI Corps of two Panzer Divisions and a Motorised Infantry division and of 9th Army's XV Corps of similar strength. Clearly the beachhead had been set up to land these units and give them a jumping-off point for a dramatic sweep through England. It therefore remained vital to confine the Germans' gateway to the narrow length of coast they now held, or even to lessen it, and seek to draw them into positions from which counter-attack would be possible. Orders were therefore given for the 42nd Division to move from its position west of London to reinforce the North Downs south-east of the capital, adding 1st Army Tank Brigade to their strength on the way. The Canadian Division and the 1st Armoured Division were to remain east of Guildford. The reserves north of London, 43rd and 2nd

Armoured Divisions were to take position west of London and V Corps was to push the 4th Division and 21st Army Tank Brigade towards Petersfield and Chichester to deny the Germans progress towards Portsmouth and the west while the 3rd Division, under the command of Bernard Montgomery one of the most reliable formations, and the Australian Imperial Force, one of the most aggressive, would be poised to strike from the Petersfield–Farnborough line.

The Battle of England

The Second Wave consisted of two armoured corps intended to smash around London and force surrender on the British. The 16th Army on the right had the XXXXI Corps of 8th and 10th Panzer Divisions, 29th (Motorised) Infantry Division and two motorised regiments, Grossdeutschland and SS Liebstandarte Adolf Hitler, each with an assault battery. The 8th Panzer Division consisted of 10th Panzer Regiment, 8th and 28th Panzergrenadiers and 80th Panzer Artillery regiments. Their *Wehrkreis*, their principal recruiting office, was in Berlin. The 10th Panzer Division, recruited in Stuttgart, was made up of 7th Panzer Regiment, 69th and 86th Panzergrenadiers and 90th Panzer Artillery regiments.

The 9th Army's XV Corps consisted of 4th and 7th Panzer Divisions and the 20th (Motorised) Infantry Division. The 4th Panzer Division, Nuremberg, had been a stronger formation with 35th and 36th Panzer Regiments, but the 36th was transferred to become the spearhead of the 14th Division that summer. The 12th and 33rd Panzergrenadiers and 103rd Panzer Artillery completed the formation. Erwin Rommel spent much of the time from the surrender of France until the first week of September training the 7th Panzer Division for Sealion, but he was not to lead them in England. Shortly before S-Day he was called to Berlin and told to immerse himself in information about North Africa.[12] This was, in fact, an invented task at the time. Rommel's conduct in France had scared many of his colleagues and most of his superiors, including the commander of XV Corps, General Hermann Hoth. Although the divisional commander's gallop across northern France had succeeded, many thought it was evidence of good fortune rather than mature calculation and the thought of his cavalier behaviour being repeated was too much. He was, to his subsequent relief, but immediate fury, replaced. The formation, based on Kassel, consisted of 25th Panzer regiment, 6th and 7th Panzergrenadiers and 78th Panzer Artillery regiments.[13]

Figure 44 A horse-drawn German supply column in 1940. (Tank Museum)

The Panzergrenadier regiment consisted of five companies with truck transportation. One company was equipped with anti-tank guns and light field and anti-aircraft guns, one company with heavy machine-guns and 8cm mortars, and three companies with light machine-guns, mortars and anti-tank rifles. There were variations. The artillery regiments were also motorised and were made up of three battalions of three companies each. One battalion had four 15cm guns in each company while the other two had 10.5cm guns. The divisions also had an anti-tank battalion each with ten 3.7cm guns, a reconnaissance battalion in armoured cars and a signals battalion with a radio company and a telephone company.[14] The divisions were thus largely self-supporting fighting units, but a great limitation was their range. Without refuelling the Panzer II tank could travel only 60 miles (100km) cross country, the Panzer III 72 miles (120km) and the Panzer IV 100 miles (160km). On roads these ranges were significantly improved, up to half as far again. Self-propelled artillery frequently made use of Panzer I or Panzer II bodies and was similarly limited in range. Thus, in theory, a Panzer II landed at Pevensey was able to drive clockwise around the Weald to Guildford and one landed at Rye could go anti-clockwise as far as Dorking, assuming a cross-country route and no need to deviate from a convenient route. Resupply of petrol, assuming none could be scavenged *en route*, was dependent on the delivery of fuel in drums, brought up by truck or by horse-drawn wagon; petrol-free transport.[15]

The original concept of the use of the armoured divisions in England was, quite simply, that the 16th Army's Panzers would go north of the Weald and the 9th's south of it. However, the situation had developed along different lines and the concentration of effort now had to be directed along the southerly route. The northern one was not ruled out altogether; the 10th Panzer Division and SS Liebstandarte Adolf Hitler were to be held near Tenterden until the development of the attack became clear.

The last drive

Early in the morning of Thursday 26 September the landings began. It was cloudy with a northerly wind and fair visibility. Rommel or no Rommel, they wasted no time before getting on the move. Brushing aside the trains of horse-drawn wagons moving food and other basic supplies west in the wake of the bridgehead forces, the 4th and 7th Divisions roared off from Pevensey,

Figure 45 A snapshot made by a German soldier of armour crossing a temporary pontoon bridge. (Tank Museum)

the 4th taking the Lewes road after Polegate and the 7th heading further inland, through East Hoathly and Uckfield, where it had to cross the Ouse, and on towards Haywards Heath and Horsham. The style remained the same as that used in northern France; where resistance was met the Panzergrenadiers engaged their adversaries and the tanks went round the flank. Occasional probing diversions northwards tried out the land; the terrain classified in the handbook as 'Low mountain country ... away from tracks ground presents considerable difficulties for vehicles, horse-drawn artillery and motorised troops.' It did not seem so bad, but they hesitated to try a short cut. Presumably those who had studied the matter and written the evaluations knew what they were doing. They decided to stick to the book.

To their left the column of 4th Panzer was held up in its drive along the open, exposed road beneath the Downs by the RAF. The Germans were using their radios to communicate with each other and it was no problem for the radio direction finding units which had become so adept at pin-pointing their own aircraft to fix the positions of these invaders. Nor was it hard for the British to figure out the broad gist of their brief conversations, code-words or no. Thus the Germans had no warning of the squadron of Blenheims that suddenly appeared with their 2000lb (900kg) bomb-loads and 0.303 inch (7.7mm) machine-guns. The aircraft were not fast, but the Germans had no cover. The airfields so thoroughly bombed by the Luftwaffe but now in German hands, Lympne and Lydd, principally, were not yet back in service and alarm calls required response from France. Regular patrolling was not even attempted as the RAF was still, inexplicably in the eyes of the invaders, capable of response. Fortunately for 4th Panzer the bombing did little more than scatter the column and force it to deploy its anti-aircraft guns, but a number of trucks were hit and some vehicles damaged in the act of taking to the fields across well-maintained ditches.

The blown bridges at Beddingham had been recommissioned with pontoons by the engineers of the 8th Infantry Division who waved them through. At Lewes the decision had to be made on which direction to go next. Reports from the 28th Infantry said that the high ground as far west as the London to Brighton road was held, but that the hills west between the town and the Devil's Dyke had numerous concrete installations on them and aerial reconnaissance had reported movement of men and equipment up there a couple of days before. It was decided to stay on the low ground through Plumpton and hurry forward in the knowledge that their left flank was secured by the 28th. By evening the 9th Army's Panzers had reached a line approximating to the London road and were in Burgess Hill and Clayton with the 28th Infantry holding the hills to the south. Attempts to refuel from service stations in Burgess Hill and Lewes had been unsuccessful; the pumps were empty. One tank had tried using a petrol pump in Ditchling. It ran for a few miles before stuttering to a halt, a sticky, black mess fouling the engine. Orders were given for all fuel to be tested before it was put in the tanks. In their tracks a column of trucks laden with petrol drums was coming up from Pevensey to resupply them that evening, and more trucks were being filled from a transport ship alongside the jetty created from the pier at St Leonards. That night a man on a bicycle hurried north by back lanes to the clandestine radio station near Cross-in-Hand, north of the Pevensey Levels and the report was duly processed through the Auxiliary Unit network to the RAF. The transport was sunk at dawn the next day and the train of trucks on the promenade went up at the same time.

From the landing area east of Hastings 8th Panzer was following the 9th Army's force. It was also harassed by air attack, but was lucky in having a squadron of its own fighters on hand to drive off the slow-moving Blenheims and inflict the loss of half their aircraft on the British. Meanwhile 10th Panzer was making cautious moves between Tenterden and Ashford, but was ordered to limit itself to reconnaissance for the time being.

On Friday the task given to 4th Panzer was to drive for Portsmouth while 7th and 8th Panzer were to push on towards the Guildford and Godalming area and break through the defence line towards Windsor and Reading. To distract the British, 10th Panzer was released to go for Maidstone and then turn west past Sevenoaks and Limpsfield.

The problem 4th Panzer ran into was two-fold. First, they encountered conventional resistance from the British 4th Division and 21st Army Tank Brigade, but then, as they tried their familiar flanking tactics by using valleys and gullies in the hills to their left, they ran into a series of ambushes. The 1st Independent Infantry Brigade was, with the advice of officers of the Indian Army provided by Brigadier Gubbins, employing the methods of the ancient opponents on India's north-west frontier. In the narrow valleys the first and last machine in their flanking force was hit, the column halted and, from concealed positions on the hillsides, small-arms fire accounted for the Panzergrenadiers. Courageous counter-attacks up the hillsides found empty fox-holes and scatterings of used cartridges. It was a frustrating business and expensive in fuel as the machines climbed, turned, descended and climbed again.

Figure 46 Only the dark rectangle of the gun enclosure amongst the foliage to the left of the trees and the stream below Manor Farm reveals the presence of a pillbox covering a bridge on the Chilworth to Shalford road

Figure 47 The loopholed wall at River House Cottage overlooking the green in Elstead

On the right 7th Panzer made another attempt to cut north through Bolney, but their patrol was held up by a flooded valley and pillbox and tank-trap complex at the innocent-looking village of Slaugham and the effort of assaulting the ridge at Handcross did not seem worthwhile. Just east of Cowfold the tanks halted to refuel before dusk came on. The supplies were meagre and the process laborious. A small column of trucks had completed the journey from Hastings, survivors of the air strike. The drums of fuel had to be man-handled and tipped to refill the Panzers, but there was not enough to do more than half-fill petrol tanks depleted by the series of exploratory forays off the principal route. Not a single service station had been found with fuel to be pumped into the German machines and they were entirely reliant on what was brought over from France. The resources of the flame-thrower support tankers had been exhausted by the fight at Hastings and by the need to keep other tanks and trucks mobile. About 15 per cent of the motorised transport was now out of service as a result of fuel shortage and the horse-drawn transport was straining to make up the deficiency. The Panzers decided to lay up for the night rather than risk getting lost or drawn into an action in the twilight that might further eat into their supplies.

Saturday brought no comfort. Before they were on the move the news came of the sabotage of the pontoon bridge over the Ouse at Beddingham. Some of the guards had been knifed in the night and charges had been set and blown, sinking three of the pontoons and putting the bridge out of use for at least six hours. An operation to ferry drums to Newhaven by torpedo boat had been put in hand but the payload was small and the chances of success limited. The 7th Panzer continued with the sweep around Horsham, 8th Panzer immediately to their rear. Once more RAF attacks slowed and eroded the column as they hurried across the old Roman road, Stane Street, and, on Saturday, along the valley towards Guildford. The main British force bided its time. On the left of the German advance the Australians and the 3rd Division were ready to move. The GHQ line below the hills at Shalford and Peasemarsh had been seen as a fairly feeble barrier, but it was not so much the strength of the pillboxes that did the work as the presence of water. All along the valley through Chilworth and across the flat water-meadows towards Farnham the complex of river and canal hindered the deployment of heavy machines. Even the road block at the Seahorse public house in Shalford delayed a tank long enough for a track to be blown off it, enhancing the road block until another tank shoved it aside. A flanking foray to the left through Godalming brought the spigot-mortar on the Guildford road[16] into action for a time and two Panzergrenadier trucks were set on fire before the crew of the curious weapon were killed. The advance developed westward along the river and bridges, with a series of little actions at pillboxes all along the road towards Farnham. A patrol rushing west through Elstead came under fire from the rear through, to their total disbelief, loopholes in a garden wall. They burned the house down and killed not only the uniformed Home Guard, but anyone else they saw there.

The advance of 10th Panzer from Tenterden made good progress for a while, unaware that the details of its strength in men and machines was being noted by the Auxiliary Unit in the area and that a messenger would take it to Adrian Monck-Mason's radio station at Charing, north-west of Ashford.[17] As it held to the flank of the Weald the going was good, but the descent onto the flood plain of the River Beult north of Staplehurst marked the beginning of its problems. The weirs and banks of the river had been smashed and, as they approached, or even as they were crossing, the bridges' charges were blown. The damage was not insurmountable, but as the engineers sweated away to create some sort of causeway they came under fire from field guns on the hills to the north. Once they began to clamber off the flatland the New Zealanders began their hit and run attacks again. The temper of the Liebstandarte Adolf Hitler was not improved by this and when they managed to capture a couple of dozen of their tormentors they herded them into a barn and machine-gunned them.[18] The crossing of the Medway was made on Saturday at Teston, south-west of Maidstone, where the heavy machine-gun pillbox[19] held out until a Panzergrenadier managed to crawl close enough to lob grenades through the embrasures. Their progress westwards staggered only until they reached the Limpsfield nodal point, not that the defences around this little village were particularly impressive, but because the concept of the nodal point was demonstrated in classic style. As the German formation went into hold-and-by-pass posture, part of the 1st Armoured Division fell on the Panzergrenadier element with devastating effect. With the 42nd Division on one side supported by artillery and the Canadians on the other, 10th Panzer, with the British armour now striking from their rear, soon ceased to be an operational unit. Many attempted retreat, but their way back was closed. The anti-clockwise attack had failed.

The jaws were closing on the clockwise column at the same time. As 8th Panzer explored the routes east of Shalford, through Wonersh and

Figure 48 A pillbox on the banks of the Wey, north of Somerset Bridge, on the minor road from Elstead to Peper Harow. It is so overgrown that it cannot be identified from the road

Chilworth, they came under fire from troops on Blackheath. On the sandy, high ground generations of packhorses and foot travellers trekking across the hillsides had worn sunken tracks that became perfect trenches, concealing the defenders from sight and from gunshot. Attempts to climb off the flood plain of the streams at Wonersh failed as the tank tracks cut through the turf to the sand beneath. Courageous rushes by Panzergrenadiers lured them into hollow-ways more like the trench systems of the previous war than these young men realised, but to the 'Dad's Army' of local men it was familiar territory and the Tommy-guns of the Auxiliaries proved to be excellently suited to this style of fight. The manoeuvring tanks were low on fuel and the infantry were low on morale; the constant sniping and the invisibility of their enemy were hard to endure. There was no way out of this pocket to the east.

On Saturday night word came that fuel had been landed at Newhaven and that the precious drums were even now on their way. The quantity was a disappointment, but it was better than nothing and 7th Panzer was able to give its machines between them enough to bring Reading within range, given an unopposed run. The breakthrough on the GHQ Line was achieved, to their surprise, in Guildford itself. The fortification of the approaches and along the rivers, the Wey towards Elstead in the west and the Tillingbourne to the east, hampered movement enough to limit the Germans to infantry crossings, but the tanks themselves rolled through the town on Sunday morning and emerged to push north-west towards Bagshot. Both 7th and 8th Panzer were deeply committed and entirely concentrated in the Aldershot–Guildford pocket, 7th north of the town and 8th south of it. Now was the time. The trap was sprung.

The 3rd Division poured off the higher ground from Haselemere and closed the way back to Horsham before thrusting on eastwards, chopping up the support and supply forces of the German Army while the Australians, keen as usual to make their mark, slashed into the flank of 8th Panzer. From the north-east the Canadians and 1st Armoured squeezed the intruders, advancing through Shere and Albury to block any escape to the east.

Defiantly 7th Panzer thrust on towards the north-west, but as they did so two fresh divisions stood ready for them. The 43rd held the line of the Basingstoke Canal and from the hills to the Germans' left 2nd Armoured Division swept down to cut their column in three places. Even so the invaders proved to be determined adversaries, but in the turmoil of manoeuvre and one by one the Panzers ground to a halt like exhausted beasts of prey. There is little a tank without fuel can achieve. Those within range of the British anti-aircraft guns on the canal had been knocked out and set on fire before the British realised that the machines further away had simply come to a standstill. Orders were given for the 2nd Armoured to pull back and for fire to cease. Silence fell, and then, one after another, the hatches of the enemy vehicles were thrown open and handkerchiefs appeared, waving.

Cut off from their supply lines, without air support and with fuel gone, the Germans surrendered. The Battle of England was over.

Notes and References

1 Von Brauchitsch, *Instruction . . . Operation Sealion*, in Klee, Karl, *Das Unternehmen Seelöwe, Vol. 2*, 1958, pp. 360–7, trans A. McGeoch.

2 Jeschonnek, 5 September, in Klee, pp. 370–2, trans. A. McGeoch.

3 Based on Schenk, Peter, *Invasion of England 1940*, London, Conway Maritime, 1990, p. 269.

4 Based on Swift, Doug, *On a Bright Day in May*, unpublished manuscript.

5 *Befestigungskarte Grossbritannien 1:100,000, Blatt 40*, Berlin, Generalstab des Heeres, 1940.

6 Burridge, David, *20th Century Defences in Britain: Kent*, London, Brassey's, 1997, pp. 54–5.

7 Based on the account by Major Lord Sysonby of the action at Petegem, 19 May 1940. Marix Evans, Martin, *The Fall of France*, Oxford, Osprey, 2000, pp. 85–6.

8 Based on events in Boulogne, 24 May 1940, related in letter to the author from A. J. Smithers, formerly of 5th Buffs, 21 May 2000.

9 Cox, Richard (ed.), *Operation Sea Lion*, London, Thornton Cox and Futura, 1974, p. 188.

10 Lampe, David, *The Last Ditch*, London, Cassell, 1968, pp. 75–9.

11 Adapted from Anthony Quayle in Lampe, p. 81.

12 Not true at this time. Rommel remained in command until after their transfer to Bordeaux at the end of 1940. He arrived in Tripoli with his new command on 12 February 1941.

13 Quarrie, Bruce, *Encyclopaedia of the German Army in the 20th Century*.

14 *Ibid.*, pp. 112–13.

15 Schenk, Peter, personal letter, 27 January 2004.

16 ADS Online catalogue, REFNO=10495.

17 Lampe, p. 88.

18 Based on the incident at Wormhout, 28 May 1940.

19 Burridge, p. 48.

Symbols

Explanation of symbols

A	Panzer redoubt or fort	✺
B	Bullet proof battle position (pillbox)	●
C	Small battle position (pillbox)	▲
D	Readiness area	—
E	Observation post	▲
F	Lookout	▲
G	Position of unknown type	○
H	Battery position	⌒
I	Construction site	xBA
J	Searchlight	♂
K	Foxhole; running trench; shrapnel trench	∿∿∿
L	Barbed wire	xxxxxx
M	Tank obstacle	....
N	Anti-tank ditch	═
O	Terrain unsuitable for aircraft landing due to obstacles. Size of symbol indicates extent.	▦
P	Road block; street block	‖
Q	Destroyed	⊠
R	Minefield	+⁺+
S	Radio post	ʲ●
T	Barracks	▨
U	Ammunition store Mun.	▬
V	Light anti-aircraft gun	♂
W	Anti-aircraft machine-gun	♂
X	Heavy anti-aircraft gun	♂
Y	Heavy machine-gun in anti-aircraft emplacement	♂
Z	Light machine-gun in anti-aircraft or other emplacement	灭＋火
ZA	Listening equipment	♂∿
ZB	Bunker?	○
ZC	Terrain obstacle ldhs.	

Note: on the 1 : 25000 maps symbols in solid black indicate 'safe' data while outline symbols show 'unsafe' or unconfirmed features.

Explanation of symbols to water hazards map

1	River over 1.80m [6ft] deep (regulated and partly canalised)	▬▬
2	Canal over 1.80m deep	⌒⌒⌒
3	River less than 1.80m deep (regulated and partly canalised)	▬▬
4	Canal less than 1.80m deep	▲▲▲
5	Unmaintained waterway	▬ ▬ ▬
6	Lock Schl.	

Width and depth data for canals taken from older documents (1888–1928)
Width and depth of coastal waters depends on tides

7	Trunk roads with distances	+ 55 +
8	Other trunk roads	+ 52 +
9	Main roads	+ 50 +
10	Secondary roads for motor traffic	————
11	Multi-track railway	▬▬▬
12	Single-track railway	————
13	Town over 100,000 inhabitants	▨▨
14	Town over 30,000 inhabitants	◿▨
15	Town over 10,000 inhabitants	◎
16	Town over 5000 inhabitants	⊙
17	Town under 5000 inhabitants	○
18	Smaller towns and villages	o
19	National frontiers	▬ ▪ ▬ ▪ ▬
20	Provincial frontiers within Great Britain	▬ ▪ ▬ ▪ ▬
21	Provincial frontiers in Ireland	▬ ▪ ▬ ▪ ▬
22	County boundaries	▬ ▪ ▬ ▪ ▬

Sources

The Defence of Britain database

The locations of defensive works in England are based on information in various books listed below, but also and principally on the Defence of Britain database, the result of several years of research by volunteers and of cataloguing and data entry by workers based at the Imperial War Museum, Duxford. The site is at http://ads.ahds.ac.uk/catalogue/specColl/dob. The works are classified by type of structure which did not suit my needs in constructing possible events in specific locations and I was guided to the appropriate methodology by Dr William Kilbride, User Services Manager, Archaeology Data Service. As he pointed out, the method described throws up all sites of any age in a given area and it is necessary to weed out those not wanted, but I found it very much the best approach and also came upon things irrelevant to my task but fascinating in their own right, which was fun.

The method is as follows. Open http://ads.ahds.ac.uk/catalogue/search/map.cfm and click on the broad geographical area of interest, and then on the underlying map to specify the size of the search box. This will produce a listing of short records from which those of promise can be selected and an extended record viewed or the full Defence of Britain record summoned up. In the notes to this book the reference has been abbreviated from the full screen designation, but it includes the unique 'REFNO' number.

Other websites

For tidal information the Proudman Oceanographic Laboratory site offers modern information through its Tide Prediction Service at www.pol.ac.uk/appl/tidepred.html. It kindly provided data for 1940.

The information on sunrise and sunset was found on the site of the Astronomical Applications Department, US Naval Observatory, at http://aa.usno.navy.mil/data/docs/RS_OneYear.html.

Unpublished

Bechtolsheim, Anton von, Lecture, 1932, Hamilton Howze Papers, US Army Military History Institute, Carlisle, PA, USA.

Brongers, E. H., *The Battle of the Grebbeberg*, Battlefields Trust Conference paper, 2002.

Dean, Col. Donald, VC, letter to A. J. Smithers, 30 May 1980.

Redfern, John, Thomson, Alex and Naylor, John *The Battle of Aumale*, no date, annotated by Major Redfern 2000, archives of Queen's Royal Surrey Regiment, Clandon Park, Guildford.

Smithers, A. J., correspondence with author 21 May 2000, and unpublished letter to the *Daily Telegraph*, 30 October 1997.

Sysonby, Major Lord, letters 10 May to 8 June 1940, archives of Queen's Royal Surrey Regiment, Clandon Park, Guildford.

German Army publications

Note: English titles used in this text are given in parens. All published in Berlin, by Generalstab des Heeres Abteilung für Kriegskarten und Vermessungswesen, 1940.

Befestigungskarte Grossbritannien, [The Defences Map of 3 September].

England (IV Militärgeographische Beschreibung), [The Geological Map]

Militärgeographische Angaben über England, Südküste, [The Coastal Handbook]

Militärgeographische Beschreibung von Frankreich, Teil I, Nordost-Frankreich, [The Geological Map of Northern France].

Stellungskarte Grossbritannien, [the 1: 25,000 map].

Übersichtskarte der Gewässerabschnitte in England [The Water Hazards map].

Published works

Alanbrooke, Field Marshal Lord, *War Diaries 1939–1945*, London, Weidenfeld & Nicolson, 2001.

Anon., *The Battle of Britain, August–October 1940*, London, HMSO, 1941.

Anon., *Before We Go Back: Norway's Fight Since April 1940*, London, HMSO, 1944.

Anon., *Bomber Command*, London, HMSO, 1941.

Anon., *Coastal Command*, London, HMSO, 1943.

Anon., *Notes on the German Preparations for Invasion of the United Kingdom (2nd edition)*, General Staff, War Office, M.I.14, 1942, reprinted Uckfield, Naval & Military Press, 2004.

Anon., *The Rise and Fall of the German Air Force*, London, Air Ministry Pamphlet No. 248, 1948.

Anon., *Roof over Britain*, London, HMSO, 1943.

Ansel, Walter, *Hitler Confronts England*, Durham, N.C. and London, Duke University Press and Cambridge University Press, 1960.

Bacon, Reginald, Fuller, J. F. C. and Playfair, Patrick, *Warfare Today*, London, Odhams Press, 1944.

Bond, Brian, and Taylor, Michael D., *The Battles of France and Flanders 1940*, Barnsley, Pen & Sword, 2001.

Brodhurst, Robin, 'The Royal Navy's Role in the Campaign' in Bond, Brian and Taylor, Michael D. (eds), *The Battle of France and Flanders 1940*, Barnsley, Pen & Sword, 2001.

Burridge, David, *20th Century Defences in Britain: Kent*, London, Brassey's, 1997.

Cardigan, the Earl of, *I Walked Alone*, London, Routledge & Kegan Paul, 1950.

Churchill, Winston S., compiled by Randolph S. Churchill, *Into Battle*, London, 1941.

Churchill, Winston S., *The Second World War, Volume I*, London, Cassell, 1948.

Collier, Basil, *The Defence of the United Kingdom*, London, HMSO, 1957.

Cox, Richard (ed.), *Operation Sea Lion*, London, Thornton Cox/Futura, 1974.

Cruickshank, Dan, *Invasion: Defending Britain from Attack*, London, Boxtree, 2001.

Culver, Bruce, *SDKFZ 251 Half-Track 1939–1945, New Vanguard 25*, Oxford, Osprey, 1998.

Dear, I. C. B. and Foot, M. R. D. (eds), *The Oxford Companion to World War II*, Oxford, Oxford University Press, 1995.

Dobinson, Colin, *AA Command*, London, Methuen, 2001.

Doorman, P. L. G., *Military Operations in the Netherlands*, London, Netherlands Government Information Bureau and George Allen & Unwin, 1944.

Ellis, L. F., *The War in France and Flanders 1939–1940*, London, HMSO, 1953, reprinted Imperial War Museum and Battery Press, Nashville, 1996.

Sources

Falconer, Jonathan, *RAF Fighter Airfields of World War 2*, Shepperton, Ian Allen, 1993.

Fleming, Peter, *Invasion 1940*, London, Rupert Hart-Davis, 1957.

Fletcher, David, *Matilda Infantry Tank 1938–1945, New Vanguard 8*, London, Osprey, 1991.

Fletcher, David, *Mechanised Force*, London, HMSO, 1991.

French, David, *Raising Churchill's Army*, Oxford, Oxford University Press, 2000.

German Naval History, *The U-boat War in the Atlantic 1939–1945*, London, HMSO, 1989.

Gilbert, Martin, *Finest Hour*, London, Heinemann, 1983.

Gravett, Christopher, *Hastings 1066*, Oxford, Osprey, 1992.

Guderian, Heinz, *Achtung – Panzer!*, London, Cassell, 1999.

Guderian, Heinz, *Panzer Leader*, London & New York, Michael Joseph & Dutton, 1952, new edition Da Capo Press 1996, reprinted Penguin, 2000.

Hinsley, F. H., *et al.*, *British Intelligence in the Second World War, Vol. I*, London, HMSO, 1979.

Jacobsen, Hans-Adolf, and Rohwer, Jürgen, *Decisive Battles of World War II: the German View*, London, André Deutsch, 1965.

Jane's Fighting Ships of World War II, London, Studio/Random House, 1989.

Kieser, Egbert, *Operation Sea Lion*, London, Arms and Armour, 1997.

Klee, Karl, *Das Unternehmen Seelöwe, Volumes I and II*, Göttingen, 1958.

Kleffens, E. N. van, *The Rape of the Netherlands*, London, Hodder & Stoughton, 1940.

Ladd, James, *Commandos and Rangers of World War II*, London, Macdonald and Jane's, 1978.

Lampe, David, *The Last Ditch*, London, Cassell, 1968.

Lewin, Ronald, *Hitler's Mistakes*, London, Leo Cooper, 1984.

Lowry, Bernard (ed.), *20th Century Defences in Britain*, York, British Council for Archaeology, 1995.

Macksey, Kenneth, *Invasion*, London, 1980 and Barton-under-Needwood, Wren's Park, 2001.

Macleod, R. and Kelly, D. (eds), *The Ironside Diaries 1937–1940*, London, Constable, 1962.

Marix Evans, Martin, *The Fall of France – Act with Daring*, Oxford, Osprey, 2000.

Marix Evans, Martin, 'The Error that Lost the War?', *Osprey Military Journal*, Vol. 2, Issue 3.

Maurois, André, *The Battle of France*, London, John Lane The Bodley Head, 1940.

Mondey, David, *British Aircraft of World War II*, London, Hamlyn, 1982.

Mondey, David, *Axis Aircraft of World War II*, London, Temple Press, 1984.

Moulton, J. L., *The Norwegian Campaign of 1940*, London, Eyre & Spottiswoode, 1966.

Pallud, Jean Paul, *Blitzkrieg in the West, Then and Now*, London, Battle of Britain Prints International, 1991.

Perrett, Bryan, *German Light Panzers 1932–1942, New Vanguard 26*, Oxford, Osprey, 1998.

Perrett, Bryan, *Panzerkampfwagen III Medium Tank 1936–1944, New Vanguard 27*, Oxford, Osprey, 1999.

Perrett, Bryan, *Panzerkampfwagen IV Medium Tank 1936–1945, New Vanguard 28*, Oxford, Osprey, 1999.

Perrett, Bryan, *Sturmartillerie & Panzerjäger 1939–1945, New Vanguard 34*, Oxford, Osprey, 1999.

Quarrie, Bruce, *Encyclopedia of the German Army in the 20th Century*, Wellingborough, Patrick Stephens, 1989.

Reitz, Deneys, *No Outspan*, London, Faber & Faber, 1943.

Rommel, Erwin, ed. Liddell Hart, B.H., *The Rommel Papers*, London, Collins, 1953.

Roskill, S. W., *The War at Sea 1939–1945, Volume I*, London, HMSO, 1954.

Saunders, Andrew, *Channel Defences*, London, Batsford/English Heritage, 1997.

Saunders, Andrew, *Fortress Britain*, Liphook, Beaufort Publishing, 1989.

Schatke, Werner, 'The Memories of a German Soldier', *Everyone's War No.5*, Leeds, Second World War Experience Centre, 2002.

Schellenberg, Walter, *Invasion 1940*, London, St Ermin's Press, 2000.

Schenk, Peter, *Invasion of England 1940*, London, Conway Maritime Press, 1990.

Terraine, John, *The Right of the Line*, London, Hodder & Stoughton, 1985.

Warlimont, Walter, *Inside Hitler's Headquarters 1939–45*, London, Weidenfeld & Nicolson, 1964.

Warwicker, John (ed.), *With Britain in Mortal Danger*, Bristol, Cerebus, 2002.

Weal, John, *Messerschmitt Bf110 Zerstörer Aces of World War 2*, Oxford, Osprey, 1999.

Williamson, Gordon, *German Mountain & Ski Troops 1939–45, Elite No.63*, Oxford, Osprey, 1996.

Wills, Henry, *Pillboxes: A Study of UK Defences 1940*, London, Leo Cooper, 1985.

Windrow, Martin, *The Panzer Divisions, Men-at-Arms No.24*, London, Osprey, 1982.

Wood, Derek, with Dempster, Derek, *The Narrow Margin*, London, Hutchinson, 1961.

Ziemke, Earl F., *The German Northern Theater of Operations 1940–1945*, Washington, D.C., Department of the Army Pamphlet No. 20–271, 1959, reprinted, Uckfield, Naval & Military Press, 2003.

Index

Entries in bold indicate illustrations and entries in italic refer to conjectural events in Part 2 of the book.

Aa, the 42
Abbeville 40
Ægir 18
Acasta, HMS 31
Admiral Hipper 12, 14, 16, 19, 31, 75, 140
Admiral Scheer 140
aircraft, British,
  Blackburn B–24 Skua 19, 76, *246*
  Bristol Blenheim 25, 76, *252*
  Gloster Gladiator 28
  Handley Page Heyford 57
  Hawker Hurricane 31, 49
  Supermarine Spitfire 49
Swordfish 19
aircraft, capability 6, 13, 19, 25, 42, 50, 145, **146**, *252*
aircraft, German,
  Dornier flying boat 30
  He 111, 13, 19
  Ju 52 18, 34, 181
  Ju 87 ëStukaí 13, 25, 147, *223*
  Ju 88 13, 18, 19, 147
  Messerschmitt 109, 13, 173
  Messerschmitt 110, 49
Aldershot 163, *259*
Alfriston *221*
Altmark 10
Åndalsnes 21, 24, 26, 28
Ansel, Rear Admiral Walter 81–82
anti-tank devices 59, **60–61**, 169–170, 192, *218*, **219**, 243
Antwerp 114, *191*
Appledore *240–242*
Ardennes, the 37–38
Argus, HMS 68
Ark Royal, HMS 24, 28, 31
Arras 41
ASDIC 232
Ashford 162, *253*, *257*
assault boats 115, **115**, 117–118, **117**
Ardent, HMS 31

artillery, British 139, 169–170
artillery, German 128, 138–139, *191*
Atlantis (hospital ship) 31
Auxiliary Units 72–73, *202*, *229*, *247*, *253*, *257*, *259*

Bagshot *259*
barges 118–120, **119**, 124–126
Bartels, Fregatten Kapitän Heinrich 93
Bartholomew, Lieutenant-General Sir William 233
Basingstoke Canal *259*
Batteries, Emergency Coastal 59, **61**
Battle *201*, *208*, *240*
Beachy Head *207*, *211*
Bechtolsheim, Anton von ix
Beddingham *225*, *252*, *256*
Belgium, invasion of 35–38
Bergen 11, 12, 15, 16–17, 21
Bernd von Arnim 16
Berney-Ficklin, Brigadier 25
Best, Captain Sigismund Payne 87
Beult, River *257*
Bexhill 161, 204, **207**
Bilting, Kent 73
Bishopstone Halt *222*, *223*, **224**
Bismarck 69, 76, 140
Blacker Bombard 62
Blackheath *257*
Blücher 12, 17
Bodø 30
Bock, Colonel-General Fedor von 33, 91
Bond, James 73
Boulogne 114, *204*, 215
bows and arrows 73
Boyes anti-tank rifles 26, *239*
Branchitsch, Colonel-General Walter von 33, 85
Brede Levels *201*, *202*, *242*
bren-gun carriers *240*, **241**
bridge, pontoon **251**, 252
Brighton 162, 217

Britain, Battle of 48–52
British Army 77, *234*, *247–248*
Corps V 65, 77, *248*
  VII 77
  XI *229*
  XII 73
Divisions 1st (London) 77, *182*, *229*,
    238–240
  3rd 66, 77, *234*, *248*, *259*
  4th 65, 77, *248*, *253*
  5th 67
  9th 67
  42nd 77, *234*, *247*, *257*
  43rd 77, *247*, *259*
  45th 77, *194*, *208*, *229*, *234*
  46th 67
  48th 65
  50th 65
  52nd 65
  1st Armoured 77, *234*, *247*, *257*, *259*
  2nd Armoured 77, *234*, *247*, *259*
  Australian Imperial Force 65, 77, *234*,
    248
  Canadian 65, 77, *234*, *247*, *257*, *259*
  New Zealand 77, *228*, *234*, *240*, *257*
Brigades 1st Independent 77, *229*, *253*
  21st 77
  29th 77, *229*
  1st Tank 77, *234*, *247*
  21st Tank 77, *234*, *248*, *253*
Other Units Auxiliary Military Pioneer
    Service *245*
British Expeditionary Force, France 4,
    7, 36
  losses 48
  1st Armoured Division 45
  51st (Highland) Division 45
  52nd Division 45
  5th Kings Own Scottish Borderers
    46–47
  1st/5th Queenís Royal 36
  1st Royal Canadian Horse Artillery 47
  7th Royal Sussex 40
  7th Royal West Kent 40
British Expeditionary Force, Norway
    13, 30
  Royal Marines 26
  49th Infantry Division 13
  15th Infantry Brigade 27
  24th Guards Brigade 13
  146th Infantry Brigade 24

147th Infantry Brigade 24
148th Infantry Brigade 13, 24, 26
1st Green Howards 27
Independent Companies 29–30, 72
1st Irish Guards 30
1st Kingís Own Yorkshire Light
    Infantry 27
1st/4th Kingís Own Yorkshire Light
    Infantry 25
1st/5th Leicestershire 26
1st/4th Royal Lincolnshire 25
5th Scots Guards 10, 23, 30
1st/8th Sherwood Foresters 26
2nd South Wales Borderers 30–31
1st York and Lancaster 27
Brooke, General Sir Alan 45–46, 64–65,
    66–67, 71, 74, 77, *170*, *228–229*,
    234, *247*
Burgess Hill 161, *253*

Calais 74, *191*
Calvert, Captain Michael 73
Canaris, Admiral Wilhelm 89
Chain Home *see also* radar 57, 169,
    177, *228*
Chamberlain, Neville 8
Cherbourg, fall of 47
Chilworth **254**, *256*, *257*
Churchill, Winston 15, 23, 24, 47–48,
    51–52, 66, 72, 74
Ciano di Cortellazzo, Count Galeazzo
    90
Cliff End (nr. Hastings) *192*
Clyde, the 13
Clyde, HMS 68
Code-breaking, British *see also* ULTRA
    49, 70
  German 90–91
Combined Intelligence Committee
    (CIC) 70
Commandos 72
Communications, British 233
convoys 67–68
Cork and Orrery, Admiral the Earl of
    23–24
Court-at-Street *187*
Cradle Hill 217, *221*, *227*
'Cromwell', 71–72
Cross, Squadron-Leader Kenneth 31
Cross-in-Hand *253*

Cuckmerehaven 161, 215, *217–221*, **216, 219**
Cuckmere River 161, *218*, **220**, *243*

Daventry 57
defence, British air 56–58
  coastal 59
  ground 58–64, 66
  sea 67–69
Denmark Straits 75
Dietl, Major-General Eduard 21, 28
Dill, General Sir John 45
direction finding (DF) 58
Dönitz, Rear Admiral Karl 142–143, *233*
Dombås 26
Douglas, Air Vice-Marshal William Sholto 67
Dover 74, **88**, **105**, 156, 160, *179*, 184, *228*, *240*
  tide 176, 184
Dowding, Air Chief Marshal Sir Hugh 50, 56, *168*
Dungeness 74, 160, *179*, *199*, *231*
Dunkirk 74, 114, 127, 173, *175*
Dymchurch *177*, *179*
Dymchurch (Grand) Redoubt *177*, *179*, *184*

Eagle Day (*Adlerangriff*) 49
Eastbourne 161, 204, *210*, *211–212*, *221*
East Hoathly *243*, *252*
Eastleigh *233*
Eban Emael 35
Eden, Anthony 7, 66
Ellis, Colonel C.H. 87
Elstead **255**, *257*, **258**, *259*
Emden 12, 18, 140
Engelbrecht, Major-General 17
Enigma machine 49, 70, *229*, *247*
England, Battle of *248–260*
evacuation of civilians 64

Falkenhorst, General Nikolaus von 14, 21
Farnham *256–257*
Ferries, Herbert 122, **122**, 127, *205*, 215, *217*
  Siebel 122, *205*
Fischer, Colonel Hermann 27, 28
Flame Fougasse 62, *202*

Fleming, Ian 73
Fleming, Captain Peter 73, 89
Folkestone 160
  Racecourse *182*
Forbes, Admiral Sir Charles 15, 19, 69, 141, *232*
Franklin, Major-General Harold 41
French Army 4, 44
  2nd Army Group 5
  3rd Army Group 45
  2nd Army 37
  Cavalry Corps 36
  X Corps 37
  3rd Brigade of Spahis 38
  1st Armoured Division 39
  4th Armoured Division 39
  2nd Division Légère Mèchanique 36
  3rd Division Légère Mèchanique 36
French Army, Norway, 5th Demi-Brigade Chasseurs Alpins 24, 25, 28, 29
Freyberg, Major-General Bernard *228*
Fricke, Rear Admiral Kurt 80, 83, 99
Führer Directive No.9 81
  No.16 85, 91
  No.17 49
fuel, destruction of supplies 64, *229*, *253*, *256*
Furious, HMS 19

Gaulle, Colonel Charles de 39, 51
German air force, *see Luftwaffe*
German Army, France 33, 44
  Army Group A 33, 38, 44
    B 33, 44
    C 33, 44
  12th Army 39
  Gruppe von Kleist 37, 43
  XIX Panzer Corps 37
  XV Panzer Corps 37
  Divisions, 22nd Infantry 34
    207th Infantry 34
    1st Panzer 38
    2nd Panzer 38, 40
    3rd Panzer 36
    4th Panzer 35, 36
    7th Panzer 39–40, 44, 46
    9th Panzer 34
  Other Units, SS Standarte ëDer F,hrerí 35
German Army, Norway,

69th Infantry Division 18
163rd Infantry Division 17
196th Infantry Division 22
138th Mountain Regiment 30
German Army, Sealion 83, 126–129
Army Group, A 91, 102
orders of 14.Sept.'40 129–136, B, 91, 103
Army, 9th 131, 159, 161, 175, *202, 204, 247, 248*
16th 127, 130–131, 159, 160, 175, *247, 248*
Corps XV, *247, 248*
XXXVIII *205*
XXXXI Armoured 175, *247, 248*
Division, 7th Infantry *194, 240–241, 242*
8th Infantry *215, 221, 223, 252*
17th Infantry *175, 176, 234, 237, 240*
26th Infantry *204, 207, 208, 221, 243*
28th Infantry *215, 221–222, 225, 252*
34th Infantry *204, 210, 212, 243*
20th (Motorized) Infantry *248*
29th (Motorized) Infantry 175, *248*
1st Mountain *194–195, 201, 212, 240, 243*
6th Mountain *212, 215, 217–221, 227, 229, 243*
4th Panzer *248, 253*
7th Panzer *248, 256, 259–260*
8th Panzer 175, *248, 253, 256, 257–260*
10th Panzer 175, *248, 250, 253, 257*
Regiment, 19th Infantry *195–196, 199, 201, 242*
21st Infantry *177, 238*
39th Infantry *205*
49th Infantry *225*
55th Infantry *177, 240*
62nd Infantry *195–196, 199, 201, 242*
78th Infantry *205*
80th Infantry *205*
107th Infantry *205*
28th Jäger *223*
84th Jäger *225*
98th Mountain *194–195*
99th Mountain *194, 199*
6th Panzergrenadier *248*

7th Panzergrenadier *248*
8th Panzergrenadier *248*
12th Panzergrenadier *248*
33rd Panzergrenadier *248*
Grossdeutschland 175
SS Liebstandarte Adolf Hitler 175, *250*
Battalion, 1st Brandenburg *184–187, 207, 210–212*
Engineer 47 119, 121
Engineer Training 1, 115
11th, Artillery Regiment 67, *238*
Tank Detachment, (Fl) 100, *195, 201–202*
(U)A *194, 199*
(U)B *179, 189, 238*
(U)C *205, 212, 243*
(U)D *180, 184, 186–187, 215, 218, 221, 238, 243–245*
attached from the Luftwaffe, 7th Airborne Division 160, *176–177, 181–183, 234*
2nd Regiment *183*
3rd Regiment *183*
Bräuer Detachment *177*
Meindl Detachment *176, 181–182, 187–189, 239*
Stentzler Detachment *176, 182*
German Navy, Norway 12, 19, 20
German Navy, Sealion 92–93, 98, 140–144, **143**, 214–215
destroyers 144
minesweepers *192*
submarine 142–144, **143**, *232–233*
torpedo boats 143
Trials Command 115
GHQ Line 59, **61**, 163, *256–257, 259*
Glorious, HMS 24, 28, 31–32
Glowworm, HMS 16
Glynde 225
Gneisenau 12, 14, 16, 19, 31, 68, 140
Godalming *257*
Göring, Reichsmarschall Hermann 46, 47, 82, 119
Gravelines 126, *191*
Gubbins, Brigadier Colin 29, 30, 31, 72, *202, 253*
Gudbrandsdal 21, 26, 27
Guderian, Major-General Heinz 3, 32, 37, 8–39, 41–42, 44, 120, 173
on tank warfare 4

on terrain, Dunkirk 43, 175
Guildford 163, *256, 259*
gunboats 123
Gurkha, HMS 19, 68

Haakon, King 20
Halder, General Franz 33, 38, 83, 91, 93, 127
Harstad 11, 24
Hartmann, Lieutenant Dr *184*
Harwich 76
Haslemere *259*
Hastings 160, 191, *194, 231, 240*
Hawkinge *182, 239–240*
Hitler, Adolf 3, 11, 14, 33, 44, 82, 84–85, 91, 99, *167*
Halt Order 24 May 42–43, *173*
Hoffmeister, Colonel *238–240*
Holland, Colonel John 72
Home Guard *see also* Auxiliary Units 59, 71, 72, *181, 238*
Hood, HMS 73
Horsebridge *243*
horses 104, 126, 128, *175,* **249**
Horsham 161, *252, 256, 259*
Horton, Vice-Admiral Sir Max 14
hospital ships 123
Hotblack, Major-General 24
Huntzinger, General Charles 37
Hythe 160, *176, 183, 239*
intelligence, British 69–70, 140–141, *229, 230–231, 247*
intelligence, German 89–91, 130, 136
Ironside, General Lord 23, 24, 58

Jeschonnek, General Hans 111
Jodl, General Alfried 83, 92
on Sealion, 12 July 84
13 August 97–99
Joint Intelligence Committee (JIC) 70

Karlsruhe 12, 18, 20
Kennedy, Lieutenant-Colonel 169–170
Kesselring, Field Marshal Albrecht 145
Kingston *225*
Kleikamp, Captain 191
Kleist, General Ewald von 37, 38–39
Köln 12, 16, 19, 76, 140
Königsberg 12, 17, 19
Kristiansand 11, 12, 18–19

Laake, Major-General Kristian 21
Lancastria 47
Landing Area, A 114
B 114, 149, *173–189*, **178**, *231, 237–240*
C 114, 149, *191–202*, **193**, *240–243*
D 114, 150, *204–213*, **206**, *243*
E 150, *214–227*, **216**
landing craft, German 93, 114, 118–120
land-tows 123
Langney Point 204, 207, 208
leads, the 10, 13
Leeb, Colonel-General Wilhelm Ritter von 33
Le Havre 114, *214*
Leigh-Mallery, Air Vice-Marshal Sir Trafford 58
Leipzig 140
Lewes 161, 215, *225, 243–245, 252*
Lillehammer 21, 26
Limpsfield *257*
List, Colonel-General Wilhelm 39
Local Defence Volunteers *see also* Home Guard 59
Loch, Major-General Herbert *176*
Lofoten Islands 11, 24
London 6, 167
London Defence Positions 163
loop-holed wall 64, **255**, *257, 259*
Ludlow-Hewitt, Air Chief Marshal Sir Edgar 231–232
Lütjens, Vice-Admiral G.nther von 15, 16
Lützow 12, 18, 20, 140
Luftwaffe, France, etc. 48–49, 91
5th Luftflotten 50
7th Airborne Division 34
Luftwaffe, Norway 12–13, 18
X Air Corps 12
Paratroops 17, 18, 22
Luftwaffe, Sealion 91, 92, 98, 115, 133–134, 144–147
deployment 145
orders of 5 Sept'40 109–111
Luftflotte 2 145
Luftflotte 3 145
Luftflotte 5 145
Lyme Bay 91, 97, 114
Lyminge 160, *182, 239*
Lympne **61**, *182, 183, 187, 237–238*

Mackesy, Major-General P.J. 23, 24
Maginot Line 5, 7–8
Maidstone 162, *228*
Manstein, General Erich von 32–33, *205–207*
mapping, German 85–87, 148–159
Marschall, Admiral Wilhelm 31
Medway, river 162
Michelham Priory *243*
Military Co-ordination Committee 23
Military Intelligence 14 (MI 14) *230–231*
minefields 139–140, **143**
minesweeping devices 232
Mjøsa, Lake 21, 22
Molotov Cocktail 62
Monck-Mason, Adrian *257*
Montgomery, General Bernard 66, *248*
Morgan, Brigadier 26
Mosjøen 29, 30

Namsos 21, 25
Narvik 10, 11, 13, 15, 23, 28, 29
Nebelwerfer 129
Nelson, HMS 73
Netherlands, invasion of 34–35
Newhaven 161, 162, 215, *222–225*, **222, 226**, *227, 231*
tide 217
Newhaven Redoubt 217, **223**
Nieuport 126
Normanís Bay 204, **207**
Norway **9**, 10, 75, 81
invasion of 11–32
invasion warning 14
Norwegian Army 11, 22, 29, 30
2nd Division 22
Norwegian Navy 11
Nürnberg 76, 140

Oberkommando der Wehrmacht (OKW) 32, 39, 81, 92
Intelligence (*Abwehr*) 89–91
Orders of 3 Sept. í40 108–109
Section L 83
Oberkommando des Heeres (OKH) 32, 33, 38, 39, 81
Memo of 10 Aug. '40 93–97
Orders of 30 Aug. '40 100–108
Observer Corps, 57–58 *169, 229*
Østerdal 21, 27

Operation Dynamo (Dunkirk) 43–44
Operation *Fall Rot* (Red) 44–48
Operation Hammer (Trondheim) 24–26
Operation *Herbstreise* (Autumn Journey) 75–76, 141–142, *229*
Operation *Seelöwe* (Sealion), execution of,
defeat of *250–260*
evening 21 Sept. '40 *229–230, 236–237*
evening 22 Sept. '40 *245–246*
Second Operational Objective *236*
Second Wave *236, 248, 250*
Operation *Seelöwe* (Sealion), planning of 80–111
Army orders of 30 Aug. '40 100–108
of 14 Sept. í40 129–136
beachhead 159
British defences 149, 156–163, **154**
delay order 108–109
First Operational Objective 102, 109, 130–131, 150, 155, 162
fleet assembly 123–126
frontage dispute 93–97
German army strength 91
German fleet strength 99, 113–115
preparations ordered 85
preconditions 81, 82, 84, 91, 95, 98
publications for 85–89
Second Operational Objective 162
Study England 83
Study *Nordwest* 81–82
Study Red 80–81, 82
terrain evaluation 95, 149–156, **151, 153, 157, 158**
Operation *Weserübing* 11, 14
Orzel 15
Oscarsborg Fort 17
Oslo 11, 12, 18, 20, 21
Oslofjord 15, 17
Ostend 114, 126, *175*
Ouse, River 161, 215, *225, 245*
Oxney, Isle of *196, 201, 242*

Paddlesworth *182, 239*
Paget, Major-General 25
Panzer division, strength of 248–250
parachute troops 82
Park, Air Vice-Marshal Sir Keith 52, 58, *228*
Pétain, Marshal Henri 37

Petroleum Warfare Department 62
Pevensey Bay, tide 205
Pevensey Castle 63, 64, 161, *208, 210*
Pevensey Levels 161, 204, **209**, *250*
Pile, Major-General Sir Frederick 170
pillboxes 59, **60**, 64, **197, 219, 220,
258**
pimples 59, **61**
Plan D 36
Plunkett-Ernle-Erle-Drax, Admiral the
Hon. Sir R. 69
Plymouth 73, 76, 139
Poland, invasion of 3
Portsmouth 76, 139, *214, 253*
Postling *183*
Pound, Admiral Sir Dudley 15, 23
Prähme, see barges 118
Prinz Eugen 140

Quisling, Major Vidkun 11, 20

radar 49, 56–57, *169*
radio, clandestine 73, *229, 253*
Raeder, Grand Admiral Erich 11, 80,
82–83, 84, 91, 144, *227*
rafts, seagoing *see also* ferries 121–122
Ramsay, Vice-Admiral Bertram 43
Red Cross, the 123
Reinden Wood *239–240*
Reinhardt, General Georg Hans 91, 93,
114
Reitz, Denys 5–8
Renown, HMS 13, 16
reprisals *247, 257*
Revenge, HMS 73
Ribbentrop-Molotov Pact 8
Rio de Janiero 15
rocket launcher, *see* Nebelwerfer 129
Roda 18
Rodney, HMS 19, 68
Rommel, Major-General Erwin 38, 39,
44, 46–47, *248*
Romney Marsh 155, *173, 237*
Rookery Hill 222, *225*
Roskill, Captain S.W. 15
Rosyth 13, 73
Rother, River 160, 191, *196*, 200
Rotterdam 34–35, *175*
Rottingdean 162, 217, *221*
Royal Air Force (RAF) 49, 50–51,
167–169

Bomber Command 67, 74, 231–232,
237, 242
Coastal Command 70, 73–74, *177, 232*
Fighter Command 50, 52, 56, 58, *228*
10 Group 58, *168*
11 Group 52, 58
12 Group 58
13 Group 50, 58
72 Squadron 50
605 Squadron 50
RAF Regiment *238*
Royal Air Force, Norway 28
Bomber Command 15
Fighter Command, 46 Squadron 31
262 Squadron 28, 31
Royal Military Canal 160, *176, 183,
186*, 192, *237*
Royal Navy 67–69, 73, 74, 76, 139,
232–233, 246
Home Fleet 68
Nore Command 68
Northern Patrol 75
Western Approaches Command 68
2nd Cruiser Squadron 74
21st Flotilla 74
Fleet Air Arm 76, *233*
800 Squadron 76
803 Squadron 76
806 Squadron *233*
Royal Navy, Norway 12, 13, 21, 32
air attacks on 19, 25, 68
Fleet Air Arm 19
800 Squadron 28
801 Squadron 28
submarines 14, 20
1st Cruiser Squadron 15
2nd Cruiser Squadron 15
rubber dinghies 117–118, **118**
Ruge, Major-General Otto 21, 22, 24
Rundstedt, Field Marshal Gerd von 32,
33, 91
Russo-Finnish War 8–10
Rye 160, **196, 197**, *199, 231*

Saltdean 217, *221*
Saltwood Castle *189, 239, 240*
Sandgate *179, 189*
Scapa Flow 15
Scharnhorst 12, 14, 16, 19, 31, 68, 140
Schatke, Werner 127–128
Schellenberg, SS General Walter 87

Schniewind, Vice Admiral Otto 80, 83, 93, 114, 123
Schuten see barges 118
Scissorforce 29–30
S-Day 108–109
  21 Sept '40 173, *175, 229–230*
Seaford 161, 215, *221, 222–223, 231*
Secret Intelligence Service (British) 87
Sedan 37
Seeleichter see barges 118
Seven Sisters *217, 218*
Shalford **254,** *256,* 257
Sheerness 76
Shere **60,** *259*
Shorncliffe 74
Shorncliffe Camp *189, 239*
Siebel, Major Fritz 115, 119, 121–122
Slaugham *256*
Sola airfield 13, 18, 25
sound mirrors 56
South Heighton 222, 225
Spearfish, HMS 20
Sperrle, Field Marshal Hugo 145
spies, *see* intelligence
spigot mortar 62–64, **62,** *257*
Staplehurst *257*
Stavanger 12, 13, 18, 25
Stedingen 18
Steiff, Major Helmuth 81
Steinkjer 25, 26
Stevens, Major Richard 87
Straight, Squadron-Leader Whitney 28
Student, Lieutenant-General Kurt 34, *176*
Stülpnagel, Colonel Heinrich 81
Suffolk, HMS 25, 68
supply, British 68
supply, German
  in Norway 20, 21, 28
  in Sealion 116, 124–125, *230–231, 253, 256, 259*
Sysonby, Major Lord 36

tactics, British 30, *233, 234, 253*
tactics, French 44
tactics, German ix, 22–23, 30, 37–38, 103–104, 108, 233, 238, 252
  in air 50
tanks, British 65–66

tanks, German *see also* Panzer division 26–27
  amphibious and underwater 103, 120–121, 175, **180**
  flame-throwers 128–129
  range 250
Tenterden *196, 240, 257*
terrain, German assessment of,
  Dunkirk 42–43
  England 149–156, *252*
Teviot Bank, HMS 13
Thorne, General Andrew 73
Tillingbourne, river *259*
Tizard, H.T. 56
Tommy guns 72, *259*
Tow groups 116
transport ships 116–117
Triton, HMS 18
Tromsö 21, 29
Trondheim 11, 12, 15, 19, 21, 23, 24–26, 29
Truant, HMS 20

Uckfield *230, 252*
ULTRA 49, 70
United States of America 51–52
USSR, 8
  plan to attack 92

Vian, Captain Philip 10

Warlimont, Colonel Walter 83, 92, 114, 141
Warspite, HMS 21
Watson-Watt, Robert 56–57
Wavell, General Archibald 6, 67
Weald, the 152, 162, *257*
West Hythe *187–189*
Wey, River **258,** *259*
Weygand, General Maxime 44–45
Whitworth, Vice-Admiral Sir J.W. 16, 21, 23
Winchelsea *194, 195, 199, 247*
Winkelman, General Henri G. 35
Wolverine, HMS 31
Wonersh *257–259*

Zieb, Captain Paul 120